A FIELD GUIDE TO

WHALES, PORPOISES, AND SEALS

FROM CAPE COD TO NEWFOUNDLAND

A FIELD GUIDE TO
WHALES, PORPOISES, AND SEALS
FROM CAPE COD TO NEWFOUNDLAND

STEVEN K. KATONA, VALERIE ROUGH, AND DAVID T. RICHARDSON

FOURTH EDITION, REVISED

SMITHSONIAN INSTITUTION PRESS
Washington and London

Library of Congress Catalog Number 93-84473
ISBN 1-56098-333-7

British Library Cataloguing-in-Publication Data is available

Manufactured in the United States of America

00 99 98 97   5 4 3

David Richardson's

love of Maine's seals helped to make this book possible. His field research provided the first detailed record of the distribution and abundance of harbor and gray seals along the Maine coast. He brought to the study of marine mammals both an emotional appreciation for the animals he observed and a desire for scientific precision in recording his observations. David's accomplishments were not won easily, because he had cystic fibrosis. His will to continue learning and working was an inspiration to everyone who knew him. We dedicate this book to his memory.

CONTENTS

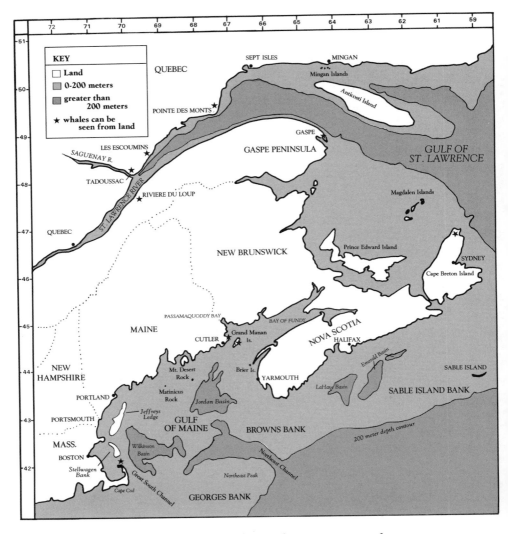

Cape Cod to Nova Scotia, showing locations mentioned in text

PREFACE

On July 4, 1990, a 30-foot-long humpback whale swam into Lowell's Cove at Orr's Island, Maine. The whale was unable to swim out because a long net called a stop seine had been placed across the mouth of the cove to capture menhaden (pogies), a type of herring that is used commercially to produce oil, fish meal, and fertilizer. The whale had apparently been able to swim through the door of the net but could not—or would not—leave. For the next 5 weeks the whale remained in the cove while officials from the National Marine Fisheries Service (NMFS), the state of Maine, and concerned citizens considered what to do.

The seine owner, Alden Leeman, did not want to hurt the whale, but he also did not want to lower his net to release it because he feared losing the estimated 800,000 pounds of pogies, worth nearly $100,000, he had trapped to sell for lobster bait. Some Orr's Island residents urged him to keep the whale because the tourists who came to see it purchased hundreds of T-shirts celebrating the whale, meals, fuel, or other sundries. Income from sales bolstered an otherwise slow economy. Local entrepreneurs took tourists to see the whale by boat. On some days the cove was packed with dozens of boats, and the whale's behavior was affected by noise and crowding.

Marine wardens from the Maine Department of Marine Resources at first refused to act, claiming that NMFS was responsible for marine mammals. NMFS stationed two agents and a boat at the scene for 9 hours each day, at substantial cost, to prevent overeager spectators from harassing the whale. The Marine Mammal Protection Act of 1972, as amended, defines harassment in such broad language that NMFS agents were not certain whether the seine owner, fishermen, or onlookers were violating the law. Furthermore, since NMFS administers marine fisheries in addition to marine mammals, the agency probably did not want to antagonize a fisherman unnecessarily. It was still not clear whether the whale remained voluntarily or was at risk. In the net, the whale had abundant food, but twice it became entangled in ropes or mesh and could have drowned.

Maine's Department of Marine Resources responded to rising concern by passing a temporary law prohibiting boats from entering the cove. Following a month of frustration, NMFS urged Leeman to release the whale. On August 3, assisted by whale experts from the Center for Coastal Studies and the New England Aquarium, fishermen successfully released the whale without losing the pogies. The whale breached (jumped) 30 times as it swam away. Some observers thought the whale was jumping for joy to celebrate its freedom, but other explanations are possible. The main question of whether the whale benefited or was harmed remained unanswered.

This incident highlights many issues that concern anyone interested in whales, dolphins, and porpoises. Whales can never again enjoy the full sweep of the seas. Our fisheries, fishnets, garbage, debris, and noise are now facts of life for them. Yet we humans cannot use and abuse the seas and their resources as freely and thoughtlessly as we once did. Many nations now prohibit particularly blatant abuses, and marine mammals, birds, and other species are gaining human allies determined to improve the quality of marine habitats. With luck, there is still time to make the ethical and economic adjustments necessary for people, whales, porpoises, seals, and other animals to share the ocean's resources. The large potential revenue from whale-watching and seal-watching tours offers strong economic incentive to do so. If we do not make those adjustments, our generation will surely be one of the last to enjoy the magnificent experiences now available to readers of this book.

This book is intended for whale watchers, seal watchers, yachtsmen, mariners, or anyone else who ventures to sea in coastal or continental shelf waters between Cape Cod and the northern tip of Newfoundland. It contains information on all marine mammals that routinely or occasionally occur in these waters, plus descriptions of their main prey species and of other large sea animals often seen on whale-watching trips.

Seventeen years have passed since the first edition of this book was published. Interest in marine mammals has grown each year, as has the number of books and articles devoted to them. This fourth edition contains accounts of 22 species of whales and 7 species of seals that have been seen at sea or stranded on a beach between Cape Cod and northern Newfoundland. Field marks for species identification are emphasized in text and illustrations. Field marks are outstanding color patterns, body shapes, or behavior traits that observers can use to distinguish species rapidly and accurately in the wild. As in bird-watching, it pays to know these features well because different whales or seals are sometimes difficult to tell apart, especially when seen briefly or when only part of the body is visible. Since most whales or seals will be seen from a distance, a good binocular (7 to 10 power × 35 to 50 mm) will usually be necessary. Instruments with greater magnification can be used on land but are hard to hold on a rocking boat.

Insofar as possible, all descriptions, photographs, and literature citations are drawn from waters between Cape Cod and northern Newfoundland. The text emphasizes information most useful to people observing animals in the wild within that region. New lists of locations for watching whales and seals have been prepared. Each species description has been updated with new information gained during the past 8 years, and one species has been added since the previous edition. We are confident that this new edition will make your experiences with the animals more informative and more enjoyable.

Rising public interest in marine mammals has stimulated tremendous growth in research. Hundreds of papers are added to the primary scientific literature each year, in addition to numerous books, magazine articles, and unpublished technical reports or government documents. Descriptions presented here are synthesized from writings and observations of many scientists, both professional and amateur, in addition to our own experiences. In a volume like this one, however, designed primarily for amateur naturalists, citations within the text of all publications that substantiate or discuss each statement would be cumbersome. The updated bibliographies list literature used in preparing this book. Guides to references on each species are provided with the bibliographies. We beg the forbearance of any colleagues who find some of their ideas incorporated into the text without specific credit.

Accurate written reports or photographs by amateurs can provide valuable information on these animals, some of which are still poorly understood. Sample sighting report forms are provided in this guide along with instructions on how to report your observations. We would be grateful to receive accounts of all sightings of living, injured, or dead whales, porpoises, and seals from the study area. Firsthand observations or newspaper accounts may be sent to us at Allied Whale, c/o College of the Atlantic, Bar Harbor, Maine 04609. We will forward information obtained from Canadian waters to interested Canadian scientists.

All marine mammals in U.S. waters are protected by the Marine Mammal Protection Act of 1972. Many whales are also protected by the Endangered Species Act of 1973. Harassment is detrimental to animals and punishable by fines or imprisonment. Even stranded or dead specimens are protected, and special permission must be obtained to touch them. In New England, any stranded, injured, or entrapped marine mammal should be reported immediately to the local police, the coastal warden, the National Marine Fisheries Service Enforcement Division (offices in Portland, Maine, and Gloucester, Massachusetts), or the New England Aquarium, Central Wharf, Boston, Massachusetts 02110 (617-973-5247), which is a clearinghouse for such data. In Canada, such events should be reported to the Prince Edward Island Stranding Network in Charlottetown (902-569-4803), Nova Scotia Stranding Network (902-469-2420), Whale Research Program, Memorial University of Newfoundland, St. John's, Newfoundland A1C 5S7 (709-753-5495), or the nearest office of the Department of Fisheries and Oceans. All data are eventually submitted to the Marine Mammal Event Program, Smithsonian Institution, Washington, D.C. 20560, a worldwide data base for information on stranded animals.

The quest to learn more about the lives of marine mammals has provided some of our most memorable experiences. Watching hundreds of seals bask along Maine's rocky shore on a sunny summer morning; a pod of open-mouthed humpback whales bursting to the surface pursuing herring under a Nova Scotian sunset; or a school of white-sided dolphins riding the boat's bow wave and leaping exuberantly in the wake . . . these are among this planet's great wildlife spectacles. We feel privileged to have known such high moments. All readers of this book are fortunate that such opportunities are easily found, thanks to the flourishing wildlife-travel industry.

Watching whales or seals can provide observers with unique and exhilarating experiences, but those opportunities bring responsibility. We must ensure that our actions do not reduce the potential enjoyment of others in the future or the welfare of the animals we watch. Few people nowadays would deliberately hurt a marine mammal, but some actions can unintentionally affect animals. Common courtesy will eliminate most problems: crowding, startling, chasing, or trying to feed the animals are clearly out of bounds and easily avoided. Littering their habitats or creating unnecessarily loud sounds above water or underwater is just as detrimental and unpleasant to the animals as it would be to us. Respecting the animals in these ways will improve the chances for enjoying them during generations to come.

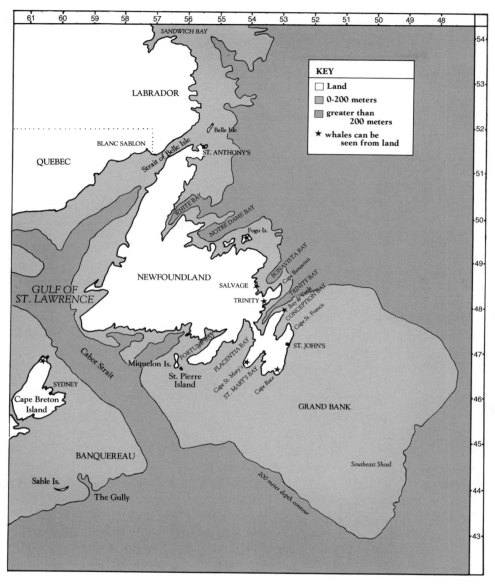

Newfoundland, showing locations mentioned in text

ACKNOWLEDGMENTS

Our debts are great. The list of people who provided encouragement, observations, published or unpublished data, photographs, or other assistance during the past 15 years is long. So is the list of individuals, foundations, and agencies whose financial assistance on particular projects provided information used in this book. Reviewing acknowledgments included in three previous editions reminds us of many stimulating friendships and associations that enriched this work.

Working with colleagues and students at College of the Atlantic has been tremendously valuable to us. It is a pleasure to acknowledge Beverly Agler, Lisa Baraff, Lydia Barnes, Ben Baxter, Sam Blanchard, Bob Bowman, Lisa Carpenter, Harriet Corbett, Gayle Cliett, Peter Cohen, Tim Cole, Kate Darling, Dan Dendanto, Steven Donoso, William H. Drury, Samuel A. Eliot, Tom Fernald, Matthew Hare, Katherine Hazard, Catherine Kiorpes, Scott Kraus, Ed Lemire, Phillip Lichtenstein, Stephanie Martin, Rebecca May, Gail McCullough, Bill McDowell, Sydney Rathbun McKay, Bill McLellan, Megan McOsker, Stephen Mullane, Paula Olsen, Cathy Ramsdell, Ann Rivers, Kim Robertson, Jenny Rock, Sentiel Rommel, Steve Savage, Rachel Snow, Nancy Gunnlaugson Stevick, Peter Stevick, Greg Stone, Porter Turnbull, Katrina Van Dine, Vicki Walsh, and Rick Waters. We give special thanks to Judith Allen, Associate Director of Allied Whale, whose skill and dedication have strengthened marine mammal research at the college since 1978.

For comments, teaching, and encouragement to create this guide we thank James G. Mead, Edward D. Mitchell, Katy Payne, Roger Payne, Clayton Ray, William E. Schevill, David E. Sergeant, William A. Watkins, and Howard E. Winn. We also thank Robin Hazard Ray, who coauthored the first two editions.

Our interest and excitement have frequently been rekindled by observations on cetaceans generously shared with us by Lisa Baraff, Edward McC. Blair, Bob Bowman, Philip Clapham, Steven Frohock, Harold Graham, Henry and Elizabeth Guthrie, Carl Haycock, Tudor Leland, John Lien, Scott Marion, David Mattila, Charles "Stormy" Mayo, Scott Mercer, Judy Perkins, Sam Sadove, Richard Sears, Mason Weinrich, Fred Wenzel, Hal Whitehead, David Wiley, and J. Michael Williamson.

For sharing information about seals we thank Beverly Agler, Doug Beattie, Bob Bowman, Oscar Bunting, Alan Costa, Bruce Cowan, Leslie Cowperthwaite, Sheila Dean, William H. Drury, Greg Early, Pat Fiorelli, Marcia Litchfield, Gail McCullough, Doreen Moser, Michael Payne, Kim Robertson, Sam Sadove, Rachel Snow, Bob Schoelkopf, Peter Stevick, Greg Stone, Peter Trull, the Maine Department of Inland Fisheries and Wildlife, and the staff at the Mystic Marine Life Aquarium. We are grateful to Edith and Clinton Andrews, Brian Beck, W. Don Bowen, Bud Fay, James R. Gilbert, Mike Hammill, Wyb Hoek, George Horonowitsch, David Houghton, Arthur Mansfield, Bob Prescott, Don Reid, Pierre Richard, Thomas G. Smith, Gary Stenson, and Susan Wilson for assisting with new information about seals for this edition.

We thank all the people who contributed photographs and artwork for use in this edition. Arthur Mansfield and Canada's Department of Fisheries and Oceans generously allowed us to use drawings from Mansfield's *Seals of Arctic and Eastern Canada.*

The first edition of this guide was begun under a National Science Foundation Student Originated Studies Grant to College of the Atlantic (GY 11454). Information obtained during projects assisted by the Bureau of Land Management; Carolyn Fund; Conservation and Research Foundation; Davis Conservation Foundation; Island Foundation; Marine Mammal Commission; Marine Mammal Conservation Program of the Maria Mitchell Association; Massachusetts Audubon Society; Massachusetts Natural Heritage Program; National Audubon Society; National Geographic Society; National Marine Fisheries Service, Nature Conservancy; the University of Massachusetts Field Station; U.S. Coast Guard, Southwest Harbor Group; U.S. Fish and Wildlife

Service; Warner-Lambert Co.; and the World Wildlife Fund has been used. For support or logistic assistance important in our fieldwork we also thank Acadian Whale Watch Co., Edward McC. Blair, Peter Dyer, Don Little and Crocker Snow, Jr., Maine Whale Watch Co., Frank and Sarah Peabody, Carlton Ray, Susan and Wes Tiffney, Jr., and Paul and Nicola Tsongas.

We welcome any suggestions about how this guide could be made more accurate or useful.

PART I

WHALES, DOLPHINS, *and* PORPOISES

Humpback whale feeding on small fishes,
with gannets diving for the leftovers.

D. D. TYLER

Introduction

T hrough the ages, whales and people have been linked in myth, literature, art, music, and commerce. Until recently, people were interested mainly in products made from whales, although some early scientists tried to gain a better understanding of the animals. The apparently high intelligence and trainability of some dolphins (which are really small whales) kindled public interest in the biology of whales. Recordings of the remarkable sounds of humpback whales, killer whales, and other marine mammals, as well as many films, books, and articles, have stimulated public attention. Dolphins are among the most popular features at marine aquariums, allowing visitors a firsthand glimpse of their fascinating skills. We know little about these creatures, but because some species are critically endangered it is urgent that we learn about them quickly.

All whales, dolphins, and porpoises belong to the order of mammals called cetaceans. Like other mammals, they breathe air with lungs, have warm blood, bear live young, and suckle the young with milk from mammary glands. But they differ from nearly all other mammals in that they have no hind legs and no fur, except for a few hairs on the head. The manatees and dugongs (Order Sirenia) are also hairless and have no rear limbs, but they evolved those features independently of cetaceans, although in response to similar environmental forces.

Evidence suggests that cetaceans started evolving at least 45 or 50 million years ago (MYA) from land mammals that had hind legs. Similarities in the number and molecular structure of chromosomes indicates that all cetaceans shared a common ancestor at that time. A developing consensus suggests that cetaceans are descended from an ungulate (cattle and their relatives, Order Artiodactyla) ancestor, perhaps a form similar to the hippopotamus, rather than from a primitive carnivore. In addition to similarities in the molecular makeup of their bodies, the cetaceans' chambered stomach resembles that of ungulates. Other features confuse the issue, however. For example, the teeth of cetaceans, and their exclusively carnivorous diet, indicate that their ancestor must not have resembled today's ungulates.

Why did cetaceans evolve at all? What made their early ancestors leave secure land habitats and take to the sea? We can never know for certain, but the following speculations seem possible. About 50 MYA shallow seas covered much of the earth. At certain places, such as the coast of what is now North Africa, competition for food may have been intense on land. Some animals may have found more food in the shallow water at land's edge. After a while competition may have reduced the abundance of easily available foods, favoring individuals that could swim better, feed in deeper water, or remain in the water longer. Natural selection has worked along those lines several times, starting with different ancestors, to produce the other marine mammals that we see today: the seals and sea lions, sea otter, polar bear, manatees, and dugongs. In the case of the cetaceans, the tail evolved into the major organ of locomotion. Wide flukes made of connective tissues and tendons developed on the sides of the tail for propulsion and steering. The cetacean tail beats up and down, rather than from side to side as in fish, mainly because the muscles used are basically the same as those used by the ancestral mammal for flexing the backbone up and down during running. Cetaceans, however, followed a completely different evolutionary path from that of their running ancestor, and they lost the hind limbs. All that remains of the legs is a pair of small bones, vestiges of the pelvis, located near where the rear limbs of a land mammal would connect with the backbone. Meanwhile, the forelimbs evolved into flippers, used mainly as stabilizers or for steering, but also to regulate body temperature. Most cetaceans have a dorsal fin that perhaps stabilizes the body during swimming but also helps regulate body temperature by acting as a heat radiator when necessary.

The smooth, streamlined form of a whale or dolphin is created in large part by a thick layer of blubber, which makes up the innermost layer of skin. The blubber padding may be only an inch thick in dolphins or porpoises—which are usually less than 10 feet (3 m) long and weigh several hundred pounds—but it may be up to 2 feet (61 cm) thick in some of the larger whales, which may approach 100 feet (30 m) in length and 150 tons (136 metric tons) in weight. When a cetacean eats more than it needs for daily survival, the excess food is converted into fat and stored as blubber. If the cetacean eats less than its daily metabolism requires, fats are drawn from the blubber for immediate use. A cetacean must maintain a certain blubber thickness, not just for streamlining and food reserves, but also for thermal insulation. If the animal cannot catch enough prey, it will ultimately deplete its blubber thickness so much that it will be unable to maintain normal body temperature and will die. Body temperature in dolphins is about the same as ours (98.6°F, 37°C); whales are a bit cooler (about 96°F, 35.5°C). Finally, blubber provides buoyancy because it is lighter than water, so a well-nourished animal can stay afloat more easily than a poorly nourished one. Blubber was boiled down in times past to make oil for burning in lamps, for lubrication, and, more recently, for use in food products such as margarine.

The ancestors of whales must have breathed as land mammals do today, but the respiratory system underwent considerable modification during cetacean evolution. The nostrils are located on top of the head in most modern species, rather than at the snout tip as in other mammals. As a result, a whale can continue to swim while it breathes through this blowhole, because only the very top of the head must break the water surface. In most large whales, the rostrum forward of the blowhole is elevated as a splashguard to keep water from entering the nostrils. The specialized epiglottis separates the trachea and esophagus so effectively that cetaceans can breathe and swallow simultaneously. Cetaceans fill and empty their lungs more quickly and completely than do other mammals, thus minimizing the amount of time spent at the surface. Large amounts of respiratory pigments in the blood (hemoglobin) and muscle (myoglobin) bind oxygen to maximize dive times.

Whales and porpoises always fill their lungs with air before submerging, but they probably never get "the bends," no matter how often or deep they dive. Two factors protect them. First, at depth the air is compressed to a very small volume. As water pressure increases, the ribs, most of which are not firmly connected to the breastbone, collapse inward compressing the lungs and forcing air into nonabsorptive portions of the lung (bronchioles, bronchi, and trachea)

BODY FEATURES OF BALEEN AND TOOTHED WHALES

D. D. TYLER

GENERALIZED WHALE TYPES

baleen · blowhole · dorsal fin
throat grooves · flipper · flukes

BALEEN WHALE

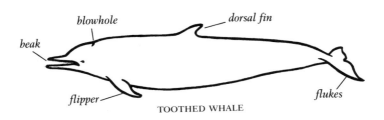

blowhole · dorsal fin
beak
flipper · flukes

TOOTHED WHALE

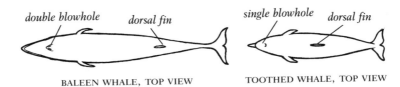

double blowhole · dorsal fin · single blowhole · dorsal fin

BALEEN WHALE, TOP VIEW   TOOTHED WHALE, TOP VIEW

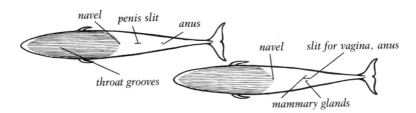

navel · penis slit · anus
throat grooves
navel · slit for vagina, anus
mammary glands

MALE AND FEMALE BALEEN WHALES, SEEN FROM BELOW

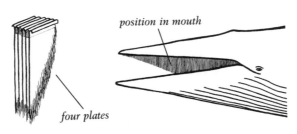

position in mouth
four plates

BALEEN

and—in toothed whales—air sacs near the blowhole. Second, lung compression reduces blood flow to the lungs. Both processes (and perhaps others) minimize absorption of air into the blood, preventing excessive quantities of nitrogen from dissolving in the blood. As the whale ascends, the compressed air expands again, refills the lung, and blood flow and gas exchange resume.

At the surface, the whale's exhaled breath is often visible as a spout, probably caused by atomization of residual water from in or around the blowhole. In addition, the warm, moist, slightly compressed air from the lungs probably condenses when it encounters cold sea air saturated with water vapor. The sudden blast of exhaled breath can be heard for up to a mile on a quiet day, and whales can often be located from a boat if one stops the engine in a favorable location and listens for blows. Blows of dolphins or porpoises are usually not visible, but they can be heard at close range.

The mammalian Order Cetacea is divided into two suborders, the Odontoceti (from the Greek *odontos*, tooth, and *ketos*, whale) and the Mysticeti (Gr. *mystax*, mustache, referring to the hairy appearance of the baleen). Sketches of cetaceans from the two groups are shown below to familiarize readers with their shapes and the locations of external body parts.

Odontocetes, or toothed cetaceans, are usually well under 30 feet (9.1 m) in length. They generally pursue individual prey, such as squid, fish, or—very rarely—birds or mammals. Some species have been shown to use echolocation to find food, and others probably have that ability. They can also locate food by listening for any sound emitted by prey or by other cetaceans feeding. Nearly 70 species of toothed cetaceans have been named and described scientifically, the most recent in 1991, and perhaps a few more will be discovered as we learn more about the oceans. The smaller types are known as dolphins or porpoises. People frequently ask which term is correct. Technically, dolphins and porpoises are classified in separate families, as are cats and dogs. The only consistent difference between odontocetes in the families Delphinidae (Gr. *delphos*, dolphin) and (Phocoenidae, Gr. *phokos*, seal, referring to the seal-like shape of the nominate species, the harbor porpoise) is that delphinids have pointed teeth and phocoenids have teeth that are flattened laterally. This difference cannot be observed at sea. Adult delphinids are usually bigger (generally 8–12 feet, or 2.4–3.7 m) than phocoenids (generally about 5 feet or 1.5 m). The rostrum of the skull is drawn out as a beak in both families, but its protrusion is visible externally only in dolphins. A fatty pad of tissue (the melon) makes the phocoenids appear blunt-snouted. The melon of delphinids is usually small enough so that the jaw protrusion can still be seen. Finally, although both groups contain species that lack a dorsal fin, delphinids usually have large, curved fins and phocoenids small, triangular fins. In keeping with these differences, we recommend the use of the name *dolphin* in reference to any delphinid and *porpoise* in reference to a phocoenid. Either name can be used informally to refer to an unspecified small odontocete. There is a popular warm-water game fish, *Coryphaena hippurus*, whose common name is dolphin, so if you use that name please specify that you are talking about mammals.

The skulls and "foreheads" of all odontocetes show anatomical modifications that are probably associated with sound production, hearing, and echolocation. In all species, but especially in sperm whales (family Physeteridae), beaked whales (family Ziphiidae), and river dolphins (family Platanistidae), the front of the skull has evolved to be a sound reflector or wave guide for sound pulses. Similar modifications can be seen in other species. The forehead in most species contains oil-saturated tissues. Some species, such as the pilot or pothead whale (family Globicephalidae), have so much of this tissue that the front of the head bulges forward beyond the tip of the drawn-out jaws. The tissue is called the melon because it is rounded and has a firm, fibrous appearance when sliced open. Experiments suggest that the dense, oily melon tissue acts as an acoustic lens to focus sound pulses. The foreheads of sperm whales and some of the beaked whales have been modified even further to contain waxy liquid that may be used for modifying sounds. Observations and calculations suggest that odontocetes can produce sonar pulses intense enough to disorient, stun, or kill prey, but further experiments are needed to prove this theory.

Mysticetes have no teeth, but instead possess a series of horny plates, called baleen or whalebone, which hang from the gums of the upper jaw and whose frayed inner edges filter food from the water. This type of whale first appeared about 30 MYA, according to the fossil record. Rudimentary tooth buds have been found in embryos of modern baleen whales, further evidence that mysticetes are descended from toothed ancestors. Fragments of the jaw of a fossil whale from the late Eocene (perhaps 40 or 45 MYA), *Llanocetus denticrenatus*, found in Antarctica and recently described (Mitchell, 1989) show a possible pathway by which baleen may have evolved. The teeth in that species closely resemble the lobed teeth of crabeater seals, *Lobodon carcinophagus*, which are used to strain krill from the water, although the teeth of *Llanocetus* were about 4 inches (10 cm) apart. Mitchell (1989) suggests that flaps of gum tissue probably grew between the teeth to make filter-feeding more efficient. As later species evolved, the gum tissue replaced teeth as the primary filtering structure, eventually evolving into the baleen we see today.

Mysticete whales in the genus *Balaenoptera* (the blue whale and its relatives) all have a number of folds or grooves on the throat and chest. When cut in cross section, the ridge between each two grooves looks vaguely like a tube. Whalers named such whales "rorquals" from the Norwegian *ror*, tube, and *hval*, whale. The approximate maximum number of grooves in blue, finback, sei, and minke whales is, respectively, 88, 100, 56, and 70. In sei and minke whales the grooves do not extend far beyond the flippers, but in the other two species they reach the navel. The humpback whale has up to 25 wide grooves that extend to the navel, so it, too, is a rorqual whale, although its morphology is sufficiently different from those other species that it is classified as a separate genus. Rorqual whales usually feed by gulping single mouthfuls of water containing food. As water enters the mouth, the ventral grooves stretch, allowing the floor of the mouth to balloon outward so that the largest possible volume of water and food is trapped. The water is then squirted out through the baleen, leaving the food in the mouth and on the inner surfaces of the baleen. You can get a feeling for the process by taking a mouthful of breakfast cereal and milk, closing your jaws, and squeezing the milk through your teeth to concentrate the cereal. A baleen whale probably uses its large tongue to squeeze out water, assisted by contraction of the elastic ventral grooves.

Not all baleen whales are rorquals. The right whale and bowhead whale (family Balaenidae) and the pygmy right whale (family Neobalaenidae) do not have ventral grooves. They filter single mouthfuls of water on occasion but usually strain food continuously while swimming through shoals of small plankton, such as copepods or krill. Gray whales (family Eschrichtidae), usually feed by sucking amphipods and other bottom organisms from shallow, muddy sea floors and have only two ventral grooves.

Although some published evidence suggests the possibility that mysticete whales may produce sounds that could be used for echolocation, most researchers now doubt that those animals use echo-location to find food. Echoes of their sounds are probably useful for navigating under ice (bowhead whale) or ascertaining depth of the bottom. Sounds produced underwater (and occasionally above water) by various mysticetes probably help maintain communication between individuals during migration or other activities; synchronize feeding rushes during coordinated feeding; and communicate information about individual identity, gender, location, dominance, fitness, and receptiveness during courtship.

In both the American and Canadian portions of our study area, whales have been important to people since aboriginal times and the earliest days of European settlement. As early as the 1500s, Basque whalers sailed to the waters of Newfoundland looking for right whales, having hunted the species nearly to extinction along the European coast during the previous several hundred years. Over subsequent centuries, whales and porpoises occasionally supplemented the predominantly fish diet of coastal residents in eastern Canada. Whaling from shore stations took place at several locations in the Gulf of St. Lawrence during the 1800s. Large-scale hunting did not begin until 1947, when a fishery for minke whales opened at Dildo, Newfoundland, and began operations in Conception, Trinity, and Bonavista bays. This was joined by a fishery operating out of Blandford, Nova Scotia, which hunted minke whales from 1962 to 1964, then concentrated on finback and sei whales. Starting in 1951, the Dildo fishery also took pilot whales, and the catch of over 48,000 individuals during the subsequent decade caused the stock to decline sharply. All commercial whaling in Canada ceased in 1972. Coastal people still take meat from whales or porpoises caught accidentally in shore-fast nets or weirs, and a few dolphins and porpoises are still hunted locally.

Coastal American Indians, including Wampanoags in Nantucket, Pequot on Martha's Vineyard, Mashpee on Cape Cod, Passamaquoddy and Penobscot in Maine, and Micmacs in New Brunswick and Nova Scotia, hunted porpoises, dolphins, and whales using canoes and spears. They also made good use of any carcasses that washed ashore. English colonists who settled in Massachusetts quickly noticed the large number of whale spouts along that coast, promising them a good supply of meat and oil. Enlisting the aid of Indian harpooners, the settlers lost no time in starting to hunt right whales from shore stations around Cape Cod and adjoining waters, and they successfully pursued this fishery all along the American East Coast during the 1600s and

Humpback whale snout, showing outside edges of approximately 125 baleen plates.
MASON WEINRICH

Minke whale, head on. South Harpswell, Maine, 1980. Whale drowned after entanglement in lobster fishing gear. Stomach contained seven mackerel.
STEVEN KATONA

Blows of three finback whales. Blows are usually the first cue to a whale's presence.
STEVEN KATONA

Humpback whale lunge-feeding. Note water pouring from mouth and expanded floor of mouth. Mt. Desert Rock, Maine, July 1976.
BEN BAXTER

early 1700s. Porpoises and pilot whales were also hunted or driven ashore during those years. As a result of this early whaling, right whales became rare along the U.S. coast as early as 1750, and they remain so today. During the nineteenth century, coastal whaling for humpback and finback whales was carried out from New Brunswick ports in the Bay of Fundy and along the Maine coast from ports such as Winter Harbor, Prospect Harbor, and Tremont. An average of 6 to 7 whales, mostly finbacks, was taken annually from Prospect Harbor during 1835 to 1840, the peak whaling years in that area. Many pilot whales were driven ashore from Cape Cod Bay and Massachusetts Bay during the 1800s. Inshore in the Bay of Fundy, Micmac Indians hunted porpoises for their oil during the late 1800s and early into this century. Little hunting took place in the Gulf of Maine after 1900.

Since the International Whaling Commission's (IWC) indefinite moratorium on commercial hunting of whales took effect in 1986, no whales have been hunted commercially in the North Atlantic Ocean. A small take of whales still continues under IWC provisions for "scientific whaling" or "subsistence hunting." As of 1991, the only baleen whales that may be killed are up to 41 bowheads (54 struck) by Alaskan Eskimos; 169 gray whales by the U.S.S.R. for use by Siberian Eskimos; 90 minke whales and 10 finback whales for use by Greenland Eskimos; 3 humpbacks for subsistence use at Bequia Island, St. Vincent and the Grenadines; and 300 minke whales in the Southern Ocean for scientific purposes by Japan. Some smaller whales, dolphins, and porpoises are still hunted, but not in our study area. The IWC has not yet agreed to oversee fisheries that hunt small cetaceans, so they have no international protection.

Of more serious concern to cetacean populations in our area is the increasing frequency of entanglements or entrapments in fishery gear. This problem has been most urgent in Newfoundland, where shore-fast nets or gill nets set for cod, salmon, or capelin trap many whales and other species every year. During 1990, for example, scientists at Memorial University of Newfoundland documented entrapments of 75 humpbacks, 14 minke whales, 1 finback whale, 1 beluga, and 1 northern bottlenose whale. Loss of gear, fish, and fishing time are serious detriments to the fishermen, most of whom have no other source of income. Minke, humpback, and right whales, as well as other cetaceans, sometimes become trapped in herring weirs along the eastern Maine, New Brunswick, and Nova Scotia coasts, although most are freed. More significant here are gill nets, which entangle and drown many harbor porpoises, white-sided dolphins, and some minke, humpback, and right whales. Gill nets set at the surface, in midwater, or near the bottom threaten cetaceans, marine birds, and sea turtles worldwide. Lobster fishing gear also has entangled minke, finback, humpback, and right whales, as well as sea turtles. The rope ("pot warp") running from the traps to the marker buoys can catch in a whale's mouth or around the tail or flipper. The rope may cut the mouth or skin, and dragging the rope and trap through the water tires the animal. If several traps are ganged on one line, the whale will quickly tire and drown.

Fisheries can also adversely affect cetaceans by removing so much fish for human consumption that the nutrition of marine mammals is compromised. The only way to avoid such an occurrence in the future is to set aside adequate amounts of food for marine wildlife by explicitly including them in planning fishery quotas.

Other threats to the well-being of cetacean populations include increasing speed, size, and number of ships, with the attendant dangers of striking whales and causing noise or disturbance to the animals; offshore oil production and oil spills resulting from tanker casualties or other accidents; ocean pollution; and the preempting of important feeding or breeding areas by human activities. In most cases neither the magnitude of present effects nor of future threats is precisely known, but many scientists now think that these factors will grievously affect marine mammals, even in the absence of commercial hunting.

Such environmental threats may have caused severe damage to several species in our study area. At least 8 of the 25 right whales found dead in the North Atlantic Ocean between 1970 and 1989 died from collisions with ships (5) and entanglement in fishing gear (3) (Kraus, 1990). Since the entire population is probably no larger than about 350 individuals, mortality caused by human activities could slow or prevent population growth. Our smallest cetacean, the harbor porpoise, is also threatened by very high body concentrations of pesticides and heavy metals plus alarmingly high rates of entanglement in gill nets during recent years. Ingestion of plastic bags, discarded fishing gear, or other marine debris has killed whales, dolphins, marine turtles, and others. Perhaps most discouraging of all is the plight of beluga whales in the Gulf of St. Lawrence, whose population is being

Finback whale surfaces near whale watchers, showing white right lips. Scantums Ledge, Maine, October 21, 1981.
STEVEN KATONA

Humpback whale lobtailing. Stellwagen Bank, summer 1980.
DOTTE LARSEN

Humpback whales surfacing near whale watchers and showing typical dorsal fin shapes. Jeffreys Ledge, October 21, 1981.
PETER STEVICK

destroyed by chemical pollution originating in the Great Lakes. Some belugas have become so heavily contaminated that their pathetic, lesion-covered carcasses must be treated as hazardous waste.

These examples emphasize the interconnectedness of our own activities and the natural world. Marine mammals are feeling the brunt of expanding human populations and our increasing demands for food, raw materials, and manufactured goods. Rivers, winds, ocean currents, and animal migrations have spread our pesticides, insecticides, plasticizers, and other toxic products and by-products around the world. Belugas in Quebec die from chemicals produced in Ohio or New York. A ship carrying fuel oil or food or lumber kills a right whale. Harbor porpoises die in the gill net that catches codfish for our dinner or a fast-food fishburger. Can't we do a better job of sharing the planet with the plants and animals that were here first?

With these thoughts in mind, we prepared the first edition of this field guide in 1975. Nothing stimulates concern for a species or habitat more than firsthand experience, and there was little question that an afternoon in the company of a whale or a quiet period of observation at a seal ledge would foster a lifetime of enthusiasm for the animals and lasting concern for their welfare. Now, 17 years later, New England and eastern Canada are among the foremost areas for whale watching in the world. A combination of responsible self-restraint by boat owners and tour leaders and supervision by wardens entrusted with enforcing legislation to protect marine mammals and endangered species is necessary to keep us from excessive contact with the animals. We think that those efforts have been successful in our study area and that—for the most part—whale watching has benefited both whales and people. Particularly important has been the willingness of whale-watch boats to carry trained naturalists to educate passengers about the animals and their needs and to gather data and photographs essential to long-term research. A list of commercial whale-watching trips available in our study area is included in Appendix II.

For those people who own a boat suitable for whale watching, additional possibilities exist. Fishing banks are excellent places to spot whales or porpoises, especially when schools of fish are abundant. The southern Gulf of Maine, Stellwagen Bank, Old and New Scantums ledges, and Jeffreys Ledge are productive sites for observing humpback, finback, and minke whales and several species of porpoises. Whales appear near these banks earlier in the spring and later in the autumn than in the more northerly areas in the Gulf. From late June through early September, the waters around Matinicus Rock and nearby islands; Mt. Desert Rock and the Schoodic Ridges; outer Passamaquoddy Bay; Grand Manan Island and the Grand Manan Banks, New Brunswick; and Lurcher Shoal and Brier Island, Nova Scotia, are often excellent sites for whales. Right whales may be seen at those or other places in the lower Bay of Fundy during August and September. Although few yachtsmen will venture to Georges Bank or Browns Bank, the Northeast Peak of Georges and the seaward edges of both banks are good places to see whales. Extended commercial whale-watching trips or study-at-sea courses sometimes visit those waters. Our knowledge of good whale-watching areas along the eastern coast of Nova Scotia is still limited. Finback whales have been seen only a few miles offshore from Halifax during some winters. We have also received reports of memorable encounters with schools of pilot whales in several near-shore locations, although most of the whales along the Nova Scotia coast appear to swim farther offshore than in other portions of our study area. There, near the edge of the Scotian shelf, one can see finback, sei, and sperm whales, plus a variety of dolphins, during the warm months of the year. In addition, "the Gully," a deep canyon in the shelf edge about 30 miles east of Sable Island, is one of the few places where the northern bottlenose whale has been regularly spotted.

Areas farther north and east provide special opportunities. The north shore of the Gulf of St. Lawrence offers the chance to see all of the species mentioned above, plus occasional blue whales and belugas. Sites of particular interest include the confluence of the St. Lawrence and Saguenay rivers, the St. Lawrence Channel, Sept Iles, the Mingan Islands, and Blanc Sablon. Much of Newfoundland's coast offers excellent whale-watching potential, as detailed further in the section on shore lookouts, below. Finally, Newfoundland's Grand Bank is habitat for large numbers of whales during the summer, although it is beyond the reach of most readers. The Southeast Shoal of the Grand Bank is used heavily by humpback whales for feeding during early summer.

Having mentioned some of the possibilities open to boat owners, let us offer some cautions. We strongly urge people to patronize commercial whale-watching tours whenever possible, rather than taking private boats to the same areas. Minimizing the number of boats can only benefit the whales. Private expeditions to less-traveled waters do

GUIDELINES FOR WATCHING WHALES

Within American waters cetaceans are protected by the Marine Mammal Act of 1972, as amended. Within Canadian waters of our study area they receive similar protection from the Cetacean Protection Regulations of the Fisheries Act of Canada. Species designated as "endangered" or "threatened" are additionally protected by the U.S. Endangered Species Act of 1973, the Convention on International Trade in Endangered Species (CITES), and some state or provincial regulations. Guidelines published by the National Marine Fisheries Service for the Gulf of Maine and the Department of Fisheries and Oceans for the maritime provinces of Atlantic Canada are summarized below.

- Avoid excessive speed or sudden changes in speed or direction when whales are visible within 1,650 feet (500 meters).
- Aircraft must observe the FAA minimum-altitude regulation of 1,000 feet over U.S. waters and 450 m in Canada.
- Do not approach closer than 1,000 feet (300 m) to whales sleeping, resting, or feeding at the surface.
- When it is possible to get closer, parallel the course of moving whales or approach obliquely at reduced speed, avoiding sudden speed or direction changes. Avoid head-on approaches.
- Do not restrict a whale's normal movement or behavior, or take actions that evoke a reaction or result in physical contact with it.
- If more than one boat is present, boats should avoid herding or encircling the whales. Only one boat at a time should be within 300 m of the animal(s). Total time spent near any particular whale or group should be limited.
- Never actively approach closer than 100 meters (Canada) or 100 feet (U.S.). This also applies to swimmers or divers. Do not approach any individual this closely more than three times. No more than one boat should be this close to a whale or pod. Motors must be at neutral idle (or very low speed if necessary). Sailboat captains should turn on an echosounder or idle the motor (if present) to signal the boat's location to the whale. Keep clear of flukes.
- When leaving a whale, start slowly and wait until you are farther than 300 m before accelerating gradually.
- Even when you are not whale watching, be on the lookout to avoid collisions when in waters frequented by whales. If you cannot detour around a whale or pod of whales, slow down and wait until they are more than 1,000 feet (300 m) away before resuming speed.

Special Regulations

- *Beluga whales.* Do not move toward or drift toward belugas. When belugas are present, reduce speed to 5–9 knots and maintain constant reduced speed and direction until the animals are at a distance.
- *Right whales.* Massachusetts state law prohibits approaching closer than 500 meters to a right whale.

not appear to pose a problem at this time, provided boat handlers are reasonably considerate of the whales. For the safety of both the whales and the boat, it is important to maintain a respectful distance and to avoid any actions, such as gunning the motor, changing gears rapidly, chasing whales, intruding between a mother and her calf, or closely approaching sleeping, feeding, or courting whales. Your goal should be to observe the whales without causing any change in their natural behavior.

Over the years we have received many communications from boat owners asking whether they have any reason to fear the presence of whales. Several situations should be considered.

First is the chance of an accidental collision with a whale, such as striking a sleeping whale. Whales do not sleep in the same way we do, and they probably feed both day and night. At times, however, they rest motionless at the surface, breathing slowly and just barely visible. Boats can run into resting whales. Many examples are known of propeller-caused injury or mortality to right, humpback, and finback whales. Sailing vessels are especially likely to hit whales because they are quiet. But they also are slow, and a whale has a good chance of avoiding the boat if it detects it. Sailing vessels making offshore passage at night or during heavy fog face the small risk of hitting a whale, but the probability of such a collision is low, judging from the few reports.

Sometimes the whale's behavior may make it vulnerable to accidental collision. For example, during courtship right whales may be so intent on mating that they ignore the approach of a boat and do not take evasive action. Such behavior usually makes a great commotion at the surface, however, so the whales should be easily seen and avoided by skippers under good conditions. Some subsurface activities could be more problematic. In 1981, a boat was holed and sunk by a humpback whale not far off the coast of Portland, Maine. Newspaper accounts noted that the skipper reported seeing green bubbles before the collision, leaving little doubt that the boat had unintentionally been positioned right in the middle of the whale's "bubble cloud." Humpbacks often blow clouds or rings of bubbles to trap or herd schools of fish or krill, then rise open-mouthed through the center of the bubbles to eat the prey. At such times the whale probably cannot see a boat through all the fish and bubbles. Whales cannot be faulted for such a collision; it is up to skippers to avoid bubbly green water.

Whale watchers observing humpback whales flipper-slapping and rolling. Northwest Stellwagen Bank, September 3, 1982.

STEVEN KATONA

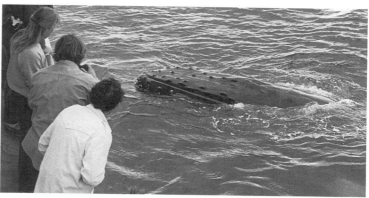

(Above) Whale watchers and humpback whale inspecting each other. (Left) Whale watchers get a close-up view of a humpback whale. Northwest Stellwagen Bank, September 3, 1982.

STEVEN KATONA

Second, humpback, finback, minke, and right whales occasionally approach boats or swim under the hull to investigate the vessel. Minke whales can tag along with sailboats or motor vessels for an hour or more. In some of these cases the sight of a whale's head on one side of the boat and its tail on the other may induce understandable fear in skipper and crew, but we have never heard of a case when an undisturbed whale approached and damaged a vessel in our study area. Our advice in this situation is to take a deep breath, relax, and enjoy the experience. The curious whale knows how to avoid your boat and will not harm it or you.

The third case involves reported attacks unprovoked by vessels. No such accounts are known for our study area. Whales have reportedly struck and sunk several small sailboats (see, for example, Dougal Robertson's *Survive the Savage Sea* or Steven Callahan's *Adrift*). Such interactions took place in remote waters. The identity of the offending whales is uncertain because the events took place quickly, sometimes at night, and skippers were usually not skilled in identifying whales. Perhaps the boats struck large floating objects such as logs. Killer whales have sometimes been blamed, but in regions where small boats commonly approach them, such as the Pacific Northwest, they have not behaved aggressively toward people.

The fourth case involves incidents that were in some way caused or provoked by the boat. There have been numerous occasions on which observers, researchers, or divers have deliberately approached whales too closely. Despite such intrusions, there are no accounts from our study area of a whale deliberately harming people or their boats, though sometimes the animals have given signals of annoyance or aggressive intention. The only instance of damage that we know of involved a small boat drifting quietly while research workers studied humpback whales. One of the whales breached and fell back onto the boat. Two people were thrown overboard, and lots of photographic equipment was lost. Luckily, nobody was hurt and the boat remained intact. The crew, all experienced whale watchers, thought that the animal simply didn't know the boat was there. The moral of that story is clear: small, silent boats should not linger near large, leaping whales.

The rise in popularity of sea kayaking or canoeing prompts an additional warning, illustrated by two incidents reported from the West Coast. In one case, a kayaker was overturned, but unharmed, by a gray whale off the coast of San Diego. In another episode, people in a small private skiff were watching gray whales in Black Warrior

Lagoon (Guerero Negro), Baja, California. A whale either jumped on or hit the skiff. One man was killed when hit with an oar and another suffered a fatal heart attack. This incident occurred in a place where commercial whale-watching boats do not go. Commercial trips have deployed skiffs to watch (and pet) gray whales since 1975 in San Ignatio Lagoon, without instances of aggression. Unless guided by experienced professionals, people in kayaks, canoes, or rowboats should not attempt to approach whales. Such boats can approach a whale so quietly as to startle it, and any turbulence from the whale's movement can tip a small craft.

Seen from a whale's perspective, the incidents described above can be explained either as accidents resulting from the boat's venturing so close that it risked accidental collision, or intruding so far into the whale's space that signals frequently used to mean "go away," such as breaching, tail slashing, flipper pounding, and raising and lowering of the head actually affected the boat by creating turbulence or physical contact.

Related to this class is a final group of incidents, in which sperm whales, gray whales, or others deliberately rammed and sank whaleboats or whaling ships after being harpooned. Such incidents, which are documented in whaling literature from the eighteenth and nineteenth centuries and in folklore of whale-hunting aboriginal peoples, are certainly understandable from a whale's point of view.

Considering all of these cases, we contend that a nearby whale presents less of a hazard to boaters than driving to the marina, rowing a dingy to and from the mooring, or falling overboard.

Some tips are in order for readers of this guide who have never been to sea or seen a whale, who don't know what to look for, and who may very well wonder why all the other people on the whale-watching boat have jumped to the rail when there is apparently nothing to see. In fact, the first trace of a whale is usually a very small, far-off, undramatic puff of a spout that seems almost illusory as it vanishes in the wind. Perhaps 15 seconds later it appears again, nearly a mile off. If you look closely in that direction, frustrated because you haven't seen it yet, you may just make out some specks in the sky. Those specks are seabirds, usually gannets, herring gulls, or terns, circling over the whales or porpoises, diving on the same fish school that the mammals are working. The birds may have drawn attention to the animals even before the spouts were seen. Experienced whale watchers look for such cues. Now that you know where to look, the next time the whale blows you will see your first spout. As the boat draws closer, you can make out a glistening black back and perhaps a dorsal fin. You will suddenly find yourself relieved, because you have seen a whale, and excited, because the boat is drawing up on the animal and the best is yet to come.

New whale watchers will find that only two things can spoil the fun—seasickness and cameras. Here are some ways to prevent or minimize seasickness. Eat a light breakfast, avoiding coffee, eggs, greasy food, and milk. Light tea and lightly buttered toast are a safe bet. Dress warmly so that you can stay above deck in the fresh air. Remember that it will be cold at sea, no matter how balmy the temperature onshore. Do not take a seasickness medication unless you have used that medication successfully before. Some pills or patches make certain people feel worse. If you take medication, do it several hours before departure; by the time you feel sick it is usually too late. Some people may want to explore alternative methods for control of seasickness. Wristbands and capsules of powdered ginger root or of vitamin B complex each have their proponents.

Stay away from cigarette smoke. Most smokers don't realize that their smoke will make others seasick. They also may not realize that many of us treasure the smell of clean sea air or the fishy odor of a whale's blow. Whale-watch boat owners should strictly limit smoking to the leeward stern quarter, if it is permitted onboard at all. This policy should be enforced by the boat's crew so as to minimize embarrassment among passengers.

Diesel exhaust can also induce seasickness. Boat captains try to pick a course that minimizes exhaust smells, but wind and sea do not always cooperate. Move if the smell bothers you.

Always eat a light lunch aboard the boat. Follow our simple rule: eat only foods that will taste as good coming up as going down. To be safe, avoid anything sour, acid, or hot-spicy. We stick with apples, saltine crackers, and mild cheese sandwiches. Thick pretzels and seltzer water can also help. If you do feel ill, either stand up in the fresh air and look at the horizon or, if necessary, lie down, preferably out of the way and above deck. Keep warm.

If you do "lose your lunch" you will probably feel better immediately. Don't be ashamed of seasickness, for it is a common malady that affects nearly everyone at some time, including the present authors. If you do throw up, drink water and eat an apple, saltines, or pretzels as soon as you feel you can hold it down.

The blow of a finback whale. Mt. Desert Rock, Maine, in background.
SCOTT KRAUS

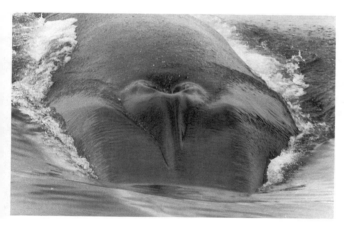

The leading edge of a whale's blowholes forms a splashguard to deflect water when the whale takes a breath. Finback whale, Mt. Desert Rock, Maine, July 20, 1988.
BEVERLY AGLER

Humpback whale, blowholes open. All baleen whales have a double blowhole.
STEVEN KATONA

Cameras may spoil your whale-watching fun if you worry about your equipment, whether you clicked the shutter too soon or too late, or whether your photos will turn out well. Nevertheless, since few people nowadays have the ability merely to experience the event without documenting it, and since photographs can be valuable for scientific purposes, the following comments should help. Telephoto lenses longer than about 300 mm for a 35-mm camera will require a combination of fast film speed, a chest mount or rifle mount, a steady hand, and a calm day. People intending to photograph cetaceans for individual identification should also consult Lien and Katona (1990). Check equipment and film before going to sea. Carry spares of the batteries required for your equipment. Use a plastic bag to keep spray and whale breath off your lens. Watch the whale for a while before you take photos. Learning the rhythm and timing of its behaviors allows you to anticipate its actions and obtain better photographs. Watch what other photographers do and learn from their successes and mistakes. If the far-off whale looks like a dot in your viewfinder, it will look like a dot in your photo. If you can't see the whale in the sun's glare, your camera can't either. Wait for better opportunities.

Sophisticated photographic equipment is now available. Newer video cameras are compact, reliable, and very useful for recording whale behavior. Auto-focus cameras have also been used successfully by some researchers, but others still prefer manual focus. Programmed exposure options in which you choose the aperture (f-stop) and the camera chooses shutter speed can cause blurred photographs unless you use high-speed film. Remember that the electronic circuits of automated cameras will be ruined by salt spray. Protect them carefully while at sea. Wipe and dry them when you return home.

Several whale-watch companies sell videocasettes showing species commonly seen in our study area and some of their more spectacular behaviors. Those and other films are listed at the end of the Bibliography.

Fortunately for those who dislike being on boats, it is sometimes possible to watch whales at selected places along our coasts. In the Gulf of Maine, observations can be made during spring and summer from the dunes on Cape Cod, especially near Wellfleet, Truro, or Provincetown, where dolphins and occasional whales can be sighted starting in April or May. During the summer, harbor porpoises can be seen from near the Bass Harbor Light and from the cliffs and headlands on Mt. Desert Island. July and August bring good chances for seeing harbor porpoises, minke whales, finback whales, and occasional right or humpback whales from vantage points in the Passamaquoddy Bay region. The cliffs at West Quoddy Head State Park, near Lubec, Maine, and Head Harbor Light or Liberty Point on Campobello Island, New Brunswick, have proven excellent places to observe harbor porpoises. The Swallowtail Light and cliffs at Northern Head and Southern Head on Grand Manan Island, New Brunswick, also offer excellent lookouts.

Across the Bay of Fundy, humpback and finback whales can be spotted from Brier Island at the tip of the Digby Neck in southwestern Nova Scotia. In Quebec, the lighthouse at Forillon National Park near the town of Gaspé and the cliffs near Les Escoumins and Tadoussac on the north shore of the Gulf of St. Lawrence yield views of finback, minke, and—from the latter two stations—occasionally blue whales. The Tadoussac site and the ferry dock at Rivière du Loup, directly across the St. Lawrence River, provide sightings of beluga whales during late summer. Finally, Newfoundland's steep and forbidding coast can be a whale-watcher's paradise, yielding sightings of humpback, finback, minke, and pilot whales, plus several species of dolphins. All of the large bays will contain whales during summer months if inshore populations of the capelin on which they feed are abundant. Shore lookouts are possible at Placentia Bay (from near Cape St. Mary's Lighthouse); at Cape Race; at Conception Bay (cliffs near Bay de Verde); at Trinity Bay (town of Trinity); at Cape Bonavista (town of Elliston); at Bonavista Bay (town of Salvage); and at Fogo Island. Other sites can be found along Newfoundland's extraordinary coast where cliffs overlook deep water.

Observers should keep in mind that not every trip to these places will yield sightings and that animals will usually be seen in the distance, visible perhaps only by their spouts. Binoculars or a 15× or 20× spotting telescope on a steady tripod will be useful.

The tall, powerful blow of a finback whale can rise 20 feet.
STEVEN KATONA

Finback whale approaches boat, showing white on right side of jaws. Mt. Desert Rock, Maine, July 20, 1988.
BEVERLY AGLER

Finback whale approaching boat, showing pale wash from right side of head rising to midline of back.
ALLIED WHALE

Species Accounts: Introduction

Our study area constitutes only a small part of the known range of most of the species described below. Many of the species have populations in other oceans that differ slightly from ours in appearance, size, reproductive rate, and even behavior. Whenever possible, the descriptions below feature information gathered from animals observed or sampled in our study area. We have noted instances where data from other locales have been used.

The twenty-two cetacean species described fall into four ecological groups, and it is largely these ecological differences between the species that account for their commonness or rarity in our study area.

GROUP I. Continental shelf, boreal. These species regularly occur on the continental shelf or near the coast in cool waters during at least part of the year, and are therefore frequently seen by whale watchers. They include finback, humpback, minke, and right whales; harbor porpoise, white-sided and white-beaked dolphins; killer whale and pilot whale.

GROUP II. Arctic or subarctic. The distribution of these species, although basically centered in very cold waters, extends south into our study area in specific places possessing favorable bottom topography, productivity, or other environmental factors. These species include the northern bottlenose whale, blue whale, and be-

27

luga. Strays of a fourth species, the narwhal, have been seen very rarely in Newfoundland. We have not included a species account for narwhals, but the bibliography will guide interested readers to further information about them.

GROUP III. Warm water, continental slope, or offshore. These species are common in the relatively warm, deep water at the edge of the continental shelf, over the continental slope, and farther offshore. They are seen inshore in our area only on rare occasions. These whales include the common, striped, bottlenose, and Risso's dolphins; sperm whale and pygmy sperm whale; and perhaps the sei whale. Whales from the first two groups may also winter in this habitat.

GROUP IV. Rare warm-water beaked whales. The Blainville's beaked whale, True's beaked whale, and Sowerby's beaked whale appear to be rare throughout their range, which is similar in extent to that described for Group III.

In the accounts that follow we discuss first the baleen whales, then the toothed whales. Within each group, the species are ordered by their apparent relative abundance within our study area. In most cases, each description of field marks begins with those characteristics visible at greatest distance. Features that are not visible at sea or not necessary for species identification are mentioned only briefly, if at all. Information on length, weight, age at sexual maturity, gestation time, interval between calves, and other vital parameters is given, where known. Some of those parameters may be expected to vary geographically or over time in relation to population size and food availability. Estimates of population abundance are also given, where available. Readers who have looked for whales at sea will appreciate the difficulties of preparing census estimates. Most estimates are only rough indications of abundance.

A key for identification of dead or stranded cetaceans is included after the species accounts.

WHALES AND PORPOISES FOUND FROM
CAPE COD TO NEWFOUNDLAND

Order
CETACEA

Suborder
MYSTICETI

Family
Balaenopteridae

finback whale
minke whale
humpback
whale
blue whale
sei whale

Family
Balaenidae

right
whale

Suborder
ODONTOCETI

Family
Phocoenidae

harbor
porpoise

Family
Delphinidae

pilot whale
white-sided
dolphin
white-beaked
dolphin
common dolphin
striped dolphin
bottlenose
dolphin
Risso's dolphin
killer whale

Family
Monodontidae

beluga
(narwhal)*

Family
Physeteridae

sperm whale
(pygmy
sperm
whale)

Family
Ziphiidae

northern bottle-
nose whale
(Blainville's beaked
whale)
(True's beaked
whale)
(Sowerby's beaked
whale)

*Note: Species in parentheses can be expected only as rare strays or strandings.

29

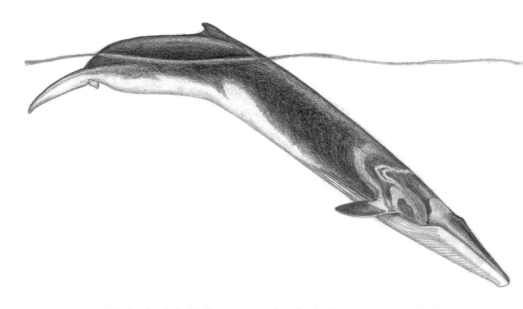

Finback whale (Balaenoptera physalus). *Size range: up to 85 feet.*
KIM ROBERTSON

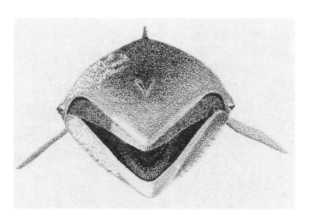

Finback whale, front view.
D. D. TYLER

Baleen Whales

FINBACK WHALE
(*Balaenoptera physalus*)

This sleek whale, second in size only to the blue whale, inhabits all oceans and is the most common large baleen whale throughout our study area. In many places it will probably be the first large whale encountered. It is often possible to judge a whale watcher's previous experience by his or her reaction to a finback. Quiet awe or an audible "Wow!" signify a novice. A blasé attitude, with sotto voce murmuring of impatience or disappointment, shows that the person has seen whales before and wants rarer or more acrobatic species. Finally, a person who remains quietly and carefully attentive is likely to be a seasoned whale watcher who realizes how little is known about the details of finback behavior, who wants to learn more firsthand, and who knows how interesting encounters with this species can be.

Finbacks are relatively easy to spot and identify at a distance because the robust spout, which rises up to 20 feet (6 m) on a windless day, and the prominent back and dorsal fin (up to 24 inches, or 60 cm) are easily seen. Finback whales often blow up to ten times at intervals of 15 to 20 seconds. Usually the whale performs a shallow dive after each breath, descending perhaps 30 or 40 feet, then surfacing a few hundred feet away for the next breath. A sequence of breaths terminates with a deeper, longer dive, often called a "terminal dive" or simply a "TD." Terminal dives of 5 to 8 minutes are most

31

*Finback whale splashes down after
lunge feeding in Frenchman Bay, Maine, July 1991.*
TOM FERNALD

common, but they can last for up to 10 minutes or more. The dorsal fin, whose shape and size varies, appears several seconds after each blow. You will know that a terminal dive is occurring when the finback hunches up its back so that the tailstock aft of the dorsal fin is exposed. When that happens you can say good-bye to the whale for 5 or 10 minutes. Start your stopwatch and time the dive. After several sequences you will be able to predict when the whale will next appear. Unlike humpback or right whales, finbacks usually do not fluke up when diving. The scientific name of this whale (L. *balaena*, whale, + Gr. *pteron*, fin, and Gr. *physa*, bellows) calls attention to the prominent dorsal fin and tall blow of the finback and its relatives.

Most people will require a closer look at the whale to confirm species identity. This may present a problem because finbacks cannot always be approached. They are often restless or "spooky." They seem to avoid noisy boats but sometimes swim near vessels idling or dead in the water. They can be watched when feeding at the surface or on occasions when they lie quietly on a calm summer day. Then the distinctive asymmetric coloration of the head can be seen. On the right side of the head the lower lip, upper lip (usually), and anterior third of the baleen are white or pale gray. The lips and baleen of the left side are all dark. The white color of the right lip continues aft as a broad, pale wash that sweeps up from the corner of the jaw to behind the blowhole. In most animals, two pale stripes called chevrons originate behind the blowhole and run aft, spreading to form a broad V along the back and upper side. The chevrons are best seen from above with good viewing conditions. The pale right lips, wash, and chevrons add fine and subtle variation to the otherwise dark back. Although the coloration of the right lip and baleen is uniform among individuals, the color, intensity, and overall appearance of the chevrons and white wash can vary considerably among different animals. The "North Atlantic Finback Whale Catalogue," maintained at College of the Atlantic, contains about 750 individuals identified by photographs of those features. If you get a close look at the sides of a finback in good light, you may see pale orange or yellowish patches that are probably caused by a film of single-celled algae of the class Bacillariophycae (diatoms). If the whale rolls, you may be able to see that the white of the belly extends farther up on the right side than on the left.

The asymmetric head and body pigmentation are unique to finback whales and may play a role in their feeding behavior. Finbacks

Finback whale, blowholes open. Note splashguard protecting blowhole, pale wash from right lips, and right chevron.
JANE M. GIBBS

Finback whale feeding, right side down, showing baleen and distended mouth. New Scantums Ledge, Maine, May 17, 1980.
STEVEN KATONA

Finback whales usually don't fluke up, but this one did, off Montauk, New York.
SAM SADOVE (OKEANOS PHOTO)

Finback whale at autopsy, showing white baleen in front third of right jaw. This is the only cetacean with this field mark. Brigantine Wildlife Refuge, New Jersey, April 15, 1975.
STEVEN KATONA

Finback mother and calf, showing white right lips and chevrons. Mt. Desert Rock, Maine, August 1975.
STEVEN KATONA

Finback whale lunge feeding. Note white baleen toward front of mouth. Frenchman Bay, Maine, July 1991.
TOM FERNALD

have a varied diet of fish, especially spawning and postspawning capelin, herring, and sand lance, supplemented by other resources such
as krill or copepods. They feed at depth or at the surface, depending
on where prey is located. Descriptions of feeding are possible for
shallow- or surface-feeding animals, but feeding methods at depth
remain a mystery. Observations at the surface indicate that a finback
frequently turns on its side when it opens its mouth. Many tend to
feed with the right side down. Side-swimming allows the whale to
turn sharply. Finbacks have also been seen circling around or through
a school of fish, often but not always in a clockwise direction. These
observations have led to speculation that the white color of the head's
right side, and perhaps the lower right flank, would startle fish and
herd them into a confined area to make feeding easier if the whale
swam in clockwise circles around its prey. It has also been suggested
that the uneven head coloration may camouflage the whale from the
fish it pursues. Both tactics could be used in different situations.

Along with the blue whale, the finback whale possesses the deepest voice on earth. The typical call is about 20 Hz (cycles per second).
The lowest note humans can hear is about 40 Hz. Loud single pulses
may call other finbacks up to 15 miles (25 km) away. Repeated 20-
Hz pulses about 8 to 12 seconds apart occur only in winter, apparently
as part of courtship or reproductive display. Slightly higher-frequency
sounds are also produced for communicating with nearby whales during feeding or diving.

Finbacks are found throughout the North Atlantic Ocean. In
our study area they are most common between New York and Labrador. This species made up 51 percent of the baleen whales sighted
during the University of Rhode Island's three-year Cetacean and Turtle Assessment Program (CETAP) survey along the continental shelf
of the U.S. East Coast* and 58 percent of all whales sighted during
surveys from 1966 to 1971 over the continental shelf from Labrador
to Cape Cod (Mitchell, 1974). Their population has the largest bio-

---

*Under the direction of Professor Howard E. Winn, intensive surveys from airplanes
and boats were carried out from November 1978 through January 1982 between Cape
Hatteras and the Canadian border and from the shoreline out to the 2,000-meter depth
contour. Surveys covered 229,000 nautical miles (424,000 km) of trackline and included
9,000 hours of observations in relatively calm waters. A total of 11,156 sightings including
170,012 cetaceans of 26 species was seen during the project. Population estimates prepared
by CETAP are usually not directly applicable to our study area, since many sightings were
made south of Cape Cod. Nevertheless, they are provided as a rough estimate of abundance
in our waters.

mass, food requirements, and impact on the ecosystem of any cetacean along the U.S. East Coast. A 50-foot (15 m) whale probably requires about 800,000 calories per day, close to 0.8 metric tons of food. At Georges Bank, where they were the most frequently seen baleen whale, finbacks made up 42 percent of the cetacean biomass and processed about 25 percent of all food eaten by whales, dolphins, or porpoises.

Finbacks prefer to feed on the continental shelf in waters 328 to 656 feet (100 to 200 meters) deep, but they also occur in shallower or deeper water. Some individuals apparently overwinter from Cape Ann to Cape Cod and around Georges Bank, but peak abundance in the Gulf of Maine is from about April through October. Winter occurrence is also reported for several Nova Scotian locations, including offshore from Halifax and in Chedabucto Bay. In the Gulf of St. Lawrence and in Newfoundland, finbacks are spotted from ice breakup in late March to freeze-up in November. Finbacks and humpbacks may frequent the same locations, but they usually remain separate, probably because finbacks are faster but cannot turn as sharply. The two occasions when we saw a finback and a humpback swimming side by side for nearly an hour near Brier Island, Nova Scotia, were exceptional. In Newfoundland, finbacks are usually found somewhat farther offshore than humpbacks. When the two species feed on the same prey schools, finbacks move faster and stay farther apart. When food is abundant, up to 40 finbacks can be seen in a small area, but feeding rushes usually include only one or a few animals.

Data from finbacks taken by Canadian whaling stations before 1972 indicated that finbacks probably became sexually mature when about 5 or 6 years old and 57 to 60 feet (17.4–18.3 m) long and that females usually bore one calf every third year. Small differences in those parameters occur geographically and over time. For example, using data from 4,570 fin whales taken off southeast Iceland from 1967 to 1989, Lockyer and Sigurjonnson (1991) calculated that females reached sexual maturity at 60 to 62 feet and ages 6 to 7 years (1967–73) or 8.5 to 10 years (1984–89). Corresponding data for males were 58 to 60 feet and 7 years (1967–73) to 11 years (1984–89). Changes in prey abundance or numbers of whales could produce the observed changes in age at sexual maturity. Thirteen photo-identified females seen in the Gulf of Maine with more than one calf had an average interval between calves of 2.7 years. A calf is about 20 feet (6 m) long when it is born between December and April after nearly a year of pregnancy. In U.S. waters, calves are most common from about Maryland to Jeffreys Ledge, Maine, but no specific area for calving has been discovered. The calf nurses for about 7 months before weaning, by which time it will be about 36 feet (11 m) long. Young whales may feed on planktonic crustaceans such as copepods before assuming the adult diet, in which fish predominate. Finbacks can attain a maximum length of 79 feet (24 m) in the Northern Hemisphere, though some individuals killed in the Antarctic were up to 85 feet (26 m) long. Finback whales are very long-lived; individuals over 90 years old were recorded in the Antarctic.

Approximately 35,000 finback whales may now inhabit the North Atlantic Ocean (*Rep. Int. Whal. Commn* 42:600, Table 1; Hain et al., 1992:663).[*]

The total population of finback whales in the North Atlantic before hunting took place has been estimated at between 30,000 and 50,000. In 1992, the International Whaling Commission gave an abundance estimate of about 10,800 finback whales in Nova Scotia, Newfoundland and Labrador, based on mark-recapture data. Kills of 3,117 (1903–15), 3,721 (1940–51), 3,250 (1945–51), and 2,092 (1964–71) were recorded from Newfoundland waters, where an annual sustainable yield of 400 whales was considered possible. A population size of 1,900 whales was estimated in 1976. An additional 1,466 finbacks were taken from Nova Scotian waters (1964–71), where the population was estimated to be 430 in 1976. It is not known whether the Newfoundland and Nova Scotia humpbacks are from the same stock. The Gulf of St. Lawrence finback population, estimated at 340 animals in 1974, was thought to be a separate subpopulation. The peak average census estimate calculated by CETAP for U.S. continental shelf waters north of Cape Hatteras was 5,423 (range 2,282–8,564), during spring; many of those animals were seen south of our study area. During recent photo-identification studies, whales from the Gulf of St. Lawrence (n = 156) were never seen in the Gulf of Maine (n = 550) and vice versa. This result agrees with the hypothesis that the finback population in the northwestern Atlantic is probably broken into three or four feeding stocks that seasonally migrate relatively

[*]Estimates of population abundance change as populations grow or shrink and as new information becomes available. Dates of estimates are included where appropriate. In most cases, estimates are a rough approximation of abundance. Confidence intervals associated with some estimates give a range within which the true population should be found 95 percent of the time.

Dorsal fins of four different finback whales photographed near Mt. Desert Rock, Maine. Nicks and scars on the dorsal fin or body help identify individual whales. (Top right) Finback photographed June 27, 1986, by Beverly Agler. (Top left) "Lunch," photographed August 5, 1986, by Beverly Agler. (Bottom right) "Trigger," photographed July 1, 1989, by Kim Robertson. Light lines are probably scars from entanglement in a rope. (Bottom left) "Grand Notch," photographed August 10, 1983, by Scott Marion.

small distances offshore-onshore and north-south with little overlap. With their great size and power, these whales could swim wherever they wish, but instead generally return to traditional areas for many years. The only evidence of very long-range movement between different stocks was a whale recovered in Iceland in 1988 nine years after it was tagged at Funk Island, Newfoundland.

Commercial hunting of finbacks in the western North Atlantic ceased in 1971. In accordance with the International Whaling Commission's unlimited moratorium, no commercial hunting of this species has taken place anywhere in the world since 1986. Nevertheless, some continued to be taken under IWC provisions for "scientific whaling," most recently 64 taken by Iceland in 1989. Furthermore, under IWC provisions for "subsistence hunting" a total of 120 (average 7 to 13 per year) have been taken from 1977 to 1989 by Danish catcher boats in western Greenland for use there by Eskimos. Nineteen (19) fin whales were caught in 1990.

Better estimates of population size and trends, more precise definition of stock structure, information on distribution during winter, and location of calving areas are needed to understand this species, which is the most important cetacean in our study area in terms of ecological energetics.

MINKE WHALE
(*Balaenoptera acutorostrata*)

The minke whale (pronounced "minky") is the smallest baleen in the study area. Its maximum length here is about 28 feet (8.5 m). Younger animals range upward from 15 feet (4.6 m), so a second look may be needed to make sure the whale is not a large dolphin. This species is seen fairly frequently but may be even more common than reports would indicate because minkes are difficult to spot: they usually swim alone, avoid boats, and do not often breach, show flukes, or make a visible spout. In general, most initial sightings of minke whales are happy accidents, when on a calm day the dorsal fin and back are seen out of the corner of the eye. Despite these generalities, minkes can surprise observers in several ways. Breaching has occasionally been reported in the Gulf of Maine and the Gulf of St. Lawrence and may be more common in some other parts of the species' range. The most unforgettable surprise for yachtsmen is the tendency of occasional

Minke whale (Balaenoptera acutorostrata). *Size range: 15–30 feet.*
HARRIET CORBETT

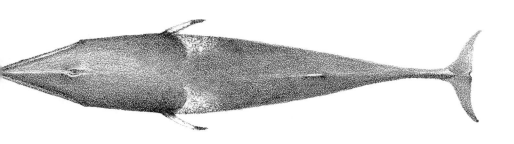

Minke whale, top view.
D. D. TYLER

individuals to approach stationary boats for a close look or to accompany a moving vessel, sometimes for many miles.

The distinctive morphological field mark—a broad white band running across each flipper—can be seen only under good conditions, but the following behaviors also identify a minke. The sharply pointed snout (the species name derives from L. *acutus*, sharp or pointed + *rostrum*, snout or bill) characteristically thrusts out of the water when the whale surfaces for air. A typical breathing pattern might be two or three breaths at intervals of about 30 seconds, followed by a terminal dive of 2 or 3 minutes. The respiration pattern of an individual will often be very regular for an hour or more as it quietly goes about its business, ignoring or avoiding observers. On several occasions we have seen minke whales vanish completely and mysteriously after a long observation period at close range in a calm sea. We understood how such escapes are accomplished after watching one minke whale hold its breath for 17 minutes while it was being freed from a small fish weir. A minke could easily swim out of sight in that time. The dorsal fin is prominent relative to the body size and is usually strongly curved or hook-shaped, with its pointed tip directed backward. The fin and back are dark gray or black, but in good light a broad, whitish, crescent-shaped wash can be seen running up each side of the whale from behind the flipper toward the back. The belly is porcelain white and may occasionally be seen through the water when a minke rolls over. The short (1 foot, 0.3 m), creamy-white baleen plates are usually visible only on stranded minkes.

The overall range of this species in the western North Atlantic Ocean is from the subtropics to northern Labrador. The population apparently winters from south of Bermuda through the West Indies and summers from Cape Cod north, but as no tagged individuals have been followed for very long, speculations about migrations are based on the distribution of sighting reports. Minke whales are common at least from April through November in the Gulf of Maine and from March through November in the Gulf of St. Lawrence. Some are said to travel past Nova Scotia in May. Sightings have been reported around Newfoundland in June or July and northern Labrador in August. Movements in Newfoundland are strongly related to the northward spread of spawning of capelin during summer months. Minke whales may remain in Labrador until sea ice forms in November or December.

Mating is thought to occur in winter or early spring but has never been observed. Males mature sexually when about 22 or 23 feet (6.7

The pointed snout of a minke whale is the first part to break water when the whale surfaces to breathe. Near Mt. Desert Island, Maine, September 1, 1990.
PETER STEVICK

Minke whale surfacing near boat. Note pointed snout.
DAHL M. DUFF

Minke whale off Provincetown, Massachusetts, April 18, 1976, showing dorsal fin and white flipper patch.
FRANK GARDNER

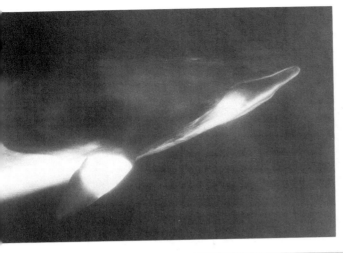

Minke whale just under the surface, showing pointed snout, white flipper patch, and pale wash extending from chest to midline of back. Near Mt. Desert Island, Maine, September 1, 1990.
PETER STEVICK

Minke whale dorsal fin. Cutler, Maine, August 1981.
STEVEN KATONA

Minke whale breaching in the Gulf of St. Lawrence, a lucky photo of behavior unusual for this species.
J. MICHAEL WILLIAMSON, MINGAN ISLANDS CETACEAN STUDY

Minke whale stranded at Plum Island, Massachusetts.
Note white baleen, white patch on flipper.
JANE M. GIBBS

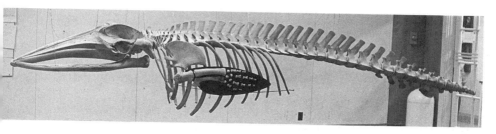

Skeleton of minke whale.
STEVEN KATONA

or 7 m) long. Females mature when about 24 feet (7.3 m) long and 4 years old, then bear a 9-foot (2.8 m) calf approximately every year, probably during October to March, after 10 to 11 months of pregnancy. Nursing lasts for less than 6 months. The maximum weight of a minke whale is about 11 tons (10 metric tons). A 21-foot (6.4 m) animal that we autopsied weighed 8,000 pounds (3,628 kg). Nearly all stranded individuals from the Gulf of Maine and farther south have been immature, whereas in more northerly habitats a higher percentage of mature specimens is found. Longevity is not known for minke whales in our study area, but the oldest individuals from the Southern Hemisphere appear to have been about 50 years of age.

Fish make up a larger proportion of the diet of minke whales than for any other baleen whale. Herring, capelin, cod, pollock, salmon, mackerel, and sand lance are eaten, along with some squid, krill, and even copepods. During summer, when schools of fish are inshore, minke whales can be found very near the coast in bays and shallow water. Data from the Newfoundland minke whale fishery suggest that juveniles and pregnant females come farther inshore than do adult males. Individuals sometimes become entangled in fishing gear, including gill nets, weirs, and line from lobster pots.

In 1969 researchers south of Newfoundland recorded sounds from a 1.8–2.1 foot (6–7 m) minke whale circling their ship at close range. During nearly three hours of observation approximately 200 clicks in 50 distinct series were recorded. Click repetition rate averaged 6.75 per second, and the sounds were in a narrow bandwidth between 4 and 7.5 kilohertz. The researchers (Beamish and Mitchell, 1973) concluded that the clicks might be suitable for echolocation. Those results have not yet been duplicated.

The minke is the most abundant baleen whale, with an estimated population of 760,000 in the Southern Hemisphere alone. Between 74,700 and 145,200 inhabit the North Atlantic from western Greenland eastward (*Rep. Int. Whal. Commn* 41:138). No estimate is available for eastern Canadian waters. CETAP survey data estimated 2,006 minke whales for continental shelf waters from Cape Hatteras to the Canadian border and out to the 3,280 foot (1,000 m) depth contour. Between 1955 and 1969, about 530 minke whales were caught in Newfoundland waters. Annual quotas of about 2,500 minke whales from the entire North Atlantic were in effect from 1978 through 1982, with most of the animals taken in the eastern North Atlantic by Norway or Iceland. Greenland Eskimos kill up to 115 per year. Proposals to take small numbers of minke whales under IWC provisions for scientific research have generated substantial controversy.

HUMPBACK WHALE
(*Megaptera novaeangliae*)

Acrobatic, vocal, often gregarious, and sometimes as curious about us as we are about them, humpbacks are a whale watcher's delight. Furthermore, it is the easiest baleen whale to identify in the field because it possesses and generously displays a set of field marks that are unmistakable. It is also the only whale named for a portion of our study area. Even though it is found in all oceans, the first specimen formally described scientifically was obtained along the Maine coast in 1846, hence the species name, *novaeangliae*, from the Latin for New England.

The first glimpse of a humpback might be the spout, which is about 10 feet (3 m) high and squatter and bushier than that of a finback. Breaching, lobtailing, spyhopping (poking the head out of the water), or waving the long white flippers may also be seen from a mile or more away under good conditions. At close range, the following features can be seen. The dark gray or black body, up to 60 feet (18 m) long, is somewhat stouter than that of the other rorqual whales. The head bears sensory knobs, each about the size of a tennis ball and containing one stout hair. These knobs, located along both the upper and lower jaws, may detect vibrations, water currents, or movements of nearby prey. The dorsal fin is shorter than the finback's, and its base is expanded as a thick, fleshy hump. The name *humpback* may refer to the shape of the fin or to the series of small bumps, actually the tops of the neural spines of the caudal vertebrae, which appear on the back, aft of the fin, in some individuals. Those bumps are usually concealed by blubber in well-nourished individuals, but may be more prominent early in the feeding season, perhaps in females whose blubber was drawn down by pregnancy and lactation. The dorsal fin is also more variably shaped than in other baleen whales and is often scarred or notched. Dorsal fins of males may be more heavily scarred as a result of skirmishes during courtship. The whale's genus name (L. *mega*, big, + *pteron*, fin or wing) refers to the enormous flippers, which are about one-third of the body length and may be used to maneuver, herd fish, guide calves, or pound the water for

Humpback whale
(Megaptera novaeangliae).
Size range: 30–60 feet.
JOHN R. QUINN

Humpback whale, full breach. Stellwagen Bank, summer 1985.
PETER STEVICK

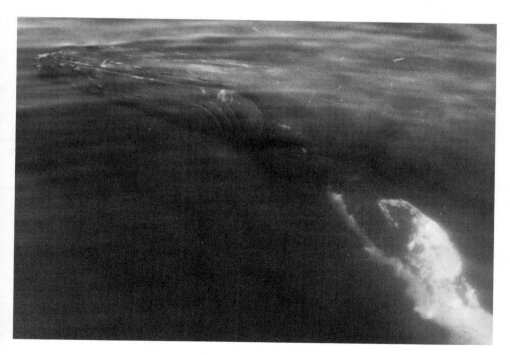

Humpback whale just under the surface.
STEVEN KATONA

signaling position, showing aggression, or stunning fish. The long flippers may also help to cool the whale, which might be necessary at times in the subtropical waters of the humpback's breeding range, where temperature is usually at least 85°F (28°C), or after vigorous exertion. In humpbacks from the North Atlantic, the flippers are usually white both dorsally and ventrally, but the dorsal surface of the flipper is dark in significant percentages of whales from other oceans. When the whale dives following a sequence of breaths, the flukes are often raised nearly vertically out of the water. Fluking up helps the humpback and other relatively fat, "stubby" species (right, bowhead, and gray whales) dive more easily. The trailing edges are always irregular, and their saw-toothed pattern of notches is slightly different in each whale. The flukes' pigmentation, probably influenced by inheritance from the parents, varies among individuals from all black to all white, with every grade in between. Superimposed on the basic pattern are scars from injuries acquired during fights with other individuals, attacks by killer whales or sharks, or attachment of parasites such as barnacles, parasitic copepods, lampreys, or others. Injuries to white skin cause black scars and vice versa. After the first year or so of life, patterns are generally constant and long-lasting, so individual whales can be recognized for many years from photographs of the fluke pigmentation and trailing edges. The shape and scar pattern of the dorsal fin are also distinctive and very useful in keeping track of individual whales in the field.

The "North Atlantic Humpback Whale Catalogue" maintained at College of the Atlantic contains photographs of more than 4,000 individual humpbacks submitted by research workers from many countries. That collection, as well as detailed photographic collections maintained for local populations by various research groups, provides excellent information on migrations, reproduction, individual life histories, and overall population abundance of this species.

Studies during the past 20 years have produced significant insights into the rich behavioral repertoire of humpback whales. The wonderful songs that first brought public attention to this species are produced only by males. All whales on a winter range sing the same song, though small differences between individuals may be heard. Whales in different oceans sing different songs. The song changes gradually during the winter months. Whales usually do not sing on the summer grounds, although grunts and whoops made during feeding and social interactions sound like song fragments. A few full songs

Humpback feeding open-mouthed at surface. Water can be seen moving through the baleen.
BOB BOWMAN

This humpback whale is closing its mouth after a feeding gulp to catch sand lance. Stellwagen Bank, August 1989.
SCOTT MARION (SEAFARERS EXPEDITIONS)

Humpback whales feeding at surface near whale watchers.
PETER STEVICK

may again be heard on the feeding range during late autumn and during migration south. When the whales arrive at the winter range, males once again share a common song, but it is different from that of the previous year. Somewhat like bird songs, these vocalizations identify the presence and location of adult males. They may attract females and offer a challenge to other males. Songs can last up to 30 minutes, each male singing nearly continuously, day and night, pausing only for breath or to interact with females or challengers. Other whales could possibly evaluate a male's physical condition, dominance status, or experience by some qualities of his song. The whales can probably hear each other for at least 10 miles (16 km) or more if the sea is quiet. Songs produced within a mile or so can be heard directly by a human swimmer, and within a hundred yards a whale's song can carry through the hull of a boat or through the air.

All humpbacks from the western North Atlantic breed and calve during January through March, principally in the warm, shallow water of Silver, Navidad, and (less commonly) Mouchoir banks, north of the Dominican Republic, and also around the Virgin Islands and along the northern coast of Puerto Rico. During courtship on the winter range, up to 8 or 10 males cluster around a female or female and calf, butting, ramming each other, or slashing with flukes or flippers while competing for the female. At such times humpbacks are not "gentle giants." Blows incurred during these scuffles leave sensory knobs raw and bleeding and scar the dorsal fins, backs, and flukes. Such competitions may continue off and on for days, with escorts (the male closest to the female) changing every few hours, until a female is ready to mate. No photograph or reliable account of copulation in this species has been published. This lack suggests that copulation is brief and perhaps occurs underwater.

Data gathered from years of photo-identification studies of humpback whales in the Gulf of Maine have revealed many details about the reproductive cycle. Females become sexually mature as early as 4 years of age, but usually at 5 or 6 years. Most females give birth every two or three years, but several females have borne calves annually. Pregnancy lasts for 11 to 12 months, and the calf, usually about 13 to 15 feet (3.75–4.5 m) long at birth, nurses for up to a year and grows about 1.5 feet (45 cm) per month. Protective of her calf, a mother will not abandon it, even in extreme danger. Early whale hunters took advantage of this behavior, first killing a calf, then killing the mother, who refused to leave the carcass.

After calving and mating, the whales migrate to feeding ranges at higher latitudes, separating into feeding herds in five areas: the Gulf of Maine–Scotian Shelf; the Gulf of St. Lawrence; Newfoundland-Labrador; southwestern Greenland; and Iceland–Denmark Strait. An individual whale returns to the same region every summer. Only rarely have individuals been observed to visit more than one feeding region. A possible explanation for these subdivisions of the population is that each whale follows the same migration route it learned as a calf, when it followed its mother north for the first time.

On the summer ground, humpback whales use an extraordinarily varied range of feeding methods to catch their prey, which consists mainly of sand lance, herring, capelin, or krill. The whale drives prey into a concentrated ball before engulfing it. The feeding method used on a particular occasion depends on prey type, depth and abundance of prey concentrations, and local conditions. Fish may be herded or stunned by lobtailing, flipper-slapping on the water surface, or flipper display underwater. When food is abundant near the surface, humpbacks often lunge partially out of the water, jaws agape, water and fish streaming out of the mouth. Individual whales have been observed to patrol local areas in a regular feeding pattern for a week or more at a time. When fish schools are concentrated in summer and autumn, one can see 10 or 20 humpbacks within a few hours at locations in the Gulf of Maine, such as Stellwagen Bank, off Cape Ann, on Jeffreys Ledge, or around Grand Manan Island, New Brunswick, or Brier Island, Nova Scotia. Similarly, a Newfoundland bay may sometimes host a hundred or more humpbacks, depending on capelin distribution, affording observers some truly spectacular whale watching. At such times, several whales may together work a school of fish at depth or at the surface, each animal benefiting from limiting the directions of escape for the prey. On the Alaskan summer range, small groups of individuals sometimes feed in a manner that appears to be cooperative, both for long portions of a single summer and during several summers. Group members maintain constant positions and use vocalizations to coordinate a feeding rush. The same individual leads each feeding rush. This behavior has not yet been noted in our study area.

Humpbacks are the only baleen whales known to blow bubbles during feeding. When bubble-feeding, a whale swims underneath or around a school of fish or krill while releasing a stream of bubbles. The rising bubbles form a temporary corral that retains or concentrates the prey as the whale swims vertically upward with its mouth open.

Humpback whale flukes up for a dive. Mt. Desert Rock, Maine, July 29, 1976.
STEVEN KATONA

A good look at the dorsal fin and bumpy back of a humpback whale.
PETER STEVICK

Right whale? Wrong! It's a humpback, whose bushy spout can resemble that of a right whale when seen from astern. Bermuda, April 1977.
BILL CONRAD (ORES)

Humpback whale snout, showing sensory knobs, each bearing a coarse hair. Jeffreys Ledge, summer 1981.
JANE M. GIBBS

Humpback whales, showing individually distinctive dorsal fins. Stellwagen Bank, 1981.
PORTER TURNBULL

Examples of pattern variation in humpback whale flukes.
STEVEN KATONA

When the bubbles come to the surface they are visible as a foamy patch of light greenish water about 20 feet (6 m) across, through which the whale will usually lunge. Boat operators should keep away from such bubble patches to avoid a surfacing whale.

Beginning in 1955, the International Whaling Commission officially protected humpback whales in the North Atlantic Ocean from commercial hunting. A subsistence fishery along the Greenland coast was allowed to take up to 10 per year for use by Eskimos, but finback whales or others were substituted during the 1980s. A subsistence fishery at Bequia Island, St. Vincent and the Grenadines, took up to 3 whales per year until 1987. None have been taken subsequently, although the 3-whale quota remains in effect.

The humpback is classified as "endangered" in U.S. waters and "vulnerable" in Canada. Since humpback whales are seen more easily from boats and airplanes than are other species, better population estimates are available for them than for other whales. Census studies carried out on the winter range during the early 1980s yielded estimates of between 2,000 and 4,000 animals for the total population of the western North Atlantic. Analysis of individual-identification photographs using capture-recapture methods provided an estimate of about 5,000 animals as of 1988. Capture-recapture population estimates for feeding aggregations in our study area are 300 to 400 humpbacks in the Gulf of Maine, approximately 200 in the Gulf of St. Lawrence, and about 2,000 to 2,500 in the Newfoundland-Labrador region. The CETAP census survey estimated peak average abundance during spring of 658 humpbacks (range 68 to 1,248) in U.S. shelf waters north of Cape Hatteras. Some of those animals could have been bound for Canadian waters, Greenland, or other locations. Adding the 5,000 North Atlantic humpbacks to recent estimates of 2,000 in the North Pacific Ocean and 5,000 for the entire Southern Hemisphere would give a world population of only 12,000.

During 1992 and 1993, scientists from the U.S., Canada, Iceland, Denmark, Norway, Puerto Rico, and the Dominican Republic are cooperating to study humpback whales using photographic and genetic sampling at all major North Atlantic feeding ranges and on the Caribbean breeding range. This project, YONAH (Years of the North Atlantic Humpback), will yield the best data on abundance, migrations, and population biology available for any baleen whale.

Right whale
(Eubalaena glacialis).
Size range: 20–50 feet.
JOHN R. QUINN

RIGHT WHALE
(*Eubalaena glacialis*)

Sighting a right whale is one of the most exciting events in whale watching, both because the species is so rare and because it is so different from the other whales in our study area. The genus name, "true whale" (Gr. *eu*, good + L. *balaena*, whale) signifies that it was the whale most familiar to people at the time it was named. It was one of the first species pursued by early hunters because it frequently came close to shore; swam slowly enough to be approached by sail or rowing; usually floated when killed, owing to the thick layer of blubber in well-fed individuals; and yielded many barrels of oil and very long pieces of baleen. Thus the "true whale" or "good whale" also came to be known as the "right" whale to catch. But many centuries of hunting, starting about A.D. 1000 along the coast of Spain, spreading across the ocean to Newfoundland by about A.D. 1500, and continuing along the coast of the American colonies during the seventeenth and eighteenth centuries, took its toll on the North Atlantic population. What had once been a common species along the coasts of western Europe and eastern North America became by the end of the eighteenth century the rarest baleen whale population in the world. Fewer than 350 remain in the western North Atlantic, and the eastern North Atlantic stock is near extinction. Other populations of right whales, also tragically depleted, are found along the coasts of South Africa (400–600 animals), Argentina (400–600), southwestern Australia (100–300), and the North Pacific Ocean (very rare).

This whale belongs to the family Balaenidae, which also includes the bowhead or Greenland right whale (*Balaena mysticetus*), found only in the Arctic Ocean. The pygmy right whale (*Caperea marginata*), found in boreal and temperate waters of the Southern Hemisphere, used to be included in this family but has recently been classified into its own family, Neobalaenidae.

The right whale's species name, L. *glacialis*, meaning "of the ice," is somewhat inappropriate because these animals rarely encounter ice. In the Atlantic, they feed in temperate or boreal waters as far north as Newfoundland, Iceland, and Norway during summer and breed in temperate or subtropical waters as far south as Florida and sub-Saharan Africa. The name *glacialis* would refer better to the bowhead whale, which lives in close association with the Arctic sea ice and has never been reported in North America farther south than Hudson Bay.

At a distance, the first clue to a right whale's identity is the low, bushy spout, which is V-shaped when seen from fore or aft, owing to the wide separation between the two blowholes. Right whales usually breathe from 5 to 10 times at intervals of 15 to 30 seconds before diving for 5 to 20 minutes. During the terminal dive, they often fluke

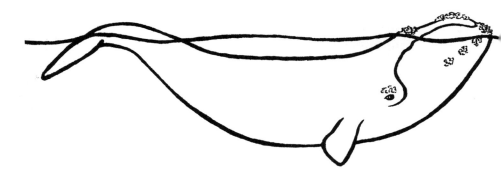

Right whale posturing at surface.
D. D. TYLER

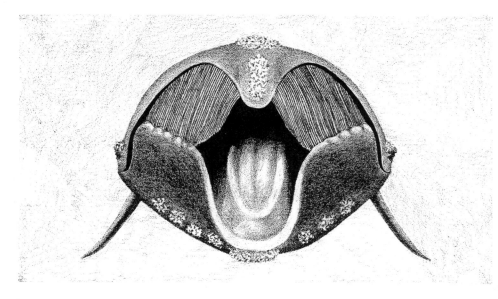

Filter feeding, front view.
D. D. TYLER

Heads of two right whales. These belly-to-belly whales may have been mating.
BOB BOWMAN

Enlarged view of callosities of right whale, showing cyamid amphipods ("whale lice").
STEVEN KATONA

V-shaped blow of approaching right whale. Mt. Desert Rock, Maine.
BOB BOWMAN

Right whale, showing closed blowholes, callosities, and broad, fat back. Offshore from Grand Manan Island, New Brunswick, August 19, 1981.
STEVEN KATONA

up. The flukes are very large, all black (except for occasional white scars), and have smooth margins, pointed tips, and a deep central cleft. If you are waiting for a whale to surface again and suspect that it could be a right whale, don't give up too soon. Wait for at least 20 minutes.

Closer up, the right whale's field marks are unmistakable. There is no dorsal fin, and the broad, fat back puts one in mind of a gargantuan hippopotamus. Right whales in our area range from about 30 feet (9 m) long for animals in their first summer to nearly 55 feet (17 m) for adults. Body color is dark, often mottled, with large patches of brown or light areas of sloughed skin. The huge head bears rough light-colored growths called "callosities" on the snout, around the blowholes, above the eyes, and along the lower jaws. The creamy or orange-pink color of the callosities is caused by infestations of several species of cyamid amphipods, commonly called whale lice. Callosity size, distribution, and number vary among individuals. Photographs of the head have been used to distinguish individuals over periods of more than 20 years here and in the Southern Hemisphere.

Although right whales have been reported from the Gulf of St. Lawrence or Newfoundland during recent years, the place to see them is in the Gulf of Maine or off Nova Scotia. They often swim in Cape Cod Bay, Massachusetts Bay, on Stellwagen Bank, on Scantum's or Jeffreys Ledge, and off Cape Ann during February to early May. In July through September they can be found in deep water offshore from Grand Manan Island and in the Roseway Basin, near Brown's Bank. In October and November they can again be seen in ones or twos on Jeffreys Ledge or off Cape Ann. The CETAP aerial surveys made numerous sightings of right whales on and inside of Georges Bank.

The Gulf of Maine is used by right whales both for feeding and courtship. More than any other whale in our area, this species feeds primarily on small planktonic crustaceans, especially the copepod *Calanus finmarchicus* and probably some krill. The copepods *Pseudocalanus elongatus* and *Centropages* spp. and larvae of barnacles are also important foods at times. Individuals select, by unknown means, areas of high plankton concentration, such as along windrows or slicks caused by tides. Whales strain food from the water continuously while slowly swimming open-mouthed through dense patches of plankton. Feeding in this manner is often called "skimming," whether it occurs at the surface or, as appears to be more frequent in the Bay of Fundy, at depth. Right whales sometimes surface with muddy snouts, indicating that they fed very near or on the bottom at depths to 892 feet (272 m).

A whale weighing 50 tons (45.5 metric tons) or more could subsist on copepods only if it had a large filtering apparatus because it takes about 4,000 of them to fill a teaspoon. The massive head with its long, arched jaw contains on each side up to 390 plates of finely fringed, dark gray baleen, increasing in length to about 7 feet (2.1 m) long posteriorly. Baleen plates near the tip of the snout are very short, leaving an opening through which water enters the mouth continuously if the whale opens its mouth while swimming. The opening is about 11 square feet (1 m²) in a 50-foot (15 m) whale, so during every yard of forward movement the copepods contained in about one cubic yard of water deposit on the fringes of the baleen plates. A right whale opens its mouth only when plankton is sufficiently abundant (usually more than 4,000 organisms per m³) to make filter-feeding worthwhile. The mouth remains closed during normal swimming. A feeding right whale swims in a convoluted path, turning frequently to stay in the patch of thick plankton. Nonfeeding whales swim in straighter lines.

Courtship behavior has been seen during August and September in water 525 to 656 feet (160 to 200 meters) deep, most frequently in the Grand Manan Basin, Lower Bay of Fundy, and in or near Roseway Basin on the Scotian Shelf. Pairs of animals sometimes lie quietly together for hours at a time, occasionally touching each other with the head or flipper. More often, pairs, trios, or larger groups of up to 30 whales roll or splash energetically, at which time males with erect penises can be seen. The mating system of right whales is fundamentally different from that of humpbacks. Right whale males do not fight to keep others away from the female. Instead, they devote energy to reproduction itself. The female apparently resists males by turning upside down with her belly and genital opening above water. If a male gets in the right position, his 11-foot-long penis may be able to arch over her for copulation. He will also try to mate when the female rolls over to breathe. A male's testes, which can weigh over a ton—almost as much as a small car—produce huge quantities of sperm. A female probably chooses certain males for mating, but in the scramble many may mate with her. Probably the male who can first deliver most sperm deepest into the female will father her calf. Thus right whale males compete with genitalia and sperm, whereas

Right whale mother and calf in herring weir. Grand Manan Island, New Brunswick, August 2, 1976.
SYDNEY RATHBUN MCKAY

Right whale breaching. Lower Bay of Fundy, summer 1982.
GREG STONE

Flukes of a right whale. Bay of Fundy, August 17, 1983.
SCOTT KRAUS (NEW ENGLAND AQUARIUM)

humpback males, whose sexual parts are much smaller, compete by fighting for exclusive mating with a female.

From December through March, right whales are scarce in the Gulf of Maine, but sightings are reported from the coasts of Florida, Georgia, and the Carolinas and very rarely from Bermuda, the Caribbean, and the Gulf of Mexico. Most animals observed off Florida and Georgia are mothers with new calves. Calves measure about 13 feet (4 m) long at birth, which occurs from about October through winter, after about 1 year of gestation. Some births may occur during the southward migration. Calves will follow their mothers north starting in about March or April and will continue to nurse until about 1 year old. A female calf will become sexually mature at age 7 to 10 years, after which time it will bear a calf every 3 or 4 years. Males and nonpregnant females apparently do not migrate to Florida and Georgia, but their winter range is not known.

Probably only 250 to 350 right whales remain alive in the western North Atlantic Ocean. The highest single count, 70, was obtained on April 13, 1970, in Cape Cod Bay by scientists from the Woods Hole Oceanographic Institution. The "North Atlantic Right Whale Catalogue," maintained at the New England Aquarium, now contains 286 identified individuals, and except for new calves, nearly every whale photographed in New England or Canadian waters has been seen previously. Since right whales have been fully protected from hunting since 1937 by international treaties, one must wonder why the population is still so small. It may be that only a dozen or two whales survived hunting and that the population is growing as quickly as its slow reproductive rate allows. Study of the cause of death of 25 right whale carcasses found between 1970 and 1989, however, indicates that collisions with ships and entanglement in fishery gear are together responsible for at least one-third of those deaths. Over 50 percent of right whales bear scars on their bodies from entanglement with nets or ropes. Since only about a dozen new calves are observed each year in the whole population, human-caused deaths could be slowing or even preventing the recovery of this population.

Two individuals photographed in different years off the coast of Iceland proved to be already known from U.S. waters. Exciting as those findings are, they suggest that right whales in the entire western North Atlantic might comprise only one population. If the few hundred animals remaining in our study area were to disappear, there may be no others to take their places.

BLUE WHALE
(*Balaenoptera musculus*)

Perhaps more than any single animal, the blue whale stimulated the resurgence of public interest in ecology that led to Earthday 1970 and the Save the Whales movement. *The Blue Whale*, by George Small, published in 1967, suggested that only about 300 blue whales remained alive, so few that males and females would not be able to find each other to mate. The thought of the sad, lonely calls of those giants spreading through the ocean, but finding none of their own kind in the great emptiness, was a powerful image that galvanized all of us to action. Fortunately, however, blue whales had the good sense not to distribute themselves randomly throughout the ocean and stayed together feeding and having babies in places where they can be seen today.

At a distance, a blue whale would look like a very big finback whale, showing a very tall, powerful, straight spout of up to 20 feet (6 m) or more in still air, a very long back, and a small dorsal fin. Observers familiar with the appearance of finback whales would notice the following differences: the spout is taller and straighter; since the whale is so long (adults to 85 feet [26 m] or more in our area) and the dorsal fin is situated so far aft, much more time elapses (up to 3 or 4 seconds) between the spout and the appearance of the dorsal fin; the dorsal fin, less than 1 foot (25 cm) high, is smaller, both absolutely and relative to the huge body; and the flukes often clear the water briefly as the whale dives. Drawing closer, suspicions aroused, one would need to note the following characteristics. The blue-gray color of the sides is mottled with irregular light spots, sometimes to the extent that the entire animal appears light gray. The overall impression is of an animal much lighter in color than a finback. Close up you can see that the blowholes are shielded by a conspicuously raised splashguard that continues forward as a rostral ridge. The rostral ridge is noticeably shorter than in the finback, and the rostrum itself is broader and more rounded. Also in contrast to the finback, both sides of the head are equally dark, and chevrons are less conspicuous or absent entirely.

If the animal you spotted really was a blue whale, you would undoubtedly be impressed by its size, for this is the largest animal

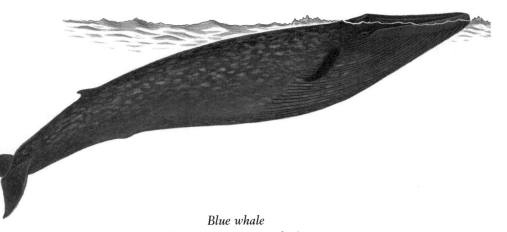

Blue whale
(Balaenoptera musculus).
Size range: 25–100 feet.
JOHN R. QUINN

alive today and almost certainly the largest that ever lived. The longest measured specimen was a female from the Antarctic 106 feet (32.3 m) long, which is supposed to have weighed over 150 tons (136 metric tons), but bigger individuals may have existed. For comparison, that female was about as long as three school buses and weighed nearly fourteen times as much as the biggest elephant on record. As is true in all baleen whale species, Northern Hemisphere individuals are somewhat smaller than those from the Southern Hemisphere. Adults grow to about 85 feet (26 m) in Newfoundland waters, averaging about 70 feet (21 meters). There can be little doubt that Linnaeus was making a pun when he gave the blue whale its Latin name, *musculus*, because it can be translated in two ways—muscular, or little mouse.

The distribution of blue whales in summer is determined largely by the abundance of krill, their exclusive food. Krill concentrations dense enough to support a blue whale are found where deep water rich in nutrients upwells to the surface, nourishing heavy blooms of phytoplankton and a productive planktonic food chain. The outflow of the mighty St. Lawrence River, which equals the total flow of all other rivers on the East Coast of North America, provides nutrients and also helps to create upwelling along the north shore of the Gulf of St. Lawrence as deep water replaces the outflowing surface layer. Here and in other productive spots, a medium-sized blue whale weighing 100 tons (91 metric tons) would eat up to 4 tons (3.6 metric tons) of krill each day during the feeding season, gulp-feeding, then straining water out through the 3-foot (91 cm) dark, coarse-bristled baleen. Scientists at the Mingan Islands Cetacean Study in the Gulf of St. Lawrence have observed blue whales feeding on their sides, ventral grooves ballooned out to enclose tremendous mouthfuls of 50 to 70 tons of water plus krill.

Measurements of animals killed in the Southern Hemisphere indicate that baby blue whales measure from 23 to 27 feet (7 to 8.2 m) long and weigh 3 to 4 tons (2.7 to 3.6 metric tons). They gain up to 200 pounds (90 kg) each day during nursing, which lasts about 7 or 8 months. At weaning the young whale will be about 50 feet (15 m) long and weigh 25 tons (23 metric tons). Scars on the ovaries show that females give birth about every 2 to 3 years, starting as early as age 5. Gestation lasts approximately 1 year. Photo-identification studies of blue whales in the Gulf of St. Lawrence are beginning to provide information on reproduction in our region. Potential longevity is prob-

Blue whale, showing huge size, mottling, and small dorsal fin. Differences in pattern of mottling and in dorsal fin shape are used to identify individuals. Mingan Islands, Gulf of St. Lawrence.
RICHARD SEARS (MINGAN ISLANDS CETACEAN STUDY)

Blue whale, showing distinctive dorsal fin shape and typical skin mottling. Mingan Islands, Gulf of St. Lawrence.
RICHARD SEARS (MINGAN ISLANDS CETACEAN STUDY)

Blue whale, showing rounded rostrum with short rostral ridge, large rostral splashguard, and mottling on back. Gulf of St. Lawrence, 1981.
RICHARD SEARS (MINGAN ISLANDS CETACEAN STUDY)

Blue whale flukes, showing some scars that can be used for individual identification. Mingan Islands, Gulf of St. Lawrence.
RICHARD SEARS (MINGAN ISLANDS CETACEAN STUDY)

ably comparable to a human lifetime, but few data are available. No information is available on the winter range of western North Atlantic blue whales, but it is thought that they migrate offshore and perhaps south to warmer oceanic waters. Mating and calving probably take place on the winter range.

Fortunately, earlier fears that blue whales might already be doomed to immediate extinction by excessive commercial hunting were premature. The latest estimates suggest that at least a thousand or more individuals still inhabit each of the major oceans. Whether or not this number is correct, it is important to remember that more blue whales were killed in the 1930–31 Antarctic whaling season alone than now remain in the entire world ocean. It is a great tragedy that this species has been so severely reduced from a prewhaling population of perhaps 300,000 individuals. The hunting of blue whales has been prohibited in all regions since 1967 by the International Whaling Commission. After nearly a quarter-century of protection it is worrisome that blue whales are hardly ever seen now in the Antarctic. The total Southern Hemisphere population is estimated at 10,000 to 12,000 blue whales. By contrast, sighting reports have become more frequent in the Northern Hemisphere during the last 10 years, partly because people are looking harder. The total Northern Hemisphere population is estimated to be 3,000. It is still too early to predict whether blue whales can escape a slow decline leading to extinction during coming centuries.

An important source of natural mortality for blue whales in our study area is entrapment in pack ice along the southwestern coast of Newfoundland during late winter. Up to 10 have been killed in years when sudden shifts in wind or currents jam the ice against the coast, trapping the whales.

No single estimate exists for the number of blue whales in the western North Atlantic Ocean. Between 1898 and 1915, Newfoundland and Quebec whalers killed a total of about 1,500 blue whales, mainly during June and July, off the south and west coasts of Newfoundland and in the northern Gulf of St. Lawrence. Rough estimates of the prewhaling population based largely on those data range from 1,100 to 1,500. More than 200 individual blue whales have been photo-identified in the Gulf of St. Lawrence during the years 1983–90. Blue whales are rare in U.S. shelf waters north of Cape Hatteras and out to 656 feet (200 meters). Extensive aerial surveys throughout that region during 1979–81 by CETAP sighted only 2 individuals,

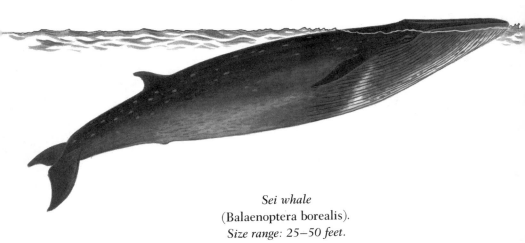

Sei whale
(Balaenoptera borealis).
Size range: 25–50 feet.
JOHN R. QUINN

both southeast of Nova Scotia. Only 3 blue whales have been reported from the Gulf of Maine.

SEI WHALE
(Balaenoptera borealis)

Sei (pronounced "say") whales are found throughout the world ocean. Here in the western North Atlantic they range from Davis Strait to Venezuela and the Gulf of Mexico. They are seen much less frequently and predictably than the other baleen whales of our area. Few amateur whale watchers have seen and identified this species, and probably only experienced whale hunters could at a distance reliably discriminate the shorter, less dense blow of a sei whale from that of a finback whale or separate the two species by profiles or behavior. Anyone else would be well cautioned to get a good close look and make certain of the following characteristics before crying "Sei!"

The sei is smaller than the finback, rarely exceeding 50 feet (15 m) long. Its head is uniformly dark on both sides, in contrast to the asymmetric coloration of the finback's head. The body is dark above, lighter below. In Antarctic and Pacific sei whales, the dark skin of the sides is dotted with many light oblong spots, each about 4 inches (10 cm) long by 1 inch (2.5 cm wide), perhaps caused by a parasitic copepod or by lampreys. In comparison, finback flanks are rarely spotted, and the light mottling of the skin of a blue whale does not usually have the spotted appearance attributed to sei whales. Sei whales in the Atlantic Ocean appear to be uniformly darker in color than finbacks.

Whalers used to identify sei whales mainly by their swimming behavior. These whales usually swim faster and change direction more erratically than other rorqual whales. Sei whales observed from the air when three other species of baleen whales were also present swam in that same way while searching for food or feeding. A sei whale may show its snout when it surfaces, but it usually reveals little of itself above water and does not arch its back when diving. The dorsal fin appears simultaneously with the blow and is usually relatively taller, thinner, and more deeply hooked than in the finback. One should be cautious in identifying balaenopterid whales by dorsal fin alone, however, because some overlap in fin shape occurs between

Sei whale on cutting deck at Blandford, Nova Scotia, September 1970. Note that right side of head is dark, as is the baleen, and that the flank is not noticeably spotted.

EVERETT BOUTILIER

Sei whale at surface.
Note that right side of jaws and head are dark.
PETER STEVICK

Dorsal fin of sei whale seen off
Ocean City, Maryland. Fin shape alone should
not be used to identify rorqual whales.
PEGGY EDDS

species. We made a mistake in the third edition, wrongly identifying the dorsal fins of two sei whales shown below as finback whales. Sei whales have been individually identified by slight differences in fin shape and scarring. A catalog of sei whales containing 29 individuals was assembled by workers at the Cetacean Research Unit (CRU), Gloucester, Massachusetts, during summer 1986 when the species was unusually common in the Gulf of Maine.

Unlike other balaenopterid whales, sei whales often skim feed as right whales do, continuously filtering small planktonic crustaceans such as copepods (*Calanus* spp.) and several species of krill. The black baleen has a fine silky fringe of white bristles that allow the whale to filter those small animals. Over 75 percent of the sei whales killed off Nova Scotia in summer had copepods in their stomachs. Krill was also an important food. Sei whales have been observed swimming slowly just below the surface, with mouths slightly open, presumably skimming plankton, covering several hundred feet between breaths, but not selecting the richest plankton patches as right whales do. CRU workers observed that feeding whales often swam with the right side down, the whale having rotated between 45° and 90° along its axis. The 1986 invasion of sei whales into the southern Gulf of Maine correlated with a decline in sand lance abundance and consequent release of copepods that the fish would otherwise have eaten. When the whales are skimming plankton, breathing is slow and regular, a single breath following one or two minutes of feeding. A sei whale spouting in this manner might be harder to notice than a whale that spouts several times in succession. A sei whale can also make longer dives for food, followed by multiple breaths. The existence of ventral grooves suggests that gulp-feeding must occur frequently. Two sudden feeding lunges were seen in the southern Gulf of Maine when the whales were probably feeding on krill. Stomachs of whales killed in Newfoundland contained capelin and krill, which are hard to catch by skimming, but no copepods.

Postmortem examination of about 400 sei whales caught by the Blandford, Nova Scotia, whaling station from 1967 to 1970 showed that sei whales mate in January and February after they have attained lengths of 40 to 45 feet (12 to 14 m). Pregnancy lasts 10 to 12 months, and females may bear a calf every 2 or 3 years. The 15-foot (4.5 m) calf nurses for about 7 months, growing nearly 1 inch (2.5 cm) in length per day. The potential longevity of a sei whale may be roughly 70 years.

Recent population estimates include 13,000 for the North Pacific Ocean in 1974; 24,000 for the whole Southern Hemisphere in 1979; and 50,000 for both regions combined in 1985. No estimate has been made for the whole North Atlantic population.

Relatively little is known about the number of sei whales in our study area. CETAP scientists described the species as common and a regular component of the cetacean fauna of the northerly waters of the continental shelf of the eastern United States, but only 67 sightings representing 204 individuals were noted in three years of intensive surveys. Sei whales were the second most numerous baleen whale seen at Georges Bank, however, constituting 12 percent of the cetacean biomass in summer and consuming about 10 percent of the food eaten by cetaceans annually. The species is somewhat more common off Nova Scotia and farther east. Most sightings were in late spring to summer on the edge of the continental shelf southeast of Georges Bank. In 1980, CETAP personnel saw 40 sei whales feeding near finback whales and humpback whales along the continental shelf break at Hydrographer's Canyon, slightly south of our study area. Overall peak average abundance for the CETAP study area was 280 ± 313 during spring. If the figures are corrected to account for submerged individuals, approximately 2,273 animals were estimated to be present, many south of our area. Canadian census data obtained in 1969 suggested that at least 965 whales inhabited Newfoundland-Labrador waters. Capture-recapture analysis on tagged whales indicated that between 1,393 and 2,248 inhabited Nova Scotian waters between 1966 and 1972. A minimum estimate of 870 in Nova Scotia and 2,078 in the entire northwestern Atlantic was calculated from shipboard census surveys. Whales in U.S. waters probably belong to the Nova Scotian population, which may be separate from the Newfoundland-Labrador herd.

Much of the difficulty in locating or counting sei whales may result from unknown factors in the ecology of the species. In northern European waters the seasonal appearance of sei whales has frequently been described as unpredictable. It is from descriptions in those waters that the whale takes its species name (L. *borealis*, northern) and its common name. *Seje* is the Norwegian name for pollock, and sei whales tended to appear off the Norwegian coast at the time when pollock were first caught, but the number of whales seen in different years varied widely. Peak catches off Nova Scotia occurred in June to July and late August to September, suggesting that many whales moved

*Dorsal fin of sei whale.
Note large white scar aft of
dorsal fin.*
PETER STEVICK

*Sei whales showing
variation in dorsal fins
between individuals. These
two whales were mistakenly
identified as finback whales
in the third edition of this
book. Mt. Desert Rock,
Maine, summer 1979.*
BOB BOWMAN

Dorsal fin of sei whale.
PETER STEVICK

past in early summer, then returned in late summer. Sei whales were taken off northeastern Newfoundland and Labrador only in August and September. If the factors governing sei whale habitat choice and migration were properly understood, one might have a better idea of where and when to look for these animals.

Harbor porpoise
(Phocoena phocoena).
Size range: 4–6 feet.
JOHN R. QUINN

Toothed Whales

HARBOR PORPOISE
(Phocoena phocoena)

This little porpoise is found from Cape Hatteras to Greenland, but is most abundant in the Gulf of Maine and off Nova Scotia, where it is the most commonly seen cetacean. It is moderately common in the Gulf of St. Lawrence but less frequently seen in Newfoundland. Populations of harbor porpoises also inhabit cool waters in Europe and along the West Coast of the United States. This is one of the smallest cetaceans, usually reaching only 5 feet (1.5 m) and about 140 pounds (64 kg). Its small size and undemonstrative nature make it difficult to observe in any kind of sea, although on a calm day from April through October, anyone sailing along our coast and keeping a sharp lookout will have a good chance of seeing this species.

Observers must rely on relatively few characteristics for identification. Most easily seen and most definitive is the triangular dorsal fin with its sloped, slightly curved trailing edge, unlike the fin of any other small cetacean in the study area. A wash of pale gray can be seen running up the flanks forward of the dorsal fin, gradually blending into the dark gray of the rest of the body. The absence of an external beak can be noted during fast swimming when harbor porpoises tend to breast the surface. Under most conditions, harbor porpoises ignore or avoid boats under way, but they sometimes approach a stopped boat. The best way to observe harbor porpoises is

Harbor porpoise near Mt. Desert Island, Maine, summer 1978. Note blunt head without beak, and light patch on side.
SCOTT KRAUS

Triangular dorsal fin of harbor porpoise.
STEVEN KATONA

Harbor porpoise stranded at Mt. Desert Rock, Maine, September 8, 1987.
BEVERLY AGLER

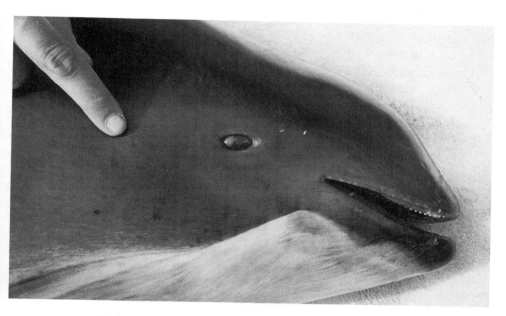

Harbor porpoise head. Finger indicates external ear opening.
STEVEN KATONA

Harbor porpoise head, showing the flattened teeth characteristic of family Phocoenidae.
STEVEN KATONA

to drift among them in a small boat on an absolutely calm, sunny day. The porpoises will sometimes come close to the boat, and as they swim around and under it you will clearly see the field marks discussed above, some of the more subtle individual markings, and also the powerful up-and-down beat of the flukes. When the sea is calm, harbor porpoises may bask motionless at the surface.

During early spring in Gulf of Maine waters, harbor porpoises appear individually or in small, loose groups, but from August through September larger groups of 20 or more are sometimes observed. Aggregations of up to 100 or 200 (in one case 800!) are seen in the Gulf of St. Lawrence from May to November. No one knows where harbor porpoises migrate in winter, but most individuals desert inshore waters. Harbor porpoise populations in the Gulf of Maine, Gulf of St. Lawrence, Newfoundland-Labrador and western Greenland probably remain separate throughout the year and do not interbreed. Evidence from strandings and sightings at sea indicates that many Gulf of Maine porpoises migrate south in winter, sometimes as far as North Carolina or northern Florida, but a few can be seen in Maine during winter, even when the water is 32°F (0°C).

Harbor porpoises do not make a visible spout, but the soft puffing sound of exhalation can be heard for perhaps a hundred yards on a quiet day, giving the animal its local name, "puffer" or "puffing pig." The term *porpoise* derives from the Latin *porcus*, pig, plus *piscus*, fish. The specific name simply comes from the Greek *phokaina*, meaning porpoise. A harbor porpoise typically breathes three to four times, then dives for several minutes.

As might be guessed from their small size and short dive times, harbor porpoises are nearly always found in relatively shallow water on the continental shelf. Even when far from shore, they will usually be on shoal banks, such as Georges Bank. In summer, they often approach shore, sometimes swimming into harbors or tidal rivers in pursuit of herring. Maine fishermen used to call them herring hogs. Mackerel, capelin, hake, cod, pollock, and whiting are also important foods. Squid and some bottom-living invertebrates are occasionally taken. Calves also eat krill. Each harbor porpoise will eat about 35 to 40 times its body weight each year.

Because harbor porpoises come close to shore and specimens have been obtained from accidental entanglements in fishery gear and transported to laboratories for careful dissection, scientists have been able to learn much about their physiology, anatomy, and ecology. Young

Harbor porpoise swimming near surface. Great Cranberry Island, Maine, July 17, 1986.
BEVERLY AGLER

Harbor porpoise swimming near surface. Great Cranberry Island, Maine, August 1986.
BEVERLY AGLER

are born from April through July, after nearly 11 months of pregnancy. Most births occur in mid-May in the Bay of Fundy. A calf is about 3 feet 4 inches (1 m) long at birth. Sexual maturity is reached at ages 3.15 to 6 years (average 3.76 years in the Bay of Fundy). Females probably bear a calf annually, starting several years after they become mature. This is one of the shortest-lived of all cetaceans, with few animals living longer than 10 years and a maximum longevity of about 13 years. Thus a female may give birth to only three or four calves during her lifetime. Despite their undemonstrative nature in the wild, a few harbor porpoises have been trained at aquariums in the United States and Europe, but most individuals do poorly in captivity.

Unfortunately, the very accessibility that provided such understanding may now endanger populations of harbor porpoises throughout their range. The increasing number of gill nets set in the Gulf of Maine and other waters to catch cod, haddock, and other species have entangled and drowned hundreds of porpoises each year. Most porpoises appear to become entangled in nets set on the bottom. Fishermen did not report those deaths, perhaps because of the animals' small size and apparent insignificance, but also because they feared prosecution for taking marine mammals in violation of the Marine Mammal Protection Act. Scientists and fishery managers first realized the apparent seriousness of the situation in the late 1980s, by which time some populations of harbor porpoises were probably already threatened.

New census surveys conducted by NMFS in the summer of 1991 gave a preliminary estimate of 45,000 to 66,000 harbor porpoises in the Gulf of Maine and Bay of Fundy (Smith et al., 1991), substantially more than previously believed. However, research also indicated that more porpoises were killed annually in fisheries gear than had been previously suspected, at least 1,250 per year. Consequently, NMFS has proposed listing this species as "threatened" in U.S. waters. This little porpoise is designated as "threatened" in Canadian waters, where there could be 11,900 to 28,800 in the Gulf of St. Lawrence and 34,415 to 57,360 in Newfoundland-Labrador (Gaskin, 1992a).

The inshore habitat of the harbor porpoise increases its vulnerability to environmental pollution. During the late 1960s tissues of harbor porpoises in the Bay of Fundy were found to contain the highest concentrations of mercury and DDT ever measured in any wild animal. The effect of these and other pollutants on the porpoises was not known, but it is not likely that they helped the animals. Although the concentrations of these particular contaminants appear to have declined somewhat, others, including organochlorines such as PCBs, are of increasing concern.

PILOT WHALE
(*Globicephala melaena*)

Although they can reach about 20 feet (6 m) in length and a weight of 3 tons (2.7 metric tons), pilot whales average about 13 feet (4 m) and 1,800 pounds (816 kg). Their normal distribution at sea is usually determined by the location of schools of squid, but they also eat cod, mackerel, and other fish. During most of the year, pilot whales swim in the warm waters at the edge of the continental shelf, where water depths quickly descend from about 656 feet (200 meters) to the ocean floor and where squid are abundant. The most common squid in our study area, *Ilex illecebrosus*, migrates over the shelf toward inshore waters during summer and early autumn, feeding on herring, mackerel, and capelin. Large schools of pilot whales follow the squid into Newfoundland waters and, to a somewhat lesser degree, into the Gulf of St. Lawrence, the Scotian Shelf, and the Gulf of Maine. During each year a pilot whale will eat between 15 and 18 times its body weight in squid, and the 50 tons (45 metric tons) or so that a big male annually requires might include nearly 250,000 squid.

Pilot whales are relatively easy to identify. They are entirely jet black (hence their species name, *melaena*, from Gr. *melas*, black, and their local name, blackfish), except for a light-colored, anchor-shaped patch on the chest, which is only rarely visible at sea. Unmistakable in shape, the dorsal fin is large, very long at the base, strongly curved, and rounded at the tip. Fin shape is sexually dimorphic (males develop longer-based, blunter-tipped fins with thickened leading edges), as is body size (body length of males averages about 20 percent longer than for females). The head is bulbous, owing to the large rounded melon, giving the whale its common name "pothead" and its species name (L. *globus*, ball, + Gr. *kephale*, head). In large animals the melon protrudes beyond the snout. Pilot whales can be seen singly or in schools of up to several hundred or more, but the average school size is between about 20 and 80. Lobtailing, spyhopping, and basking at

Pilot whale
(Globicephala melaena).
Size range: 10–20 feet.
JOHN R. QUINN

the surface are frequently seen behaviors, but bowriding and breaching are not common. Pilot whales have been seen together with bottlenose dolphins (*Tursiops truncatus*) offshore and with right whales near Browns Bank and near Mt. Desert Rock. White-sided dolphins (*Lagenorhynchus acutus*) school with them on occasion in Newfoundland. Reasons for these associations are not yet known.

This species is known from both sides of the North Atlantic Ocean, and a nearly identical form exists in the South Atlantic Ocean. In the western North Atlantic it ranges from North Carolina to Greenland. Another very closely related species, the short-finned pilot whale (*G. machrorhynchus*), extends from about New York south. The two species are indistinguishable at sea, but the rather diffuse boundary is far enough south of our study area that animals seen north of Cape Cod are almost certainly *G. melaena*.

Tragically, in some locations people have nearly as good a chance of seeing this species on land as at sea. In Cape Cod Bay, for example, pilot whales often approach close to shore during November or December, perhaps following schools of mackerel. All too frequently, a school becomes trapped in the shoal waters of a salt marsh or on a beach. In times past, these animals would either have died unnoticed or, if found, been cut up for meat and oil. Nowadays, researchers and conservation workers from Boston to Provincetown stand ready to assist the animals while the public follows the events through newspaper and television coverage. Similar mass strandings have occurred in Maine, Nova Scotia, Prince Edward Island, and Newfoundland.

These sad events raise a frequently asked question, Why do whales strand? Two types of strandings may be distinguished: occasions when a single individual comes ashore, and instances when many animals strand. Single individuals found on a beach are usually very young, very old, sick, or injured or killed by accidents such as collision with a ship or asphyxiation or drowning following entanglement in a net or rope. Animals involved in mass strandings usually appear to be generally healthy and in the prime of life, although all species that strand en masse share the characteristic that they live in herds (often called pods) that are usually segregated by age, sex, or reproductive condition and are bound by strong social ties. Such species, which include pilot whales, sperm whales, false killer whales, and white-sided dolphins, are the most frequent victims of mass strandings. Such species may normally approach coastlines during part of their seasonal movements, whereas other strongly social animals, such as common dolphins, probably do not. The approach to land may reflect a tendency of the animals to hunt food along sharp topographic boundaries, such as steep-sided channels.

Many other factors appear to be involved in a mass stranding. In some locations, such as along the gently sloping sandy shores of Cape Cod, the animals have some difficulty navigating because their sonar clicks may not echo strongly. Infestations of roundworms (nematodes) in the ears and sinuses could also interfere with echolocation. The situation may at times be exacerbated by extraordinary tidal amplitude in some locations; storms that produce rough, turbid, noisy water; or inattention to depth or bottom topography during frenzied feeding on dense schools of prey. Some or possibly all cetaceans may be able to use the earth's magnetic field for navigation, and it has been hypothesized that strandings occur more frequently at locations where local geological features cause strong changes (anomalies) in the magnetic field.

The overwhelming factor in mass strandings, however, appears to be social behavior. Pods appear to be led by one or a few animals that are larger, older, or perhaps more experienced than the others. The group will follow its leaders even if they become lost or disoriented.

Pilot whales, like all odontocetes, have a rich repertoire of species-specific vocalizations that identify individuals and communicate their location and state of excitement and probably give information on their behavior. Included in that vocabulary are sounds for communicating distress. If a school member emits distress calls, other members of the school will stand by it. If, for example, the initial distress calls sounded when an individual grounded on a beach or sandbar, and the tide was ebbing, all individuals standing by would probably also ground. Thus behavior that would be very helpful at sea, when, for example, group members could protect a sick or wounded individual from a shark or could support it at the surface to breathe until it regained strength, would in this instance endanger the entire school. This behavior is probably responsible for the tragic determination of school members to come ashore time and again, to the puzzlement and dismay of people trying to rescue them. As is the case with most cetacean mass strandings, once pilot whales beach themselves, efforts to return them immediately to the water merely result in the animals' coming ashore again. The primary technique

*This pilot whale was unexpectedly taken by rod and reel from
a sport fishing boat out of Round Pond, Maine, on August 28, 1966.*
EVERETT BOUTILIER

*Some of the approximately forty pilot whales that swam into the harbor at
Castine, Maine, on July 29, 1981. The whales were successfully driven out.*
ARTHUR B. LAYTON, JR.

Pilot whales offshore from Mt. Desert Island, Maine, September 9, 1982.
SCOTT MARION

Pilot whales coming ashore in mass stranding at Wellfleet, Massachusetts, autumn 1982.
THERESA FRARE

now used for stranded animals is to hold them for as long as possible (perhaps 6 or 8 hours) in shallow water, stabilizing and supporting them upright until they regain strength and physiological equilibrium. This resembles the way the animals would care for each other. It is also possible that under some circumstances the most effective way to prevent mass death when a school begins to strand might be to isolate or shoot beached animals immediately so that they do not draw other school members ashore with their distress cries.

There are undoubtedly other factors involved in mass strandings. These events bring suffering and pain to the animals and to the humans who attempt to help them. It is some consolation that the events at least teach us much about the whales and the way they use the sea. Whales that die are carefully measured and analyzed to determine age and see whether chemical contaminants, viruses, or other parasites or pathogens could have contributed to the stranding. It may be possible one day to prevent strandings by deploying sound reflectors or perhaps broadcasting sounds locally to herd the animals to safety.

Some animals have been tagged with visible markers or radio transmitters before release so that they could be tracked at sea or identified if they stranded again. Three pilot whales from a school that stranded near Wellfleet, Massachusetts, in winter 1986 were cared for at the New England Aquarium in association with researchers from Oregon State University. They were equipped with radio tags (one satellite-tracked) and released in June 1987 100 km east of Cape Cod. During 95 days of monitoring, the whales traveled about 4,720 miles (7,600 km), averaging 50 miles (80 km) per day and 2 miles (3.3 km) per hour. The tags monitored 187,000 dives, ranging from 6 seconds to 9 minutes long. During the night, the whales dove deeper, probably to catch short-fin squid that were migrating toward the surface. During the day they may have fed on mackerel or other fishes near the surface. The whales slept or rested quietly at the surface every 4 to 7 days.

The same social characteristics that contribute to mass strandings were traditionally manipulated by humans to herd the animals and hunt them for meat and oil. The standard method was to surround a school near shore with several boats, then drive the animals toward the coast by making noise and commotion. The whales clustered closer and closer until no escape was possible. This technique is still used in some places, such as the Faroes Islands in the eastern North

Atlantic, and was probably also employed by the aboriginal inhabitants of our coasts. Hunting in the Gulf of Maine took place mainly in Massachusetts, where pilot whales occur more abundantly and regularly than elsewhere. Thousands were driven ashore on Cape Cod from the 1700s to the 1920s. For example, a herd of 2,300 was killed in 1874, a year in which at least 3,000 animals were caught. Hunting also took place in Canada. More than 47,000 potheads were taken from 1951 to 1961 in Newfoundland waters, probably lowering the population markedly from an estimated prewhaling abundance of 50,000 or 60,000 animals. No recent population estimates have been prepared for Canadian waters. The peak average abundance in the CETAP study area was 12,391 (± 18,625), in autumn. Pilot whales were the most important toothed whale by weight seen at Georges Bank. Approximately 4,000 whales represented about 16 percent of cetacean biomass in summer and consumed about 16 percent of all food eaten annually by cetaceans.

Examination of pilot whales taken during hunting or at mass strandings has provided good information on their reproductive cycle. Females mature sexually at about age 6 and males at age 12 or 13. Apparent courtship and copulation were observed in mid-August 1981 in Trinity Bay. A male would rush at a female and put his head on her back, behind the dorsal fin, perhaps at times holding the fin in his teeth. The male then arched his body around the female so that his head was near her flipper, perhaps at times holding on to it with his teeth. Carcasses examined in Newfoundland indicated that pregnancy lasts about 16 months, and the calf, 5.5 feet (1.7 m) long at birth, nurses for about 20 months. A female can probably give birth to 5 or 6 calves during her lifetime. The maximum life span has been estimated to be approximately 25 years.

WHITE-SIDED DOLPHIN
(*Lagenorhynchus acutus*)

This lovely, energetic dolphin is common throughout our study area, although not usually seen close to shore. It ranges in size from about 6.5 to 9 feet (1.9 to 2.8 m), which is close enough to the size of other local dolphin species to make identification by size impossible. It is always necessary to get a good look at the color pattern on a dolphin's sides to identify it. The field marks are distinctive enough on the

White-sided dolphin
(Lagenorhynchus acutus).
Size range: 7–9 feet.
HARRIET CORBETT

dolphins in our area so that observers will have no difficulty in separating the species.

The distinguishing mark in this species is the sharply defined,
narrow white patch on the side, which begins below the dorsal fin
and runs aft. Several feet back, the white patch terminates abruptly,
to be continued by an equally sharply defined patch of yellow or tan.
The yellow patch runs up toward, but not over, the dorsal ridge of
the tail. The short beak, back, and dorsal fin and flippers are black;
the flanks are light gray and the belly white. The species name comes
from the Latin *acutus*, sharp, and refers to the sharply pointed dorsal
fin.

Found only in the North Atlantic Ocean, this species is most
common in the western North Atlantic, where it ranges from about
Cape Cod (with some stragglers to Chesapeake Bay) to Davis Strait
and Greenland. Many can be seen from spring through autumn in
waters surrounding Cape Cod and in summer and early autumn
throughout the rest of the Gulf of Maine, lower Bay of Fundy, Gulf
of St. Lawrence, and Canadian Maritimes. Most sightings occur in
waters with temperature below 12°C; the mean temperature for sightings in U.S. waters was 7°C.

The white-sided dolphin is quite social, and although it may
sometimes be seen singly or in small groups, schools of 50 are often
seen and schools up to 500 are fairly common. Since the animals can
probably hear one another over distances of a mile or more, scattered
individuals or groups may be part of one loose school, joining and
splitting for social reasons or to feed more efficiently.

The only part of our study area where the abundance of this species
has been studied is in U.S. waters north of Cape Hatteras, where
in the CETAP surveys the total number of animals seen during three
years (31,276) was greater than for any other species. White-sides
made up 13 percent of the odontocetes observed. They were also by
far the most numerous and trophically important odontocete seen at
Georges Bank, consuming 16 percent of food eaten by cetaceans,
though constituting only 7 percent of cetacean biomass during summer.

This species has not always been so abundant in the Gulf of
Maine. Until about 1975, the white-sided dolphin was rarely seen,
and instead its close relative the white-beaked dolphin (*L. albirostris*)
was common. The change may be explained by a substantial rise in
abundance of sand lance during the same period. That could have

Two white-sided dolphins breaching in the lower Bay of Fundy, July 1991.
STEVEN KATONA

White-sided dolphin. Mt. Desert Rock, Maine, August 1981.
ANN RIVERS

White-sided dolphin, close-up of head,
showing pointed teeth. Cuts around mouth
were caused by entanglement in a gill net.
STEVEN KATONA

been advantageous to white-sides, which are mainly fish eaters. Stomachs of specimens inspected during summer and early autumn in the Gulf of Maine have contained herring, silver hake, smelt, and short-finned squid. White-beaked dolphins, which eat more squid, may not have benefited as much from the increase in sand lance.

Despite their preference for waters at least 165 feet (50 meters) deep, schools of white-sided dolphins sometimes become stranded. Although these are sad occasions for dolphins and humans alike, they have provided most of the details available on the species. The most comprehensive data came from analysis of 57 dolphins that stranded in Cobscook Bay, Maine, in September 1974. The dolphins were part of a large school that had perhaps followed thick schools of herring up a channel toward a shallow salt marsh. When the 20-foot tide ebbed, the dolphins grounded in the mud. The largest adult male was 8.75 feet (2.67 m) long, 514 pounds (233 kg), and 22 years old. The largest female was 7.75 feet (2.36 m) long, 400 pounds (181 kg), and about 13 years old. Many of the females had recently given birth or contained fetuses that were nearly full term. The life cycle inferred from that study includes breeding from May to August by males older than 4 to 6 years and longer than 7.5 feet (2.3 m) with females older than 5 to 8 years; 11 months of gestation; birth of calves (length 3.4–4.25 feet, or 1.0–1.3 m) in June and July; and nursing for up to 18 months. Females give birth about every 2.5 years. White-sides have also mass stranded at Cape Cod, Prince Edward Island, the Gaspé Peninsula, Gulf of St. Lawrence, and Newfoundland.

Observations of white-sided dolphins at sea have not yielded as much data as have those tragic mass strandings, but they have stimulated several extremely interesting behavioral questions.

On two occasions in different years observers near Mt. Desert Rock have seen a harbor porpoise calf swimming with white-sided dolphins, raising the question of whether interspecies adoption had occurred. Off Brier Island, Nova Scotia, we watched humpback whales feed on herring that these dolphins had herded into large balls about 10 feet (3 meters) in diameter and so thick that we were able to scoop up 15 fish in one dip of a 5-gallon bucket. We wondered why the dolphins needed to accumulate so much more food than they could themselves eat and whether the dolphins and whales might have been cooperating in some way. On other occasions these dolphins have been seen swimming in formation near the head or tail of a whale, apparently playing or riding the whale's pressure wave.

White-sided dolphins swimming near Mt. Desert Rock, Maine.
BOB BOWMAN

White-sided dolphins, mother and calf.
BOB BOWMAN

White-sided dolphin breaching near Mt. Desert Rock, Maine, August 1980.
BOB BOWMAN

White-sided dolphins. Mt. Desert Rock, Maine, September 16, 1989.
BOB BOWMAN

Regardless of data gathered or questions raised, it is a memorable experience to drift quietly while these spirited dolphins breach or lobtail, see them dash about pursuing fish, or watch them effortlessly ride the bow wave of your boat. Adding to the excitement, when white-sides are seen, humpback or finback whales are often nearby.

WHITE-BEAKED DOLPHIN
(*Lagenorhynchus albirostris*)

Whale watchers would be better served if this animal were named the white-*backed* dolphin because the salient field mark is the white patch on the side starting just below and behind the dorsal fin and continuing aft onto the light saddle covering the animal's back. At sea the two blend together into one large field of white. Another white patch can be seen on the flank forward of the dorsal fin. Light patches above the flippers and forward of the blowhole may also be visible. The upper portions of the rest of the animal are black, and the belly is white. The white of the belly continues forward onto the short beak in nearly all of these dolphins, but a few individuals in the western North Atlantic are said to have dark snouts. Nevertheless, the scientific name (Gr. *lagenos*, bottle, + *rhynchus*, nose; L. *albus*, white, + *rostrum*, snout) translates as "white-snouted bottlenose," which is reasonably close to the common name. The white beak can be seen at sea, although it is much less visible than the white back. This dolphin grows to a maximum length of about 10 feet (3 m).

White-beaked dolphins are somewhat less playful than their relatives, white-sided dolphins, but they can still put on a good show of breaching and lobtailing. Some Newfoundland fishermen call these dolphins "jumpers." A loose group of about 20 white-beaks three miles east of Cape Ann, Massachusetts, on May 16, 1982, showed frequent acrobatics and featured several individuals that continually jumped clear of the water, smacking the surface with their flukes upon reentry while moving in a general circular pattern. We suspected that fluke-smacking was used to herd fish to the middle of the circle.

This species is found only in the North Atlantic Ocean, and it may be more common in European than in American waters. The western North Atlantic range extends from about Cape Cod to Davis Strait and Greenland. Groups of a few to several dozen may be encountered in our study area, but herds of up to 1,500 occur in the

White-beaked dolphin
(Lagenorhynchus albirostris).
Size range: 8–10 feet.
JOHN R. QUINN

White-beaked dolphin breaching. Mingan Islands, Gulf of St. Lawrence, summer 1980.
RICHARD SEARS (MINGAN ISLANDS CETACEAN STUDY)

White-beaked dolphin, close-up of head, Newfoundland, 1976. Note white color of snout and eye ring.
JUDY PERKINS

White-beaked dolphins, showing white beaks and white backs. Old Scantum Ledge, Maine, May 21, 1977.
STEVEN KATONA

Gulf of St. Lawrence or Newfoundland. Within the Gulf of Maine, waters from Cape Cod to Cape Ann have yielded sightings from April through November, and there are records from Mt. Desert Rock in September and the Bay of Fundy. Sightings of white-beaks in the Gulf of Maine are much less common now than they were up to the late 1970s. They are said to have been more common around Cape Cod during the 1950s than they are at present. While sightings of white-beaks have declined, sightings of white-sided dolphins have become more common.

A population estimate of 3,486 dolphins from St. Anthony, Newfoundland, to Nain, Labrador, and out to the 656-foot (200-meter) depth contour was determined from a two-week census survey during August 1982. The species was infrequently observed during CETAP surveys, with only 33 sightings of 523 individuals representing 1 percent of the odontocetes observed.

The differences in distribution between white-beaked and white-sided dolphins undoubtedly reflect differences in their ecological preferences. White-beaks have a more northerly distribution and a diet that includes more squid (Newfoundlanders also call them "squid-hounds"), but they also take cod, capelin, and other fish or crustaceans. Although these two dolphin species may be found together on occasion, there is some suggestion that their populations are separated seasonally or spatially by water temperatures and ecologically by diet. Information on reproduction and growth rate is not yet available for the white-beaked dolphin. One reason for this data gap is that this species does not strand en masse, as white-sided dolphins do. Perhaps this reflects differences in social organization or behavior. Since so much remains to be learned about these animals, photographs and descriptions of observations by whale watchers could be welcome contributions.

COMMON DOLPHIN
(*Delphinus delphis*)

The scientific name of this species (Gr. *delphis*, dolphin) and its common name both signify the worldwide abundance of this animal in warm waters. Dolphins of this species figure in Greek and Roman art and writing, evidence that they have cheered the hearts of sailors

Common dolphin
(Delphinus delphis).
Size range: 6–8 feet.
JOHN R. QUINN

for a very long time, leaping and dashing from up to a mile away toward a ship to bowride.

The common dolphin's western North Atlantic range extends from Venezuela and the Gulf of Mexico to Newfoundland. Most of the population in U.S. waters is located from Georges Bank southward in a broad band over the edge of the continental shelf, where water temperatures are above 40°F (4.4°C) and where depth is 328 to 656 feet (100 to 200 meters), although the species remains common out to depths of 6,560 feet (2,000 meters) and beyond. Temperatures where common dolphins were sighted ranged from 5°C to 22.5°C, with a mean value of 11°C.

Common dolphins eat a variety of fishes and squids. This is one of three species whose populations in the eastern North Pacific Ocean have been ravaged by the purse seine fishery for tuna. There, common dolphins, along with two other species not found in our area (spotted dolphin, *Stenella attenuata*, and spinner dolphin, *S. longirostris*), swim above schools of yellowfin tuna. The tuna may take advantage of the dolphins' ability to find food using echolocation, and both species may benefit from mutual pursuit and herding of fish. Other interactions may also be involved. Fishermen find schools of dolphins in order to catch the tuna swimming below them. Until the 1960s, tuna were caught using hook and line, with no effect on the dolphins. Beginning in the late 1950s, fishermen began to surround dolphin schools with long, deep nets called purse seines. The nets are gathered together until the animals are bunched tightly together and the tuna can be hoisted on deck. Nobody could have predicted the devastation this would wreak on dolphin populations. The dolphins refuse to jump over the nets, and many become entangled and drown or simply die of shock. More than 2 million dolphins have died since the fishery was initiated. U.S. fishermen are now required to drop a panel of the net and allow dolphins to escape or force them out. This practice has substantially reduced, but not eliminated, dolphin mortality. Unfortunately, fishermen from other nations are not always required to take such precautions. Some U.S. companies, led by the A. J. Heinz Corporation, have resolved to buy only tuna caught by approved procedures that minimize dolphin mortality. We urge U.S. consumers to purchase only tuna labeled "dolphin safe," and we hope that companies in other countries will follow the lead of the Heinz Corporation so that this needless slaughter will someday end.

Within our study area, common dolphins should be looked for

Common dolphin near southeast edge of Georges Bank, April 1983.
SCOTT MARION (SEAFARERS EXPEDITIONS)

*Common dolphin. The small Band-Aid shaped mark midway
between the flipper and the dorsal fin is a scar.*
MICHAEL PAYNE (MANOMET BIRD OBSERVATORY)

during offshore passage in the Gulf of Maine seaward of Georges or Browns Bank and at sea off Nova Scotia and Newfoundland, where they occur rather commonly, usually in groups ranging from 50 to 200. Schools of up to 2,000 may be seen. Only in summer might a few be seen closer to the coast.

Common dolphins are fast, energetic swimmers that frequently jump clear of the water and also bowride or play in the wake of a ship for long periods. At those times it is easy to see the main field mark of the species, a distinct crisscross pattern on the sides. At close range the forward half of the crisscross appears tawny yellow or brown and the posterior half gray. Even if the whole flank cannot be seen, the black "point" below the dorsal fin makes identification easy. In some places this dolphin is called the "saddleback." Bowriding common dolphins sometimes turn on their sides, apparently to look up at the ship, giving one the opportunity to see their striking patterning close up. The long, pointed snout, black eye mask, and black stripe from flipper to jaw will be seen clearly.

Common dolphins were the second most abundant species observed in the CETAP survey in numbers. A total of 24,708 individuals seen in 453 sightings accounted for 10 percent of all odontocetes seen. The peak average abundance estimate in the CETAP survey area was 31,124, during winter. Many of the animals seen were south of our study area. No estimates have been published for other portions of our study area.

The biology of this species has not been investigated in detail on our side of the Atlantic, but information from other locations indicates that females give birth to one calf each year after 11 months of gestation. Calves nurse for 4 months, attain puberty at about 3 years (female) or 4 years (male), and may live for 25 to 30 years. The average adult size is about 7.5 feet (2.3 m), and the maximum size is 8.5 feet (2.6 m). The food ration for an adult common dolphin is about 10 to 20 pounds (4.5 to 9 kg) per day.

STRIPED DOLPHIN
(*Stenella coeruleoalba*)

Like the common dolphin, the striped dolphin is distributed throughout the warmer waters of all oceans, generally in deep water. It is not common in our study area and normally would be seen only from

Striped dolphin
(Stenella coeruleoalba).
Size range: 6–8 feet.
JOHN R. QUINN

vessels far offshore or else as stranded specimens. Its western North Atlantic range is from the Gulf of Mexico and the Caribbean to western Greenland. Offshore of the U.S. coast, striped dolphins were found by the CETAP survey to be most abundant over continental slope waters 650 to 6,500 feet (200 to 2,000 meters) deep, especially east of Delaware Bay and Chesapeake Bay. Peak average abundance was 4,319 (± 3,988), during spring. Within the Gulf of Maine, the species is represented mainly by individuals that have stranded along Cape Cod. Striped dolphins are only rarely encountered in eastern Canadian waters, where records exist for Cape Breton Island, Nova Scotia, and for Sable Island, St. Pierre Bank, and Newfoundland's Placentia Bay.

To identify this species at sea, the first feature to note is the pale blaze that sweeps from the flank back and up toward the dorsal fin. Next look for the "bilge stripe," a black line running along the light lower flank from the eye to the anus. Although the species takes its common name from that stripe, it is visible at sea only when the dolphins jump. Fortunately for observers, striped dolphins often clear the water in fast, low jumps as they speed along in schools of up to a few hundred animals (average size 50 to 60). They are also reported to bowride on occasion.

The genus name (Gr. *stenos*, narrow) refers to the long, slender beak, while the species name derives from Latin *caeruleus*, sky blue, and *albus*, white, because the South American specimen described in 1833 was supposedly blue above and light below. Calling the dolphin "blue" is a bit of an exaggeration; most are at best steel blue-gray or brown.

The biology of this species in the western North Atlantic is poorly known. In waters around Japan, where large schools are hunted for food, the life cycle has been detailed as follows. Males and females mature sexually at about 5 to 9 years of age and lengths of 7.2 feet (2.2 m). Females may begin to reproduce shortly thereafter, but males may have to wait for up to 4 or 5 more years for opportunities to mate. Mating males and females can be found together in "mating schools" averaging about 225 animals during the three mating seasons: January–February, May–June, and September–October. The rest of the population remains in larger nonmating schools averaging about 750 dolphins. Pregnancy lasts 12 months. The newborn calf is slightly over 3 feet (91 cm) long. By 6 months after birth the calf begins to hunt and eat some prey, but it continues to nurse until weaning at

Striped dolphins at Georges Bank, 1987.
ARMANTE CERRO (SEAFARERS EXPEDITIONS)

Striped dolphin stranded at Montauk Point, New York,
September 18, 1972, showing long snout, pointed teeth, and forward portion of "bilge stripe."
American Museum of Natural History Specimen No. 237503.
KEVIN McCANN

age 1.5 years. For up to another 1.5 years, the calf apparently stays in the mating school with its mother. At about age 2 or 3, juveniles join together into "immature" schools, where they will remain until about age 5. Individuals then join adult nonmating schools over the next several years. Females are thought to give birth every 3 years. Fish, shrimp, and squid are the main foods of striped dolphins in Japanese waters.

A die-off of this species recently occurred in European waters. Beginning in mid-July of 1990 many dead striped dolphins were seen floating along the Mediterranean coast of Spain. More than 700 carcasses were recovered by the end of 1990 from the coasts of Spain, France, and northern Italy. Additional reports from Morocco and offshore suggested that many more dolphins probably died. Carcasses contained a herpes virus and a morbillivirus. A morbillivirus similar to canine distemper virus killed at least 17,000 harbor seals in the North Sea in 1988. Dolphin carcasses also contained high levels of polychlorinated biphenyls (PCBs) and other indications that contamination could have contributed to mortality.

BOTTLENOSE DOLPHIN
(*Tursiops truncatus*)

The bottlenose dolphin is probably the most familiar and the best-loved of all marine mammals. It can be observed in temperate to tropical inshore waters throughout the world. Its playful, acrobatic nature, trainability, and apparently high intelligence have made these dolphins a favorite display in many oceanariums and even in television shows or movies.

Bottlenose dolphins are not common in the cold waters of our study area. On the East Coast of North America, they inhabit coastal and inshore waters from Cape Hatteras south to Florida and west through the Gulf of Mexico. An offshore population of slightly larger body size lives along the edge of the continental shelf as far north as New Jersey in winter and Georges Bank in warmer months. Occasional specimens living or dead have been seen in the Gulf of Maine and as far north as Newfoundland.

People familiar with the appearance of bottlenose dolphins as a result of aquarium performances, films, or pictures will be surprised to find that identification of this species at sea is not easy. In the

Bottlenose dolphin
(Tursiops truncatus).
Size range: 8–12 feet.
JOHN R. QUINN

wild, bottlenose dolphins do not routinely do tricks, nor do they often show the short-beaked, "smiling" head. Instead, one must look for the following characteristics. The robust, powerful body may be drab bluish gray or brownish above and slightly lighter below. It lacks a distinct color pattern but has subtle traces of pigment that can only be seen up close. CETAP aerial survey crews observed that offshore bottlenose dolphins have light flank markings similar to those of the *Stenella* species, sweeping up toward the dorsal fin from above the flippers. Such markings could help to reveal whether the few individuals seen north of Cape Cod, most of which are stranded specimens, might have originated from the coastal or the offshore arm of the population. The dorsal fin is similar to that of other dolphins, although a bit thicker and more blunt. Bottlenose dolphins swim in small groups of several to about 15 animals. At sea they sometimes have been seen schooling with pilot whales.

Bottlenose dolphins hunt bottom fishes, squid, and invertebrates of many different kinds. A list of what they don't eat might be shorter than a list of foods they are known to consume. The daily ration is about 10 percent of the body weight. Depending on the situation, bottlenose dolphins may hunt single prey, team up to herd fish, approach fishing boats to take scraps or discards, steal fish from fishermens' hooks, and even chase fish up salt marsh creeks and onto mud flats. As might be guessed from the range of feeding strategies they employ and the variety of tricks they can learn in captivity, bottlenose dolphins have one of the most diverse behavioral repertoires known in the animal kingdom. A large body of information is available on topics including echolocation and acoustic communication, cooperative and help-giving behavior, play, mimicry, courtship, sexual behavior, and learning. Probably more is known about the physiology and anatomy of bottlenose dolphins than about any other cetacean. Suggestions for further reading on these topics are found in the Bibliography.

Studies of inshore dolphin communities by Randy Wells and associates over a 20-year period show that bottlenose dolphins tend to segregate into groups by sex and age. Closely bonded pairs or trios of males have been seen together for periods of years, cruising between the home ranges of groups of females and sometimes cooperating to isolate and mate with them. Sexual behavior, which begins at a few months of age, plays an important social role in this species. Males

Bottlenose dolphin. Hydrographers Canyon, July 1987.
TYLER SEAVEY (SEAFARERS EXPEDITIONS)

Bottlenose dolphins at Institute for Delphinid Research,
Grassy Key, Florida, January 1982.
STEVEN KATONA

*Bottlenose dolphins jumping during performance
at Flipper Sea School, Key West, Florida, January 1982.*
STEVEN KATONA

have very large testes and high sperm counts, suggesting that the mating system may involve sperm competition.

Significant events in the life cycle of the bottlenose dolphin include mating during spring and perhaps autumn by sexually mature females about 7.5 feet (2.3 m) long and 5 to 12 years old, with males 8 feet (2.4 m) long and 10 to 13 years old. A female might give birth every other year to a single calf 3 feet (91 cm) long and weighing about 25 pounds (11.4 kg). Gestation lasts about 12 months. The calf nurses for up to 4 years. A hardy, lucky calf might grow to at least 10 feet (3 m) and 450 pounds (205 kg) and live to 25 to 35 years of age. Lengths to 14 feet (4.3 m) have been recorded. As with many porpoises and other mammals, the teeth get worn down as an animal gets older. The first bottlenose dolphin described scientifically had short, worn-down teeth, so it was given a Latin name derived from *tursio*, porpoise, and *truncatus*, cut off or shortened.

It is ironic that this dolphin, whose jaw shape makes many individuals appear to be smiling and happy, has become embroiled in many unpleasant or controversial situations.

The coastal habitat of many of these dolphins has become polluted with chemicals and human wastes, some of which are accumulated in the animals' tissues. From July 1987 until March 1988 more than 740 bottlenose dolphins were found dead on beaches from New Jersey to Florida, and many others probably died at sea. Up to 50 or 60 percent of the nearshore population may have died. After 18 months of investigations, a research team headed by Dr. Joseph Geraci of Guelph University concluded that a toxin produced by the dinoflagellate *Ptychodiscus brevis*, a single-celled plant often responsible for red tides along the southeastern coast of the United States, had caused the die-off. The dinoflagellates were thought to have been picked up by a current in the Gulf of Mexico which swept them to the east coast of Florida. There they were eaten by menhaden *Brevoortia tyrannus*, a fish in the herring family, also known as a pogie, which feeds by filtering small plankton from the water. The toxin, called brevitoxin, accumulated in their digestive organs and poisoned dolphins that fed on them. Critics noted, however, that the dolphins also had very high levels of PCB and other pollutants in their flesh. The blubber of some contained up to 620 parts per million (ppm) of PCB, and one had 6,800 ppm, the highest amount ever found in a marine mammal. Thus some people still contend that the pollutants were the primary cause of sickness or death. In any case, by the time the dolphins washed ashore they were also ravaged by bacteria and viruses, including species normally present that they should have been able to resist, indicating that their immune systems were damaged by toxins in their bodies. Whatever the primary cause of death may have been, it is probable that the dolphin's physiology was at least compromised by contaminants derived from human abuse of coastal waters.

Our direct interactions with this species have also become troublesome. Displays of captive animals, though educational and entertaining, have raised the question of whether the price paid by the dolphins is too high. Individuals can suffer from boredom, lack of exercise, and inadequate food quality or variety, particularly in substandard facilities. Capture of dolphins has reduced populations in some locations, although reproduction in captivity has reduced the need for specimens from the wild. Some hotels and other facilities now offer opportunities to swim with dolphins. These programs may fulfill powerful human fantasies, but they may be detrimental to the animals, adding stress (and possible transmission of pathogens) from the steady stream of humans entering the tank or pool to the other potential problems of captivity.

Even more vexing is the question of whether these animals should be trained for military use. During the past 30 years, dolphins have been trained to retrieve objects and lost equipment, find sunken missiles, carry messages or tools to divers, plant small explosive charges, locate mines, perform underwater surveillance, and guard submarine bases. Some dolphins may have been trained to disable an enemy diver by pushing him to the surface or pulling the air hose from his mouth. It would seem more desirable to enlist the dolphins' remarkable talents to help us learn more about the sea rather than engaging them in our conflicts.

Intentional interactions with wild bottlenose dolphins have also been problematic. At some locations along the southeastern coast of the United States, dolphin-watching tours attract bottlenose dolphins by feeding them. People have occasionally fed the animals crackers or other inappropriate foods. Dolphins habituated to feeding by humans have gotten fishhooks in their mouths while attempting to remove fish from fishermen's lines, perhaps mistakenly thinking that they were being fed. The most benign interaction, in which free-living dolphins voluntarily come to play with human swimmers at

Monkey Mia Beach, Shark Bay, Australia, has also become troublesome. Human wastes and residues from suntan lotion have begun to pollute the water, compromising the health of the dolphins.

These examples show that we must be more thoughtful in our interactions with these appealing dolphins and with all marine mammals. Probably it will never be desirable for large numbers of people to interact with the animals. At some remote coastal locations, however, including Mauritania and Brazil, bottlenose dolphins and humans have fished cooperatively for generations, showing that there can be sustained interactions under the right conditions.

RISSO'S DOLPHIN or GRAY GRAMPUS
(Grampus griseus)

The few specimens of this species reported in our study area stray from warmer waters offshore and south. There, where water depth is 656 feet (200 meters) or more, Risso's dolphin is common, as in similar habitats worldwide. The CETAP surveys found this dolphin to be most common along the continental slope from south of Cape Cod to Cape Hatteras, with some suggestion of northward movement during warmer months. Although few sighting records exist in eastern Canada, one reference notes that large schools were seen in Newfoundland, where unsuccessful attempts were made to catch them during the 1950s. The dolphins could not be herded easily.

The genus name of this dolphin, *grampus*, is a corruption of the French words *grand*, big, and *poisson*, fish. The species name, *griseus*, comes from the French *gris*, meaning gray. Hence the common name gray grampus. Fishermen used to call several odontocetes grampus, but the term should be used only for *Grampus griseus*. This species is also known as Risso's dolphin because the specimen first described scientifically was collected in 1811 at Nice, France, by an amateur naturalist named Giovanni Risso.

Despite the nondescript common name, these dolphins can usually be distinguished quite easily at sea, swimming in schools of up to 30 animals. They might first be spotted by their acrobatics: breaching, cartwheeling, lobtailing, and spyhopping. Although they cannot be distinguished from other dolphins by length—they average 10 feet (3 m) and 650 pounds (295 kg), with a maximum of 13–14 feet (3.9–4.3 m) and nearly 1,200 pounds (500 kg)—or shape of the dorsal

Risso's dolphin or gray grampus
(Grampus griseus).
Size range: 9–13 feet.
JOHN R. QUINN

Risso's dolphins, three abreast. Near Hydrographers Canyon, August 1986.
SCOTT MARION (SEAFARERS EXPEDITIONS)

Risso's dolphins. Scars on the bodies show up nicely in this photograph.
Near Hydrographers Canyon, August 1986.
SCOTT MARION (SEAFARERS EXPEDITIONS)

Risso's dolphin breaching, showing contrast between dark fin and lighter, scratch-marked body. Off Baja California, January 29, 1976.
STEVEN KATONA

Risso's dolphin, showing contrast between dark dorsal fin and lighter body. Off Baja California, January 29, 1976.
STEVEN KATONA

Risso's dolphin, dark dorsal fin contrasting with lighter scratched body.
RICHARD ROWLETT

Risso's dolphin, stranded at Monomoy Island, Massachusetts, August 1979.
BOB PRESCOTT

fin, their acquired color pattern is usually diagnostic. The gray back and sides nearly always bear numerous white scars and scratches, which may be tooth marks suffered in fights with other Risso's dolphins or may be inflicted by suckers or beaks of squid. The bodies and heads of older animals become white from accumulated scars, contrasting sharply with the dark, less-scarred dorsal fin and flippers. The white, anchor-shaped chest patch on juvenile animals may be obliterated later in life by light scars. Workers in Monterey Bay, California, and also in the Azores Islands have photo-identified individuals on the basis of distinctive scar patterns. The bulbous forehead (melon) is furrowed by a shallow vertical groove unique to this species. There is no beak.

Relatively little is known about the natural history of Risso's dolphin. It consumes some fish, but its main food is squid. Like some other squid eaters (including the sperm whale, pygmy sperm whale, and most of the beaked whales), grampus normally has teeth only in the lower jaw. Individuals may have from 2 to 7 pairs of teeth, the average being 3 or 4 pairs located at the front of the lower jaw.

Photo-identification studies show some stability in group composition. A few individuals have survived in captivity. A viable hybrid calf was produced from mating of a grampus and a bottlenose dolphin at one aquarium; a few possible hybrids have also been reported from the wild. Risso's dolphins have been hunted in many locations, either by driving them ashore or with gill nets or hand-held harpoons.

KILLER WHALE
(*Orcinus orca*)

This striking and beautiful medium-sized whale is instantly recognizable by people everywhere. Its bold black-and-white pattern emblazons T-shirts, postcards, calendars, advertisements, and sundry other products, and the whales themselves have been seen by millions of people at aquariums in North America and Europe.

Under reasonably good viewing conditions killer whales are easily identified at sea. The most visible feature at a distance is the extraordinarily tall, swordlike dorsal fin of adult males, which may reach 6 feet (1.8 m) or more in height. The dorsal fins of females and juveniles are smaller, curved, and more closely resemble the fins of other dolphins. The distinctive field mark to look for is the oval white patch

Killer whale
(Orcinus orca).
Size range: male, up to 30 feet; female, up to 22 feet.
JOHN R. QUINN

above and behind each eye. The white of the abdomen extends partway up the rear flank, and a gray "saddle" is visible behind the dorsal fin.

Killer whales are found in all oceans from the tropics to the Arctic but are most common in cooler, productive coastal waters. The normal social unit is a group ("pod") of from 3 to 25 whales of both sexes and all ages, made up largely of relatives. Nearly all pods contain at least one large male. Identification of individual whales by photographs of fin shape, nicks and scars caused by injuries, and differences in the shape of the gray saddle have permitted study of pod composition and home range in the Pacific Northwest over a period of nearly 20 years. Similar studies have been carried out for shorter periods at several locations in the northeastern Atlantic. Results show that pods are enduring social units that maintain their cohesiveness and inhabit the same home range for many years, much as do the matriarchal social groups of African elephants.

Killer whales are clearly a regular component of the cetacean fauna of the North Atlantic and of our study area, but they are not numerous here, and much more needs to be learned about their abundance, distribution, and seasonal migrations (if any). The CETAP study reported only 12 sightings totaling 85 animals during 3 years of intensive surveys from Cape Hatteras to the Canadian border. Papers in Sigurjonsson and Leatherwood's (1988) important volume *North Atlantic Killer Whales* list, map, and describe all reported live sightings or strandings of the species in this ocean. Some may migrate seasonally north and south along the northeastern coast of North America; some may remain year-round in northern waters; and others may live year-round south of about 35°N. The largest groups reported in our waters were about 30 animals in the southern Gulf of Maine during August and September 1976; 40 near Cape Ann on September 5, 1979; and up to 100 seen by whalers from Dildo, Newfoundland, in June 1970. The death of approximately 25 killer whales in Trinity Bay, Newfoundland, on April 27, 1959, probably resulted from entrapment in ice.

Although no data on reproduction are available for our study area, information from a variety of locations has been used to form a preliminary model of the cycle. Males mature sexually when about 19–22 feet (5.8–6.7 m) long, compared with about 16 feet (4.9 m) for females. In the northeastern Atlantic, age at sexual maturity was 12 to 16 years for males and 6 to 10 years for females. Males can grow to nearly 32 feet (9.75 m) long and 11.5 tons (10 metric tons),

Killer whale, half breach.
Mt. Desert Island, Maine,
June 1982.
SCOTT MARION

Killer whale, blowhole open, showing
diagnostic white patch above and behind eye.
Mt. Desert Island, Maine, June 1982.
SCOTT MARION

Killer whale, full breach. Stellwagen Bank,
May 15, 1982.
LYDA PHILLIPS *(WINSTED EVENING CITIZEN)*

but average size is perhaps 22–26 feet (6.7–8.0 m) long and 4.4–6.9 tons (4–6.3 metric tons). Females are always smaller, reaching a maximum of about 28 feet (8.5 m) long and 8.1 tons (7.4 metric tons), with average size of 18.7–21.6 feet (5.7–6.6 m) long and 2.94–4.2 tons (2.6–3.8 metric tons).

Males in pods may fertilize more than one female during the late autumn to midwinter mating season. Single calves about 6.9 to 8.2 feet (2.1–2.4 m) long weighing 375 pounds (170 kg) are born after a long pregnancy, estimated at 16 to 17 months. Nursing lasts for at least 2 years, and the length at weaning may be about 13 feet (4 m). The interval between calves is long, averaging 5 to 6 years in the northeastern Pacific. Females probably stop reproducing after about age 40, having given birth to 5 or 6 calves. Maximum longevity may be as high as 90 years for females and 60 years for males; average lifetime appears to be about 50 years for females and 30 for males.

These whales have a diverse diet, including fish, squid, birds, marine turtles, seals, dugongs or manatees, dolphins, porpoises, and baleen whales. A killer whale's daily food intake is about 4 percent of its body weight. Bluefin tuna and herring are thought to be important foods in the Gulf of Maine. Fishermen have seen orcas attacking tuna during late summer on Stellwagen Bank and at Jeffreys Ledge. The whales may regularly follow parts of the tuna's migrations, but they have also been seen in winter when no tuna would have been present. Several apparent attacks on baleen whales at Jeffreys Ledge, Maine, have also been reported to us. In eastern Canadian waters, the movements of killer whales may be closely linked with the distribution of other whales on which they prey. Workers from the Mingan Islands Cetacean Study have seen killer whales attacking minke whales on three occasions in the Gulf of St. Lawrence. Scientists from Memorial University of Newfoundland watched them attacking humpback whales on the Grand Bank in July 1982. Killer whales are also said to have preyed on beluga whales during spring and autumn in the St. Lawrence estuary.

Different pods of killer whales may differ culturally. Slight differences in vocal repertoires occur even between pods that occupy adjacent home ranges and interact (or interbreed) frequently. Larger differences exist between pods that do not interact frequently. Pods also differ in preferred types of food. Some, especially pelagic pods, may specialize in eating whales, while others concentrate on fish, seals, or other prey. The existence of different groups of animals migrating in relation to prey abundance or inhabiting traditional territories could explain why plotting of sightings produces no clear patterns.

Nevertheless, it seems likely that the basic structure of killer whale societies relates to hunting whales. Observations of such attacks have emphasized the use of strategy, group coordination, and cooperation in herding and subduing animals many times their size. Although some groups of killer whales also demonstrate those traits while herding fish or ambushing seals, small prey can be obtained by individuals, as in other odontocetes. The evolution of stable, long-lived pods; the opportunity for learning during the long period when calves are dependent on the mother; large size; long lifetime; and relatively high intelligence are all useful adaptations for producing experienced, integrated teams of animals able to tackle the largest, most powerful prey on earth. Several recordings that include echolocation and communication sounds of killer whales are listed in the Bibliography.

Some of the behavior traits mentioned above have been responsible for the popularity of captive killer whales as exhibits in many aquariums. They are easily trained, cooperative, and nearly all have been gentle and affectionate to trainers. Several trainers have been wounded when whales refused to let them leave the water, and in 1991 a trainer drowned when three orcas dragged her by the feet around their pool. Dragging people through the water can be a form of play for killer whales, perhaps analogous to the way a cat plays with a bird or mouse, but aggression could have been a component of some incidents. For example, another trainer was seriously injured when an orca named Orky breached on him, apparently deliberately. Orky, who was involved in several previous incidents, had been taken from Puget Sound when very young and possibly never received adequate socialization. Although animals normally maintain discipline learned during training, boredom, stress, and lack of opportunity for normal social interactions with other killer whales could cause frustration and aggression in captive situations. The whales could easily have cut trainers in half with a single bite but instead held or jumped on them. Causing serious injury or death may not have been their intention, but the vast differences in size and aquatic ability between our two species leave no margin for error.

There is no indication that wild killer whales bear any malice toward people or have ever intentionally harmed a human swimmer. There are several accounts of boats being deliberately rammed and

Tall dorsal fin of adult male killer whale.
Northeast Grand Manan Bank, August 1988.
SCOTT KRAUS (SEAFARERS EXPEDITIONS)

Killer whale flukes.
Mt. Desert Island,
Maine, June 1982.
BOB BOWMAN

Killer whale diving under the bow of M/V Yankee Freedom,
with Captain Jerry Hill looking on. Northeast Grand Manan Bank, August 1988.
SCOTT MARION (SEAFARERS EXPEDITIONS)

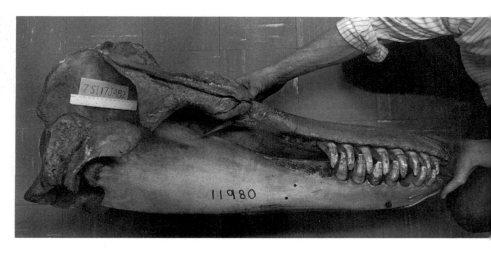

Jaws of killer whale, National Museum of Natural History,
Smithsonian Institution, Specimen 11980.
CAREY BELL

Killer whale, one of a pair of 25-foot males shot in Eastport, Maine, March 1902.
F. W. TRUE, COURTESY JAMES G. MEAD (SMITHSONIAN INSTITUTION)

sunk by killer whales, but positive identification of species (and evidence that whales really were involved) is usually lacking. It is useful to compare killer whales to social hunters like wolves or lions, which have evolved similar special structures for the same reason—to be able to take large prey—and generally leave people alone unless molested.

The issue of whether killer whales should be maintained in captivity is extremely controversial. Since the first killer whale was displayed in captivity in 1961, about 150 individuals, including 13 born in captivity, have been kept in 40 aquariums throughout the world. Concern about depleting pods, as well as practical and ethical disagreements about whether these animals should be in captivity, has eliminated live capture for display in many locations. In recent years, live capture has taken place only near Iceland, at a cost of $200,000 to $300,000 per whale. Opponents of captivity also note that captive killer whales live only about 13 years, compared to the 40 to 60 years expected for wild specimens.

Yet the performances of trained killer whales have certainly strengthened the whale protection movement, and knowledge gained from observing them closely has contributed to a better understanding of the species. These whales are no longer perceived as fierce killers of the sea, keen to devour man or beast, and many people now prefer to call them orcas rather than killer whales. (Ironically, that might translate loosely as "devil whale," since Orcus was the Roman god of the underworld.)

Can bonds with humans replace the rich social life characteristic of this species in the wild? To what extent can a challenging training program replace the stimulation of ranging freely through the ocean? Perhaps the only way to answer those questions is to give animals the choice of whether to remain captive or swim free. There are several facilities where bottlenose dolphins are free to come and go, but no facilities exist that give killer whales that choice. Some facilities where killer whales are currently displayed are certainly unsuitable, but even the best facilities, in our opinion, leave much to be desired from the perspective of the animals.

BELUGA
(*Delphinapterus leucas*)

Whale watchers in our study area have been uniquely fortunate to be able to view a small population of these "white whales" in the St. Lawrence River estuary, rather than having to travel to the remote shores of their primary habitat along Arctic coasts of Greenland, Canada, Alaska, and the Soviet Union. All North American beluga whales probably formed one continuous population during the most recent glaciation, when continental ice sheets covered all of their present range. As the ice sheet receded and the whales reoccupied their former range, a population remained in the Gulf of St. Lawrence and eventually became separated from those inhabiting sub-Arctic and Arctic waters of eastern Canada, western Greenland, and Hudson Bay.

Even whale watchers who don't go to the St. Lawrence River may someday see a free-living beluga because every few years one or two follow cold currents south around Nova Scotia and into the Bay of Fundy, or down the U.S. coast as far as Long Island. This low rate of visitation is noticeable because the animals are pure white, come close to shore, and sometimes swim into weirs or feed near fishing boats. Although belugas have evolved to live in cold seas, these strays can apparently survive and feed in warmer waters, perhaps for several years. Belugas have been kept successfully for long periods at several aquariums.

Adult males can be as long as 18 feet 8 inches (5.7 m) and weigh nearly 1.8 tons (1.6 metric tons). Females are slightly smaller. The pure white adult color may allow the whale to hide from predators among ice flows and may also reduce the rate of heat loss from the body. If the white color of adult belugas is truly adaptive, however, it is not clear why calves are dark gray or brown, lightening only slowly to become white at sexual maturity, which is about 5 years for females and 8 to 10 for males. Other adaptations for life in freezing seas are easier to understand. Absence of a dorsal fin (the scientific name means "white finless dolphin") reduces heat loss and avoids abrasion by ice. On top of the beluga's head the skin is thick and its blubber thin, probably so the whale can ram through several inches of ice to make a breathing hole when necessary. The neck vertebrae

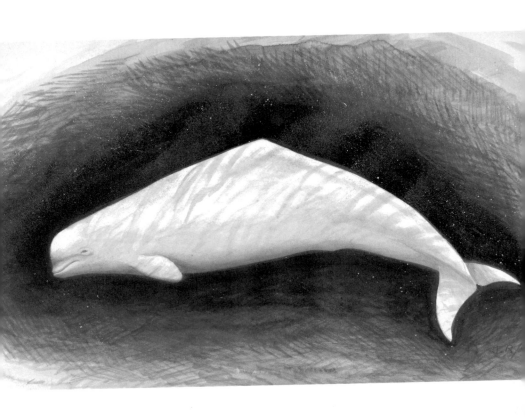

Beluga whale
(Delphinapterus leucas).
Size range: 10–15 feet.
JOHN R. QUINN

are not fused together, so the short-beaked, round-meloned head can move relatively freely, probing with sonar to find channels through pack ice or scattered breathing holes in an ice field. Belugas communicate with high-pitched trills, squeals, and whistles. Those sounds can be heard through the hull of a boat and have led to the beluga's local name, "sea canary."

The beluga's reproductive cycle is particularly interesting. Females mature sexually at age 4 to 7 years and males at age 8 to 9. Mating takes place in spring or early summer. The following summer, after about 14 months of pregnancy, the female joins large numbers of other pregnant females, plus males, in shallow water at the mouths of Arctic creeks and rivers. There, in relatively warm water (50°–60°F, or 10°–15°C), females give birth to single calves, each 4 to 5 feet (1.2–1.5 m) long and about 75 to 100 pounds (34–45 kg). Mothers nurse calves in the warm, sheltered estuaries until the calves' blubber thickens. Calves are completely dependent on nursing for a year, supplement mother's milk during the second year with food caught by hunting, and are weaned at age 2. Maximum longevity may be more than 25 years. A female gives birth every 2 or 3 years.

Within the St. Lawrence region, belugas calve and mate during spring in small bays and estuaries around the Saguenay River and around some islands. Their main summer distribution includes the St. Lawrence estuary and the northern (Iles aux Coudres to Pointe des Monts) and southern (Riviere Ouelle to Rimouski) coasts of the Gulf of St. Lawrence. During warm months, the whales approach the coast at high tide. In September and October, they can be seen near Les Escoumins, among other places. In winter they are restricted by ice to open water at the mouth of the Saguenay River and eastward to Les Escoumins. The usual size of beluga pods is 2 to 25 animals, but groups of up to 200 have been seen.

Belugas have a diverse, opportunistic diet that includes many species of fish, squid, crabs, shrimp, clams, and worms, taken on or near the bottom during dives to 1,150 feet (350 m) or more if necessary, lasting up to about 13 minutes.

These beautiful whales present zoologists with an interesting puzzle. They are adapted to Arctic conditions, but individuals can survive and feed in warmer waters. What limits them mainly to the Arctic? Competition for food in more southerly areas from well-established populations of harbor porpoises, harbor seals, and gray seals in coastal waters and from white-sided dolphins, white-beaked

Beluga in Cape Cod Canal, 1971.
BARRY T. O'NEIL

Tail of beluga whale found dead at Lubec, Maine, June 1987.
SENTIEL ROMMEL

Belugas migrating north along Arctic coast of Alaska in April 1973, showing finless back and white body. The immature animal in the middle is slightly darker.
CHESTER BEACHELL, COURTESY NATIONAL FILM BOARD OF CANADA

dolphins, pilot whales, and others in offshore waters might be an important factor. Predation by sharks, which are more numerous in warm waters, might also help to limit the beluga's range.

Sadly, the story of the St. Lawrence belugas may be entering its final chapter. When Europeans first explored North America, there were probably about 5,000 belugas in the St. Lawrence population. Hunting from the 1600s through the 1940s reduced the population to about 2,500. There has been no hunting since 1979, but the population is still declining, threatened by pollution. Contaminants from industries surrounding the Great Lakes and St. Lawrence Seaway are taking a terrible toll on the belugas. Research by Pierre Beland and colleagues at the St. Lawrence National Institute of Toxicology, Rimouski, Quebec, has identified a pitiable number of maladies afflicting these animals, including gastric ulcers, bladder cancer, hepatitis and liver cancer, mammary cancer, skin disorders, suppression of the immune system, genetic mutations, and pneumonia. Many of these disorders had never been seen before in cetaceans. Infections indicating depression of the immune system were also found. The causes appear to be chemicals such as PCBs, polycyclic aromatic hydrocarbons (PAH) such as benzo(a)pyrene (BAP), and insecticides, including DDT and mirex. Fish eaten by the belugas are contaminated by food-chain bioaccumulation of the chemicals. Up to 3,400 ppm of PCB has been found in the milk of a lactating female beluga and up to 576 ppm in blubber. By comparison, fish is unfit for human consumption if it contains 2 ppm of PCB. Eating American eels (*Anguilla rostrata*) during their spring migration from the Great Lakes down the St. Lawrence River to the sea may provide up to half of all organochlorine contaminants.

The number of belugas seen at the mouth of the Saguenay River declined steadily between 1975 and 1985. Only about 450 to 500 belugas are now estimated to remain in the St. Lawrence, and their birth rate and juvenile survival are low. Without rapid and far-reaching improvements in pollution control their future looks bleak. One justification often advanced for studying marine mammals has been that these top predators could serve as indicators of the health of marine systems. The message from these belugas is unmistakable.

Other populations have fared better, with approximately 9,000 belugas in Hudson Bay and James Bay, 10,000 to 19,000 in the Canadian High Arctic and western Greenland, 5,000 to 10,000 in Arctic waters of the northeastern Atlantic, and 25,000 to 30,000 in the

Bering and Chukchi seas. Those populations still provide Eskimos with meat and oil, although overhunting has depleted some local populations. A massive project to produce hydroelectric power by damming rivers running into James Bay threatens belugas, which use those rivers seasonally. Global warming and thinning of the ozone layer may pose special threats to belugas and other Arctic species.

To protect belugas in the St. Lawrence region, the Canadian government has prohibited whale watch vessels from approaching or drifting toward the whales. The areas of Ste. Catherine Bay, Ste. Marguerite Bay, Ste. Etienne Cove, and Southern Île-aux-Lièvres have been identified as critical habitats for beluga movement, feeding, and resting. Boats shold avoid those areas if possible and limit speed to 5 knots if passage is necessary.

SPERM WHALE
(Physeter catodon)

Sperm whales, immortalized in *Moby Dick* and the mainstay of the great American whaling fleet during the eighteenth and nineteenth centuries, are the largest of the toothed whales. Males may reach a length of 60 feet (18 m), although a size of 50 feet (15 m) and 48 tons (43 metric tons) is more common. They also have the biggest population of any large whale, with up to a million animals estimated to inhabit the North Pacific Ocean and another million in the rest of the world.

Few people would have any difficulty identifying this species if given a good look because it is one of the most distinctive and bizarre animals on earth. Unfortunately, the massive, blunt head, which is fully one-third the length of a large male, and the long, narrow, underslung lower jaw are usually not fully visible at sea. Identification must then be made on the following characteristics. The single nostril is located on the left side of the front of the head, and the 15-foot-tall (4.5 m) spout is therefore tipped forward and to the left at an angle of about 45 degrees. The dorsal fin is usually only a low hump, followed by a series of bumps along the ridge of the back and tail. Sperm whales are usually slate gray or brownish, and the skin on the flanks is usually wrinkled or corrugated. The flukes, usually visible as the whale dives, are large and triangular, with smooth edges, rounded tips, and a deep central notch. The scientific name (Gr.

Sperm whale
(Physeter catodon).
Size range: male, up to 60 feet; female, 15–38 feet.
JOHN R. QUINN

physa, bellows, and Gr. *kata*, inferior, + *odontos*, tooth) translates roughly as "spouter with teeth on the bottom," emphasizing that functional teeth are present only in the sperm whale's lower jaw.

Having learned how to identify a sperm whale, one wishes for more opportunities to see them than would be encountered in most parts of our study area. Sperm whales prefer deep water and generally stay along the edge of the continental shelf in water 3,280 or 6,560 feet (1,000 or 2,000 meters) deep or farther out to sea. In such habitats the species ranges throughout the world's oceans and from the equator to high latitudes, pursuing the squid that form its chief food.

Each day a large male sperm whale will eat about 3.5 percent of its body weight in squid. Although fish and other items are occasionally taken, the search for squid accounts for much of the behavior and biology of sperm whales. Most of the squid taken by sperm whales are only several feet long, but giant squid up to 30 feet (9 m) long have been found in sperm whales' stomachs, and sucker-inflicted scars found on some whales may bear witness to battles with enormous squid, perhaps 100 feet (30 m) long.

Many other cetaceans hunt squid, often in the same locations as do sperm whales, but extraordinary adaptations allow this species to escape competition by feeding at depths far below those attainable by any other mammal. We may never know all the reasons why sperm whales are able to hunt routinely at depths of up to 1,640 feet (500 meters) and on occasion at depths of nearly a mile (1.6 km) or more. Since feeding sperm whales are so inaccessible to human observers, we must use indirect evidence to guess how they find food.

Using underwater microphones with directional response, researchers have tracked movements of sperm whales by listening to the loud sonar clicks they produce to communicate and find food. The rhythmic clicks sound like the banging of a carpenter's hammer, but each whale can produce clicks in an individually distinctive rhythm. The different click patterns probably allow each whale to keep track of the locations of other sperm whales up to several miles away. A sperm whale may hear the echo of its clicks bouncing off a squid or fish up to half a mile (one kilometer) or more away. The huge reservoir of waxy liquid in the whale's head probably is a sound guide for focusing the whale's powerful clicks. Old whalers thought that the wax was the whale's sperm, so they called it "spermaceti" and the whale "sperm whale." Today, investigators believe an echolocation click is produced by squeezing air past a sturdy valve (the "monkey's

Sperm whale seen from rear, single spout tipped forward and left.
D. D. TYLER

Removal of stranded young sperm whale from freezing
waters at Rockport, Maine, March 1976,
for transport to New England Aquarium. Note wrinkled skin.
JOHN MARCH

muzzle") at the anterior end of the right nasal passage, near the tip of the snout. The resulting sound pulse probably bounces back and forth through the spermaceti organ, reflecting between an air sac near the monkey's muzzle and another at the rear of the brain case, focusing it and concentrating its power before releasing it to strike a target. There has been speculation that sperm whales and perhaps other odontocetes may sometimes produce clicks loud enough to startle, stun, or disable prey at close range.

In addition to conducting sound very efficiently, spermaceti has other physical characteristics that could be useful to the whale. It is liquid at 90°F (33°C), its normal temperature in a sperm whale resting at the surface, but congeals below 86°F (31°C). Its density increases by about one percent in the congealed state. Clarke (1979) calculated that the whale could regulate its buoyancy to dive more efficiently by voluntarily congealing spermaceti with seawater pumped in through the large left nostril. The whale would later need to reliquify the spermaceti by increasing blood flow to the head, thereby decreasing its density, increasing buoyancy, and either weightlessly maintaining its depth or rising more easily to the surface. Other scientists argue that the spermaceti organ is not anatomically suitable for exchanging heat so rapidly, that the process would drain too much heat from the whale, and that the whale does not need assistance for diving because it is already slightly negatively buoyant.

Other speculations were stimulated by observations that the lips and inside of the lower jaw are white and an observation that the jaws of a sperm whale carcass observed in New Zealand were luminescent as it lay alongside the catcher boat. The scientist who observed it, David Gaskin, suggested that if a sperm whale caught a squid, many species of which are luminescent, its white lips, jaw, and teeth might glow from the luminescent secretions adhering to them. If the whale then hung motionless with its mouth open, other squid might be lured close enough to be engulfed, saving the whale a lot of energy. Buoyancy regulation using the spermaceti organ, as proposed by Clarke, would help the whale remain motionless. Ingenious experiments would be required to test these interesting possibilities.

The social structure of the sperm whale population is complex and appears to vary with ecological conditions, notably food availability. Wherever sperm whales are found, they occur in groups separated by sex, age, and reproductive state. Females, including those that are pregnant or nursing, and some juveniles swim in groups called "mixed schools" or "nursery schools." Females probably form such schools so they can trade "baby-sitting" responsibilities during long dives to catch deep-living squid. By cooperating in groups, females can feed without leaving calves unattended. Some evidence suggests that a calf may nurse from several females (communal suckling), perhaps while its mother is diving. The size of those schools is related to the distribution and abundance of food but often ranges from about 20 to 40 animals. After weaning, young males may join juvenile schools; after reaching puberty at about age 9, males join a series of size-graded (and age-graded) "bachelor schools." Older schools tend to be smaller. During the breeding season in spring and early autumn, males seek to mate with sexually mature females, which are normally over 28 feet (8.5 m), 7 tons (6.3 metric tons), and 8 years old. Not all females in a school will be sexually receptive at any one time: some will already be pregnant, and some will be recovering from a previous pregnancy and may not yet be ready to ovulate. In a location where food is abundant but patchily distributed, the size of mixed or nursery schools will be large, and each school will probably contain many females ready to mate. It will then be worthwhile for the male to defend his "harem" of females against all other males. Battles over females probably occur, judging from the many tooth marks that scar the skin of large bull sperm whales and the occasional individuals seen with broken jaws. In such cases, large, experienced males would have better success monopolizing females. A smaller male would have no opportunity to breed until he achieved social maturity by deposing a "harem master" in battle. Since most harem masters are over 45 feet long (13.7 m), 30 tons (27 metric tons), and 25 years old, most males, which normally reach sexual maturity at 39 feet (11.9 m), long, 20 tons (18 metric tons), and 13 years of age, would have to wait a long time to mate, and some would never get the chance.

Hal Whitehead and colleagues (Whitehead and Waters, 1990) have shown that male sperm whales near the Galapagos Islands do not defend groups of females. Instead, they move between groups frequently. The explanation appears to be that mixed groups are smaller, owing to less abundant or more variably distributed prey. Consequently, a male will have less chance of finding many receptive females in a single school. Searching for new females in different schools is then a better strategy than fighting to monopolize a single small school. This would not require great size or strength and would give younger males more opportunities to mate.

*Large male sperm whale
stranded at Cape Cod.*
NEDRA FOSTER HECKER

*Sockets in upper jaw of female sperm whale stranded
at Seawall, Mt. Desert Island, Maine, October 21,
1966.*
PAUL FAVOUR

*Lower jaw and teeth of sperm whale in the
photo above.*

Sperm whale calf diving next to M/V Yankee Freedom. Near Georges Bank, July 1985.
SCOTT MERCER
(SEAFARERS EXPEDITIONS)

Sperm whale. Note position of blowhole and blunt, triangular dorsal fin.
PETER STEVICK

Females and young generally remain within relatively warm waters ranging from the tropics to the temperate zone, within about 45 degrees of the equator, and males must return to those waters for mating. Outside of the breeding season, or if they do not breed, individual males or small groups range into cold waters as far as 67 degrees from the equator, where females are rarely seen. For example, 99 out of 101 sperm whales taken by the Nova Scotian fishery from 1966 to 1972 were male, and the approximately 2,000 sperm whales taken near Iceland after 1948 were all male. The preferred feeding depths of males and females are also different. Because they are larger, males can dive deeper. This dimorphism may be adaptive because males and females would not compete for the same food resource.

The reproductive rate of sperm whales is one of the slowest for all mammals and is the slowest for all whales. Gestation lasts about 15 months and the 13-foot (4 m), 2,200-pound (998 kg) calf nurses for about 2 years, during which time it will grow to 22 feet (6.7 m) and about 3 tons (2.7 metric tons). One whale 13 years old had traces of milk in its stomach. A female probably does not become pregnant for at least another 9 months after weaning ends; thus the rate of calving is about once every 4 years.

Most readers of this guide will be unable to get out to the continental slope and beyond to see some of the tens of thousands of sperm whales that remain in the North Atlantic despite periods of Yankee whaling during the 1890s and modern whaling by Canada, Iceland, and other nations. CETAP's peak average census estimate for sperm whales in U.S. coastal waters north of Cape Hatteras and out to a depth of 3,280 feet (1,000 meters) was 222 (± 240) animals, during spring; most of them were seen during spring and summer along the margins of Georges Bank and into the Northeast Channel. Sightings summarized by Payne et al. (1991) indicated that a few sperm whales occur regularly in Georges Basin and along the southern edge of Browns Bank in the Northeast Channel from about July through November. Only on rare occasions do one or a few whales come into shallower waters over the continental shelf, perhaps following squid schools during their onshore-offshore migrations. The few records for the Gulf of Maine include a 31-foot (9.4 m) female that stranded alive on Mt. Desert Island, Maine, on October 20, 1966; an orphaned 15-foot (4.5 m), 3,000-pound (1,360 kg) nursing male found alive at Rockport, Maine, on March 22, 1976, which died from pneumonia on March 26 after successful transfer to the New

England Aquarium; a single sperm whale observed halfway between Grand Manan Island, New Brunswick, and Nova Scotia by New England Aquarium scientists in October 1981; and a 50-foot male stranded dead on Mosquito Island, Tenants Harbor, Maine, in late May 1991. Sperm whales are also rare in the Gulf of St. Lawrence, although several single sightings or strandings have occurred there. They are most commonly seen offshore from Nova Scotia and Newfoundland, where large males were hunted.

PYGMY SPERM WHALE
(*Kogia breviceps*)

This small whale, a resident of warm waters in the Atlantic, Pacific, and Indian oceans, has been found in our study area only on rare occasions, usually dead. A few records of live individuals suggest that the species could be encountered rarely at sea within the warmer portion of our study area.

The only definite report of a live stranding included two pygmy sperm whales just south of our area at West Yarmouth, Massachusetts, on Nantucket Sound, on December 26, 1982. A whale stranded alive in mid-November 1987 in Gouldsboro Bay, Maine, appeared to be of this species. A smaller whale swam nearby. The men who found it pushed it into deeper water, and the two whales swam away. Several days later (November 20, 1987) and not far away, a 9-foot-1-inch (2.75 m), approximately 800-pound (360 kg) female was found dead in Gouldsboro Bay at Carrying Place Inlet, Harrington, Maine. The only other record for the Gulf of Maine is a dead *Kogia* found at Nahant, Massachusetts, in 1910. Carcasses have been found in eastern Canada at Sable Island in 1969; under the ice in the harbor at Halifax, Nova Scotia, during winter of 1970; and at Miquelon Island, Gulf of St. Lawrence, in early September 1989.

Sighting records for this species display a peculiar trend. It has rarely been seen alive at sea. For example, CETAP aerial surveys from 1979 to 1981 observed only one *Kogia*, on June 8, 1981, beyond the continental shelf edge east of Delaware, where water depth was 8,400 feet (2,560 meters). Thus it is surprising how frequently pygmy sperm whales strand along tropical and subtropical shores. Records of the Marine Mammal Event Program, coordinated by the Smithsonian Institution, show pygmy sperm whales to be one of the most

Pygmy sperm whale
(Kogia breviceps).
Size range: 9–13 feet.
JOHN R. QUINN

frequently stranded cetacean species along the southeastern coast of the United States, with many alive when they first come ashore.

Most information available on these animals thus comes from specimens outside our study area. The following information is provided more in the hope of whetting zoological curiosity than with the expectation that many readers will see this species.

The average adult size of a pygmy sperm whale is about 10 feet (3 m) and 800 pounds (362 kg). Its small size is probably partly responsible for the dearth of live sightings at sea. The color is gray above, light below, sometimes with a pinkish tinge when the animal is alive. The pinkish tinge could result from increased blood flow near the skin surface so as to dump excess heat in warm water. A small dorsal fin is set toward the rear of the back. The head, only about one-seventh the body length, and the underslung lower jaw suggest a shark. The species name, from the Greek *brevis*, short, and *cepitis*, head, adequately describes the animal. Some drawings and photographs of the animal show a light crescent exactly in the place where a large fish would have a gill slit. If such a mark is common, one might consider the possibility that pygmy sperm whales capitalize on their sharklike appearance for some degree of protection from real sharks. Similarities to the sperm whale's appearance include having teeth only in the lower jaw and displacement of the blowhole slightly forward and to the left of the normal odontocete position. Furthermore, the head contains a small spermaceti organ.

The few observations of pygmy sperm whales at sea are of exceptional interest. These whales apparently occur individually or in small schools of up to perhaps 6 animals. Easy to approach, they bob quietly at the surface practically until touched, then dive suddenly while defecating a reddish-brown cloud into the water. If such behavior is normal, one must wonder whether the defecated cloud functions as a visual or olfactory decoy during escape from danger. One scientist speculated that the approachability of pygmy sperm whales might explain their apparent rarity because whaling captains might have used them as practice targets for training inexperienced crewmen while on the way to the whaling grounds.

Although stranded specimens have yielded some secrets about pygmy sperm whales—for example, that they eat squid, fish, crabs, and shrimp—the above speculations demonstrate how little we know about this pint-sized mystery of the cetacean world. Even the derivation of its genus name is a puzzle; nobody knows what *Kogia* means.

Pygmy sperm whale at New England Aquarium, 1980. Specimen MH-80-Kb. Note sharklike head with teeth in lower jaw.
SCOTT KRAUS

Pygmy sperm whale stranded in Gouldsboro Bay, Maine, showing head with underslung lower jaw. November 20, 1987.
KIM ROBERTSON

Pygmy sperm whale, 2.6-m female, showing tiny underslung lower jaw and false gill mark. Virginia Beach, Virginia, December 12, 1975.
JAMES G. MEAD

Pygmy sperm whale stranded in Gouldsboro Bay, Maine, November 20, 1987. Detail of teeth in lower jaw.
KIM ROBERTSON

Pygmy sperm whale stranded in Gouldsboro Bay, Maine, November 20, 1987. Detail of dorsal fin.
KIM ROBERTSON

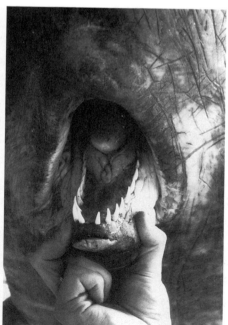

Pygmy sperm whale stranded in Gouldsboro Bay, Maine, November 20, 1987. As in the sperm whale, teeth are only present in the lower jaw.
KIM ROBERTSON

Perhaps it is derived from the Middle English *cog*, a tooth, and refers to the 12 to 16 pairs of sharp, curved teeth in the lower jaw. An obscure meaning of *cog*, however, is a deception or trick, which could refer to the animal's resemblance to a shark.

NORTHERN BOTTLENOSE WHALE
(Hyperoodon ampullatus)

The family of toothed whales to which this species belongs is known as the Ziphiidae, or beaked whales. Less is known about this group than about any of the other families of cetaceans (and perhaps less than about any other family of mammals). The group includes 19 named species, but more may be discovered. For example, a new species from Peru (*Mesoplodon peruvianus*) was described in 1991. Some species are known from only one or a few remains of stranded specimens. All ziphiids share the following characteristics: two distinct grooves on the ventral side of the jaw joining to form a forward-pointing V, a small dorsal fin set toward the rear of the back, and flukes lacking a central notch except in one species. Furthermore, all species but one have only one or two pairs of teeth located in the lower jaw and no functional teeth in the upper jaw. All beaked whales appear to feed mainly on squid, and the major evolutionary theme within this group may have been adaptive radiation to feed on different species of squid at different places or depths in the world ocean. Midwater fishes such as lantern fishes (Myctophidae) are also sometimes eaten.

Several characteristics suggest that these whales branched off quite early from the ancestral cetacean line. Their stomachs differ from those of other cetaceans. They lack a croplike forestomach; the esophagus empties directly into the main (fundic) stomach; and the fundic stomach empties into a connecting (pyloric) stomach consisting of many sacs connected by small valves. The pyloric stomach of other whales is not divided into sacs. The fats in the blubber, melon, and jaws of ziphiids share several chemical characteristics with other families thought to have branched off the main line of cetacean evolution relatively early, namely Physeteridae (sperm, pygmy sperm, and dwarf sperm whales) and Platanistidae (freshwater dolphins).

The northern bottlenose whale was commercially hunted for oil and meat by Scotland, Norway, Iceland, and Canada at various times

Northern bottlenose whale
(Hyperoodon ampullatus).
Size range: male, up to 29 feet; female, up to 26 feet.
JOHN R. QUINN

in the past century. Observations recorded by the whalers and information from the carcasses make it the best-known beaked whale in our area. The species was reasonably abundant, with more than 14,000 taken east of Greenland between 1890 and 1896 and nearly 26,000 between 1890 and 1900. More than 3,000 animals were taken annually in several of those years. During the middle 1900s, the fishery extended westward as far as Newfoundland. From 1938 through 1972, Norway took 4,870 bottlenose whales outside of Norwegian waters. At least 28,000 were estimated to exist in the North Atlantic in 1965, based on the cumulative number killed between 1965 and 1971. Hunting stopped in 1972, probably because of population decline, but also because Canada closed its whaling stations, England forbade the use of whale meat in pet food, and Norwegian fur farms switched to other foods. No population census has been done, but the stock is considered to be critically depleted.

Bottlenose whales are found mainly in deep Arctic to temperate waters of the North Atlantic Ocean. In the western North Atlantic, their range extends from Davis Strait south to Rhode Island. The chance of seeing them alive within our study area is small except at a few locations offshore. One such place is the Gully, about 130 miles east of Halifax, Nova Scotia, near Sable Island. The Gully is a narrow, steep-walled canyon cut into the Scotian Shelf, probably by a large river that drained part of the continental ice sheet during the most recent glaciation. The Gully's steep sides appear to be a good place for bottlenose whales to hunt squid throughout the year. Canadian whalers also found the Gully to be a good hunting ground, taking 87 bottlenose whales from there and the edge of the Grand Bank between 1962 and 1967. Some cruises offered by sail-training or study-at-sea programs have stopped at the Gully to study bottlenose whales in recent years. During a three-year study, Dalhousie University researchers Anika Faucher, Lindy Weilgart, and Hal Whitehead photoidentified several hundred bottlenose whales in Gully waters by distinctive scars on the body and dorsal fin.

Bottlenose whales are also sighted along the edge of the continental shelf off Newfoundland and Labrador. Live specimens have been seen in Trinity Bay, Newfoundland (two in July 1953; a group, and one released from a squid net at Dildo, in early September 1990); inshore at Cape Martin, Gulf of St. Lawrence, in 1940; and 15 miles upstream in Sydney River, Nova Scotia, October 8–15, 1992.

The frequency of strandings south of Canada during autumn and winter suggests that bottlenose whales may winter offshore from the Grand Bank south to about Cape Cod, perhaps also entering the Northeast Channel and Gulf of Maine to feed. The southernmost record for the species on this side of the Atlantic is a 27-foot (8.2 m) female at Newport, Rhode Island, in February 1867. No live bottlenose whales have been reported at sea in the Gulf of Maine. A male on the beach at North Dennis, Massachusetts, in January 1869, however, may have been alive at or shortly before stranding; and a young male and female were alive when they stranded at Beverly Farms, Massachusetts, in October 1923. The Beverly Farms whales made deep groaning and sobbing sounds that could be heard from half a mile away. A 20-foot (6 m) male found dead at Cobequid Bay, Bay of Fundy, in October 1969, was described in great detail by Mitchell (1975).

Most whale watchers won't need to remember field marks for this species, but the following information is included for completeness and zoological interest. If these descriptions lead to a report of a stranding that would otherwise have gone unnoticed, or stimulate someone to find out more about these peculiar animals or even go to see them firsthand, our effort will have been amply repaid.

Large bottlenose whales are about the same length as a minke whale but differ in many traits, such as occurring in social groups, producing visible blows up to 5 feet (1.5 m) tall, exhibiting more frequent breaching and lobtailing, and approaching boats more consistently.

The two sexes are considerably different in size, shape, and color. Males grow to about 29 feet (8.8 m) and 4 tons (3.6 metric tons), maturing at between 7 and 11 years. Females reach about 26 feet (7.9 m) and 3.5 tons (3.2 metric tons), maturing between 8 and 12 years, then bearing a calf about every 2 years after a 12-month pregnancy. Females and immature males are usually brown or gray. Older whales bear varying amounts of light or yellow color. Males, especially, frequently bear many light-colored scratches and scars, probably inflicted by other males using the two teeth found at the tip of the lower jaw. Some scars are also caused by the cookie-cutter shark (*Isistius brasiliensis*), parasitic copepods (*Penella* spp.), and perhaps lampreys. In large, old males, the upper lip protrudes, the skull develops a tall crest at the rear of each side of the upper jaw, the huge forehead (melon) bulges forward, and the head may become cream-colored. Adults of both sexes have a slight, faintly gray depression or "neck"

Northern bottlenose whale, showing light head and beak, at the Gully, Nova Scotia.
HOWARD E. WINN

Head of northern bottlenose whale photographed at the Gully.
ANIKA FAUCHER

Bulbous heads and beak of northern bottlenose whales photographed in the Gully.
ANIKA FAUCHER

*Dorsal fins of three bottlenose whales at the Gully,
showing some of the nicks and scars used to identify individuals.*
ANIKA FAUCHER

behind the melon. As in all ziphiid whales, the elongation of the jaws is visible externally as a short beak, and this species frequently shows its head and beak when breathing. The species name (L. *ampulla*, a round bottle) refers to the head shape, as does the common name bottlenose. The genus name derives from the Greek *hyperoon*, palate, + *odous*, tooth. The first specimen described seemed to have tiny teeth in the palate. Squid-eating odontocetes tend to have rough palates for holding the slippery prey, but no teeth actually grow there.

Bottlenose whales are frequently seen in small schools of 5 to 15 animals. Preliminary results from photo-identification studies at the Gully indicate that group membership is relatively stable. Sexual dimorphism in size suggests that males and females behave differently and that social structure may be complex. For example, sexes may segregate seasonally during migrations, with large males remaining in higher latitudes. Or males may dive deeper than females for feeding, perhaps taking larger prey items. Large males may fight to monopolize schools of females during the breeding season. Further studies are needed to confirm these speculations.

Catching these whales was made easier by two traits, curiosity and helpfulness. Bottlenose whales commonly approach stationary ships, especially when a generator is running or there is some other noise. Pounding on the hull or starting up the engine or propeller after lying adrift can also attract them. They have often been observed to stay with wounded school members, sometimes for hours, supporting them at the surface to aid breathing. They apparently leave abruptly if the wounded animal dies. This behavior allowed whole schools to be taken by early whalers.

Bottlenose whales feed mainly on squid, especially the deep-sea species *Gonatus fabricii*, and their stomachs may contain nearly a bushel of beaks, the only part of a squid that can't be digested. Other prey recorded include various fishes (herring, cusk, lumpfish, redfish, halibut, spiny dogfish, and skates) and bottom-living invertebrates such as sea stars and sea cucumbers. Dive times of an hour or more are apparently common, suggesting that the whales feed at great depths. Some dives of 2 hours have been observed. As in the sperm whale, the head has a spermaceti organ and a larger oil-rich melon. Both are probably involved in processing echolocation pulses. Whalers could obtain up to 200 pounds of spermaceti oil from the head of a large male, in addition to perhaps 2 tons of oil from blubber and bone.

Perhaps research will someday reveal why this species was numerous enough to have supported a whaling industry when many of the other beaked whales appear to be so rare.

BLAINVILLE'S BEAKED WHALE; DENSE-BEAKED WHALE
(*Mesoplodon densirostris*)

Twelve species of the family Ziphiidae are assigned to the genus *Mesoplodon*. Their biology is poorly understood, and some species are known only from several stranded specimens. Even experts often cannot identify these animals precisely on the few occasions when they are seen at sea. For the purposes of this book, it is sufficient to note that most *Mesoplodon* species are oceanic in warm or temperate waters. Squid of various types usually appear to be the main food. These whales have been observed swimming in groups of up to about 6 animals. All species are similar in general appearance, color, and size, with average adult lengths of about 15 feet (4.5 m).

All are medium or dark gray above and lighter gray beneath, with some body scarring, a small dorsal fin set far back, and no central notch to the flukes. The species differ strikingly in the size and placement of the one or two pairs of teeth in the lower jaw. The genus name (Gr. *mesos*, middle, *hopla*, arms, *odous*, tooth), indicating an animal armed with a tooth in the middle of the lower jaw, was created in 1850 by the French physician and zoologist Paul Gervais in his description of another species of beaked whale, *M. europaeus* (also called the Gulf Stream beaked whale or Gervais' beaked whale). That is the beaked whale most commonly stranded along the Atlantic coast of the United States, but since it has not been found north of New York on our coast, it is not described in this book.

The dense-beaked whale (L. *densus*, dense, + *rostrum*, beak) has a worldwide distribution in deep tropical to warm temperate waters. It was first described by the French zoologist Henri de Blainville in 1817. As of 1989 there were records of 22 stranded specimens from North America, including 16 from the U.S. Atlantic Coast. Records from our study area include 2 from Massachusetts (Annisquam, in 1898) and two from Nova Scotia (Peggy's Cove, in 1940 and Cape Breton Island in December 1968).

This is one of the easier *Mesoplodon* species to identify because its lower jaw swells to an enormous prominence midway along its

Blainville's beaked whale
(Mesoplodon densirostris).
Size range: up to 14 or 16 feet.
JOHN R. QUINN

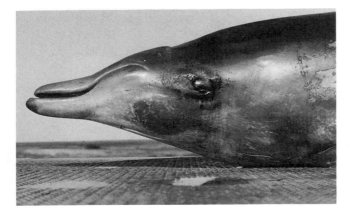

Blainville's beaked whale,
left view of head of 3.97-m
female stranded at Buxton,
North Carolina, March 4,
1975.
JAMES G. MEAD

Skull of Blainville's beaked
whale showing one huge
triangular tooth located
midway along each side of
lower jaw. Collection of the
Queensland Museum,
Brisbane, Australia.
STEVEN KATONA

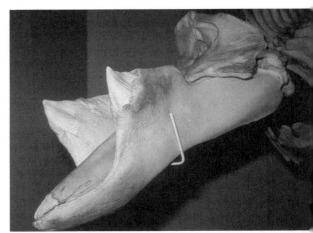

length. Each mandibular prominence contains one spectacular tooth 6 to 8 inches (15–20 cm) high, nearly 3 inches (7.5 cm) wide, and nearly 2 inches (5 cm) thick. Only the tip of each tooth protrudes from its socket, however, and only in males does it extend through the gum tissue. In females the tooth remains covered by gum.

The teeth must not be needed for feeding because females live their whole lives without them. Immature males are also toothless. Squid or other prey are probably caught by sucking them into the mouth. The V-shaped grooves on the throat probably allow the throat to expand rapidly, creating suction when the mouth is opened rapidly. The exact mechanisms by which this might occur are being investigated through dissection of stranded specimens.

Indirect evidence suggests that the primary function of teeth in most beaked whales is not for eating but for fighting. In most species, males are heavily scarred with long white lines or parallel lines. Detailed study of the size, shape, and location of scars shows that they are caused by teeth of conspecific males, probably during fights over dominance or females. Species with teeth located at the tip of the lower jaw are considered more primitive. *Mesoplodon densirostris*, with very elaborate teeth set halfway back along the jaw on a well-developed prominence, is considered one of the most advanced species in the genus. To prevent damage to the delicate jaws during ramming or raking of the body of another male during a fight, a reinforcing structure has evolved in the skull of male beaked whales. A canal within the long rostrum, the mesorostral canal, has become strengthened with very hard, heavy bone. The heavily ossified rostrum of *Mesoplodon densirostris* has the highest density of any bone in the animal kingdom. One cubic centimeter weights up to 2.4 grams, about 40 percent more than ivory in an elephant's tusk and 10 percent heavier than bone surrounding the middle and inner ear of a sperm whale. The scientific and common names of this species aptly describe this unique trait.

Mesoplodon densirostris juveniles are medium gray dorsally and white ventrally. Males are gray all over. Scientists were able to record chirps and whistles from one dense-beaked whale that came ashore alive in Florida.

True's beaked whale
(Mesoplodon mirus).
Size range: up to about 17 feet.
JOHN R. QUINN

Sowerby's beaked whale
(Mesoplodon bidens).
Size range: up to 16 feet.
SARAH LANDRY

TRUE'S BEAKED WHALE
(*Mesoplodon mirus*)

This species was first described in 1913 by Frederick True, who named it from the Latin, *mirus*, wonderful. Not much has been learned about the details of its life since True's time. Instead, we may know less about it than we thought we did.

Until recently this species was known only from temperate waters of the eastern and western North Atlantic Ocean. As of 1989, a total of 16 specimens had been found in North American waters and 6 in European waters. In the western North Atlantic, specimens have been found from Saint Anne's Bay, Cape Breton Island, Nova Scotia, south to San Salvador Island, Bahamas. The Saint Anne's Bay specimen was found on August 5, 1938, and the only other records from our study area occurred at Wells Beach, Maine, in March 1906, and at Medaket Beach, Nantucket Island, in early September 1982. The Nantucket specimen was emaciated and scars around its beak suggested that entanglement in fishnet had prevented it from eating.

In 1959 a specimen was found along the Indian Ocean coast of South Africa, and subsequently several others were found at other warm temperate shores of the Indian Ocean. The species is therefore likely to occur in the South Pacific Ocean, since the population would have had to spread through those waters to get to the Indian Ocean.

The color of specimens has been medium gray dorsally, light gray ventrally. A white patch was present around the genital slit and anus in one male, and one female apparently had similar pigmentation. A central notch has been seen in the flukes of some specimens, although this is not the usual case for ziphiid whales. The mandible contains two small, triangular, flattened teeth, located at the very tip of the lower jaw, which only extend through the gums of males.

SOWERBY'S BEAKED WHALE;
NORTH SEA BEAKED WHALE
(*Mesoplodon bidens*)

Sowerby's beaked whale is named after the man who in 1804 described the first specimen, found in Scotland in 1800. Also known as the

Heads of two Sowerby's beaked whales, probably a mother and calf, seen in a group of three adults and two calves near Hydrographers Canyon, July 1987.
SCOTT MARION (SEAFARERS EXPEDITIONS)

(Below) Sowerby's beaked whale, 3.96-m female stranded at Colleville, France, September 1975. (Left) Close-up view of head.
D. ROBINEAU, COURTESY JAMES G. MEAD

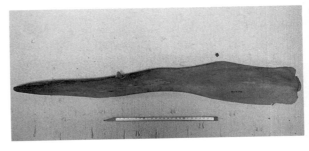

Lower left jaw of Sowerby's beaked whale, showing single tooth midway along length.
CAREY BELL

North Sea beaked whale, its distribution appears to be centered there, judging from the 77 specimens that have come ashore on European coasts up to 1989. A few live sightings at sea have also been reported. The species apparently ranges farther north than other *Mesoplodon* species, seems to inhabit cooler waters, and perhaps enters coastal waters more readily at some seasons for feeding. The specific name *bidens* (L. *bi*, two, and *dens*, tooth) refers to the two triangular teeth in the lower jaw, one on each side, that make up the entire dentition.

Records from the western North Atlantic range from Labrador (54°10'N, 58°35'W) south to Port Saint Joe, Florida, and include reports of 21 individuals distributed in 6 individual strandings, 2 mass strandings, and 3 live sightings during 120 years (1867–87). All records listed by Lien and Barry (1990) occurred from late July to October. Except for a 4.57-meter male that stranded in Florida in October 1984, all occurred within our study area or in contiguous waters. Both sexes have stranded. Two strandings occurred on Nantucket Island, Massachusetts (1867 and September 10, 1973). All others occurred in Newfoundland or Labrador. The two mass strandings, both on the northeast coast of Newfoundland, included 6 whales (August 30, 1986, at Carmenville, Newfoundland) and 3 whales (September 18, 1987, in Norris Arm, Bay of Exploits, Newfoundland). Only 3 of the 6 whales were recovered at Carmenville, and they were all males, which suggested that the species may segregate by sex, at least for part of the year.

The first of three live sightings from the western North Atlantic was a 15-foot 9-inch (4.72 m) female, harpooned in Notre Dame Bay, Newfoundland, on September 23, 1953. Next, a 13 foot-8-inch (4.1 m) long immature male became entrapped in fishing gear in Conception Bay, Newfoundland, on July 24, 1984. It stranded alive the next day, was pushed back into the bay, but came ashore dead the following day. The most recent live sighting was a group of three adults with two calves seen near Hydrographer's Canyon (40°00'N, 68°54'W) on July 18, 1987.

Adults of this species are described as dark charcoal gray or bluish gray on top with lighter streaks and spots (scars) scattered irregularly on the sides. Females listed by Lien (1990) were up to 15.75 feet (4.72 m) long, and males were up to 16.5 feet (4.95 m). Each side of the lower jaw has one flattened tooth located midway along the mandible, with its pointed crown directed slightly toward the rear. Enough stranded specimens have been recovered in Europe to indicate

that mating takes place in late winter or spring; gestation lasts about
1 year; and the 7-foot (2.1 m) calf nurses for about a year until weaning
at 10 feet (3 m) long. No population estimates are available, but the
species is classified as "vulnerable" in Canada. A new potential threat
to this species is entanglement in drift nets (gill nets) set along the
edge of the continental shelf for swordfish. Twelve of these beaked
whales died in such nets off the eastern U.S. in summer 1989 (data
cited in Payne et al. 1991).

Key for Identifying Stranded Whales, Dolphins, and Porpoises Found between Cape Cod and Newfoundland

I. Baleen in upper jaw (may be rotted out in dead specimens). No teeth. Double blowhole. Usually over 30 feet long (except minke whales and juveniles). Continue to A. BALEEN WHALES.

II. Baleen absent, teeth present (sometimes under gums). Single blowhole. Much shorter than 30 feet (except sperm and largest killer and bottlenose whales). Continue to B. TOOTHED WHALES.

A. Baleen Whales (Mysticetes)

1. a.   Dorsal fin and throat grooves present. Go to 2.
   b.   Dorsal fin and throat grooves absent. Length up to 55 feet; arched jaw 25 percent of body length; rough callosities on head; baleen dark, up to 390 plates per side, each up to 7 feet long with up to 175 bristles per inch. RIGHT WHALE.

c.   Dorsal fin and throat grooves absent. Length up to 65 feet; huge arched jaw up to 40 percent of body length; no callosities on head; baleen dark, up to 360 plates per side, each up to 15 feet long with up to about 212 bristles per inch; arctic, very rare. BOWHEAD WHALE.

2. a.   Over 30 feet long. Go to 3.

   b.   Under 30 feet long; 50–70 ventral grooves; up to 325 plates per side of short (8 inches), yellowish or cream-colored baleen with up to 63 bristles per inch; white patch on flipper, pointed snout. MINKE WHALE.

   c.   Under 30 feet, but not as in 2b. Juvenile baleen whale. Go to 3.

3. a.   Length to 55 feet; up to 25 wide throat grooves reaching to umbilicus; knobby head and jaws; white flipper up to 33 percent of body length; sawtoothed hind edges on flukes; black baleen, up to 400 plates per side, each up to 2.5 feet long, with up to 88 bristles per inch. HUMPBACK WHALE

   b.   Shorter flippers, smooth edges on flukes, over 25 throat grooves. Go to 4.

4. a.   Length to 85 feet; up to 88 throat grooves reaching to umbilicus; dorsal fin less than 12 inches high, set far back on body; light gray-blue with lighter mottling on belly, sides, and back; up to 395 wide black baleen plates per side, each up to 3 feet long with up to 75 bristles per inch. BLUE WHALE.

   b.   Length to 79 feet; up to 100 throat grooves reaching to umbilicus; prominent dorsal fin up to 24 inches high; lower-right lip and sometimes upper-right lip white; up to 473 baleen plates per side, each up to 2.5 feet long with up to 88 bristles per inch; anterior 100 or so baleen plates on right side only are light, remaining plates are dark. FINBACK WHALE.

   c.   Length to 62 feet; dark body but may have oval white spots on sides; up to 56 throat grooves reaching only slightly past flipper, not to umbilicus; up to 340 dark baleen plates per side, each up to 2.5 feet long with up to 150 fine white bristles per inch. SEI WHALE.

B. Toothed Whales (Odontocetes)

5. a.   Length to 60 feet (males) or 38 feet (females); massive square head with blowhole at left tip; narrow lower jaw with up to

25 large teeth in each side; dorsal hump; triangular flukes with deep central notch; wrinkled skin. SPERM WHALE.

b. Length under 30 feet. Go to 6.

6. a. Dorsal fin present. Go to 7.

b. No dorsal fin; length to 16 feet; body all white (juveniles gray or brown); 8–10 pairs of teeth in each jaw, up to ⅔ inch diameter. BELUGA.

c. No dorsal fin; length to 16 feet; body gray or blotched white on gray; one (rarely both) upper incisor extends as long tusk; no other teeth; arctic only. NARWHAL.

7. a. Jaws of whole animal not drawn out into beak. Go to 8.

b. Jaws of whole animal extended forward as distinct beak. Go to 11.

c. If skull is found, see 9 and 10 before continuing to 11.

8. a. Small dorsal fin. Go to 9.

b. Large dorsal fin. Go to 10.

9. a. Length to 5 feet; up to 30 pairs of small, flattened, spade-shaped teeth in each jaw; small triangular dorsal fin, often with small, rough, wartlike growths on leading edge. HARBOR PORPOISE.

b. Length to 11 feet; sharklike snout; jaw like sperm whale's with 12–16 pairs of sharp, recurved teeth, lower jaw only; upper jaw toothless. PYGMY SPERM WHALE.

10. a. Length to 30 feet; dorsal fin up to 6 feet high; body black above with white patch behind eye, gray saddle behind dorsal fin, and white of belly extending up on sides; 10–12 pairs of teeth in each jaw, up to 1 or 2 inches diameter. KILLER WHALE.

b. Length to 20 feet; rounded forehead overhangs short snout; very long-based, curved, round-tipped dorsal fin set well forward of midbody; curved and pointed flippers; jet black except for anchor-shaped gray patch on chest; 8–10 pairs of teeth in upper and lower jaws, ½ inch diameter. PILOT WHALE, POTHEAD.

c. Length to 14 feet; gray body, with many white scratches or scars; blunt snout; usually 3–7 teeth, ½ inch diameter on each side of lower jaw, usually none in upper; curved, pointed dorsal fin up to 15 inches high is usually darker than body. RISSO'S DOLPHIN.

11. a.   Distinct black-and-white color pattern and/or many teeth in both jaws. Go to 12.

   b.   Basically uniform color, usually dark gray, black, or brownish; 2–4 teeth in lower jaw only; 2 throat grooves join to form forward-pointing V; flukes without central notch; small triangular dorsal fin. Go to 13.

12. a.   Length to 10 feet; body dark above, light below, white patch on side runs aft from below dorsal fin and sweeps over the ridge of back; short snout usually white, rarely black; 22–28 teeth on each side of upper and lower jaws, ¼ inch diameter. WHITE-BEAKED DOLPHIN.

   b.   Length to 9 feet; body dark above, white on belly, white patch on side runs aft from below dorsal fin but does not reach over ridge of back; yellow or tan streak behind white patch; short, dark snout; 30–40 teeth on each side of upper and lower jaws, ³⁄₁₆ inch diameter. WHITE-SIDED DOLPHIN.

   c.   Length to 8 feet; dark above, white below, with gray or yellowish crisscross or figure-eight pattern on sides; 40–50 teeth on each side of upper and lower jaws, ¹⁄₁₀ inch diameter. COMMON DOLPHIN.

   d.   Length to 9 feet; body dark above, with white of belly sweeping up over eye and flipper toward dorsal fin and ridge of back; distinct dark line from eye along lower side to anus; 43–50 teeth on each side of upper and lower jaws, ⅛ inch diameter. STRIPED DOLPHIN.

   e.   Length to 12 feet; body gray above, lighter on belly; dark stripes run from base of short beak to eye and blowholes; no distinct color pattern; 22–26 teeth on each side of upper and lower jaws, ⅛ inch diameter. BOTTLENOSE DOLPHIN.

13. a.   Length to 30 feet; color gray to light brown or yellowish; large forehead bulges over short beak; two small teeth at tip of lower jaw; light gray indentation between head and rest of body; relatively small curved dorsal fin located behind midpoint of body. NORTHERN BOTTLENOSE WHALE.

   b.   Length to 17 feet; black above, gray on belly; small dorsal fin located toward rear of body; 2 small flattened teeth at tip of lower jaw. TRUE'S BEAKED WHALE.

   c.   Length to 15 feet; body all dark; one large tooth (up to 6 inches, only tip exposed) in massive triangular prominence midway along lower jaw; small triangular dorsal fin located

just behind midbody; flukes lack central notch. BLAIN-
VILLE'S BEAKED WHALE.

d. Length to 16 feet; body dark; one flattened tooth located midway along each side of lower jaw, tip directed posteriorly;
small dorsal fin; flukes lack central notch. SOWERBY'S
BEAKED WHALE.

FORM 80-1

GULF OF MAINE
Whale Sighting Network

Fold and mail to: **ALLIED WHALE**
College of the Atlantic
Bar Harbor, Maine 04609
(207) 288-5644 or 5015

Your name _____ Address _____ Zip _____ Phone _____

INSTRUCTIONS: Please complete this form and CIRCLE ON THE ILLUSTRATIONS ANY FEATURE THAT YOU OBSERVED. Photograph animals if possible, especially undersides of humpback flukes. Space is provided for you to sketch any unusual markings or tags or to draw species not illustrated.

Date _____, 19 _____ Time _____ am/pm. Weather and sea conditions _____ Temp. _____

Nearest land mark _____ Lat./long, Loran _____ Depth _____

Type of whale or porpoise sighted _____ Size _____ Number _____ Photographs? _____

How far were you from the animals? _____ Which direction were they swimming? _____ In a tight school? _____

The whale spouted _____ times, with _____ seconds between spouts. Then it dived for _____ minutes before spouting again. _____

Describe the animal's behavior (feeding, jumping, tail raised in air, etc.) _____

Describe any fishes, birds, or other marine life seen near the whales or porpoises. _____

COMMONLY SEEN:

finback whale
30-70 ft.

right side of jaws light, left dark

humpback whale
30-55 ft.

bumps on snout

15 ft. rough edges

flukes often raised when diving

photographs can identify individuals

white flipper-15 ft. long

minke whale
15-25 ft.

pointed snout often breaks surface

light gray sweeps up from chest

white patch on flipper

right whale
30-55 ft.

rough white patches

V-spout

12 ft. smooth edges

flukes often raised when diving

no dorsal fin

dark undersides

harbor porpoise
4-6 ft.

pothead or pilot whale
10-20 ft.

long based fin

bulbous head

OCCASIONALLY SEEN:

saddleback dolphin
6-8 ft.

criss cross pattern on side

killer whale
15-25 ft.

male fin, 5 ft.

female fin, 3 ft.

gray

white patch

white sided dolphin
7-9 ft.

tan

white

white beaked dolphin
8-10 ft.

white back

white

FOLD HERE

D.D. Tyler

Form for reporting cetaceans commonly sighted in the Gulf of Maine.

D. D. TYLER

PART 2

Bonuses for Whale Watchers:

BASKING SHARKS, SUNFISH, and LEATHERBACK TURTLES

Nearly every year we receive from whale watchers and fishermen reports of basking sharks, ocean sunfish, and leatherback turtles. Most people are surprised to learn that these animals are regular summer visitors to our study area. We include below brief accounts.

Basking shark
(Cetorhinus maximus).
Size range: up to 45 feet.
SARAH LANDRY

Species Accounts

BASKING SHARK
(Cetorhinus maximus)

This huge fish, which can grow to 45 feet (13.7 m) long, is second in size only to the whale shark,* and is frequently seen during summer in our study area by whale watchers and fishermen. Several hundred million years before baleen whales evolved, sharks like these were already straining plankton from the water.

Basking sharks inhabit temperate waters of all oceans. They range throughout the temperate and boreal waters of the North Atlantic, from Newfoundland to North Carolina, and from Norway to the Mediterranean. In the western North Atlantic, they generally occur south of our study area in winter, entering our waters during summer. In the northern Gulf of Maine they may be sighted in July or August, but their abundance is strongly linked to peak summer temperature of about 57°F (14°C) during August. On August 17, 1990, for example, basking sharks were reported at many locations along

---

*In summer of 1989, 4.5 miles southwest of Matinicus Rock, Maine, Captain John Earl observed at very close range a shark that was longer than his 40-foot (12.2 m) boat, very wide, dark in color, but with rows of white spots along its back. That description fits the whale shark, *Rhincodon typicus*, the only fish larger than the basking shark. Like the basking shark, the whale shark feeds on plankton, but it normally is found only in tropical waters. Captain Earl's sighting appears to be the first record of that species from our study area.

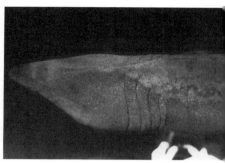

Basking shark. Note the broad dorsal fin.
The eye is also visible in this photo.
Mt. Desert Rock, Maine, August 26, 1990.
BEVERLY AGLER

Basking shark, showing pointed nose
and wrap-around gill slits. Mt. Desert Roc
Maine, August 16, 1990.
BEVERLY AGLER

Basking shark harpooned off Pemaquid Point, Maine,
July 7, 1968. Weight 1,850 pounds (839 kg).
Note gill slits extending almost completely around head.
EVERETT BOUTILIER

the eastern Maine coast, in the Grand Manan Basin, and offshore from Brier Island, Nova Scotia. They have become entangled in fishing gear along the coast of Newfoundland from July through September. The sharks may occur singly or in groups of up to 10 or more. We have seen groups of 6 or 8, head to tail, slowly swimming in a circle. Other observers have also reported this unexplained behavior.

At sea, basking sharks can be identified best by their large size —most specimens measure from 12 to 30 feet (3.7–9.7 m) long—and the large, floppy, triangular dorsal fin. Furthermore, the caudal fin often breaks the surface as the shark moves sluggishly along. These animals are very docile, almost completely harmless, and can be approached closely. They have 4 to 7 rows of teeth so small that they resemble a carpenter's rasp. The 5 large gill openings encircle the neck. Each of these openings contains a gill arch, each arch adorned with horny, bristlelike gill rakers. The gill rakers look like baleen (whalebone), and fishermen or whale hunters in times past therefore called these animals "bone sharks." The scientific name also recognizes this similarity, translating roughly as "big whale-nosed" shark. As the shark swims lazily along with its large mouth open, water streams through the gill openings and the rakers strain out copepods and other small animals. Periodically the shark must close the gill openings and "backflush" the collected plankton into the throat for swallowing. *Calanus finmarchicus* is the main food from spring though autumn. Nobody knows what these animals do in winter, although perhaps they shed their gill rakers, remain inactive on the bottom, then grow new rakers for resumption of feeding in spring.

Basking sharks have been hunted with harpoons throughout their range because the enormous liver, which constitutes up to 25 percent of the body weight, is a rich source of oil. Sharks do not have a swim bladder, and they rely on the oily liver for buoyancy. A liver can yield between 80 and 600 gallons (300–2,260 liters) of oil, which was used for burning in lamps before the discovery of petroleum. Early hunting by American colonists during the first half of the 1700s and thereafter may have reduced the abundance of this species in the Gulf of Maine to this day. Sperm whalers out of New Bedford also hunted it because its oil was about as good as sperm oil for lighting purposes.

Despite the lazy, inoffensive nature of this shark when undisturbed, harpooned specimens have proven feisty and strong. There still is a small commercial market for the meat, oil, and fins of basking sharks. The fins are used to make shark fin soup, a Chinese delicacy.

The oil, no longer needed for illumination, is rich in vitamin A and chemicals used to make cosmetics and precision lubricants. Newfoundland fishermen sell basking sharks that accidentally tangle in their nets. They are deliberately hunted off Japan and at several locations in Europe. A few are killed for sport.

Overfishing is a potential danger to basking sharks because they reproduce very slowly. A male clasps a female with his modified pelvic fins and inserts a spermatophore into the female's cloaca. Mating may occur during spring. The female's two uteri nourish the growing embryos. Circumstantial evidence suggests that babies are about 5 or 6 feet (1.5–1.8 m) long at birth, but no observations of birth or of females containing embryos have been published.

Basking sharks resemble right whales in several interesting respects. Their warm-season distributions are the same; they eat the same food and catch it in the same way; and both may have suffered a long-lasting population decline as a result of early overhunting. Furthermore, both of these huge, bizarre-looking animals often form the basis of sea monster stories. To a naive observer, a line of sharks swimming head to tail might look like a long, snakelike monster. Rotting carcasses have also been reported as those of monsters. We welcome reports of basking shark sightings in the hope that such data might reveal population trends and could provide comparisons with future sightings of right whales.

OCEAN SUNFISH
(*Mola mola*)

As a result of its large size and strange appearance, the ocean sunfish regularly generates more puzzled inquiries than any other large fish in our study area. This fish can grow to at least 11 feet (3.4 m) long and 2,000 pounds (907 kg). The oval body, with its large eye and tall, swordlike dorsal and anal fins, lacks a caudal fin. At first glance it looks like a small whale whose tail had been chopped off. More than one caller has given such a description to us. The fish gets its common name because it is often seen lazing at the surface on a sunny day. At such times it usually lies on its side or tips slowly back and forth, the tall dorsal fin waving in the air. Other local names, such as "moonfish" or "headfish," refer to the circular body and the lack of distinction between head and body.

Ocean sunfish
(Mola mola).
Size range: 8 to 11 feet or more.
SARAH LANDRY

In summer, ocean sunfish regularly visit coastal waters through-out our study area, with sightings during July and August in the Gulf of Maine, especially southern sections; along the outer Nova Scotia coast; in the Gulf of St. Lawrence; and on the Newfoundland Banks. We expect 20 or 40 reports of ocean sunfish each year in the Gulf of Maine, and many more animals probably go unreported.

Surprisingly little is known about this species, and some of the things that are known are equally surprising. The sunfish is found worldwide in tropical and temperate seas. The individuals that enter our continental shelf waters certainly come from warmer offshore waters. The listless attitude of sunfish seen in cool waters has prompted statements that they cannot survive long in our study area and will surely die by winter, at the latest. Perhaps that is true, but it is also possible that they are not in distress. Several observations support this idea. First, although sunfish in our waters are passive enough to be approached easily, fishermen who have harpooned them have been startled by their vigorous resistance to being taken. Second, plenty of food for these fish exists in our waters. The sunfish's diet apparently consists largely of jellyfish, comb jellies (ctenophores), and salps, plus some other, harder invertebrates. Exactly how a fish can grow so large feeding on such watery fare is something of a mystery, but in summer our study area provides a rich supply of these jellies, and we have obtained the remains of the common lion's mane jellyfish, *Cyanea capillata*, from a harpooned specimen. We have also watched a dying sunfish defecate a rusty red liquid that matched the color of that jellyfish. Tagging some of these curious fish to see whether any survive their forays into our waters might resolve the issue.

Not all sunfish are giants. The average size is about 3 to 5 feet (91–153 cm) long and 175 to 500 pounds (79–227 kg). We dissected a harpooned specimen that weighed 575 pounds (260 kg). The skin was exceptionally thick and tough, was covered with rough, sharklike denticles, and could be cut only with great difficulty. The entire skeleton was cartilaginous, like a shark's, even though this is a teleost (bony) fish. The skin and gills carried several dozen parasitic copepods and other crustaceans. We boiled up the fins in hopes of making a mock shark's-fin soup, but the result was poor. We had better luck with the abundant meat, which proved to be thick and fleshy, more like chicken than fish, and quite tasty when stir-fried. Several years later, we saw the ocean sunfish included in a compendium of poisonous ocean creatures, apparently because its family (Molidae) is related to

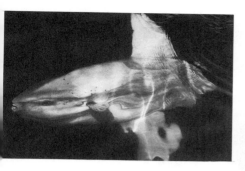

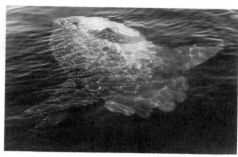

Ocean sunfish. The small oval dots on the body are parasitic crustaceans (Copepoda). Mt. Desert Rock, Maine, August 22, 1990.
BEVERLY AGLER

Ocean sunfish.
CARL HAYCOCK

Ocean sunfish caught in lobster trap lines near Isleford, Maine, by David Layton on July 29, 1982, and photographed at the J. S. Humphreys Wharf, Southwest Harbor, Maine.

Approximate weight 400 pounds (181 kg).
STEVEN KATONA

Leatherback turtle
(Dermochelys coriacea).
Size range: 6 to 11 feet or more.
SARAH LANDRY

the family of fishes (Tetraodontiformidae) that includes puffers, whose gonads are deadly poisonous. We have not been able to discover what parts of its body, if any, are actually poisonous.

LEATHERBACK TURTLE
(Dermochelys coriacea)

Whale watchers and fishermen in our study area occasionally spy the world's heaviest reptile, the leatherback turtle. The largest specimen on record, a male that weighed 2,015 pounds (916 kg) and measured 9 feet 7 inches (2.9 m) in length, died after becoming entangled in fishing nets in Cardigan Bay, Wales, on September 23, 1988.

Because it is the only turtle in the world with 5 to 7 ridges that run the full length of the shell, this species is easily identified. The leathery shell is made of thousands of nearly indistinguishably tiny bones and doesn't look at all like a normal turtle shell. The extremely long front flippers are also distinctive. Leatherbacks in our study area are usually mature and frequently measure over 6 feet (1.7 m) in length and weigh over 1,000 pounds (454 kg). They are seen singly in our area, although loose aggregations have occasionally been reported from southeastern or Gulf Coast states.

During summer, the leatherback, found in all oceans except the Antarctic, regularly visits waters around Cape Cod, the Gulf of Maine, Nova Scotia, and the cold waters around Newfoundland. It is the only marine turtle that has colonized cold waters for feeding and the only species that regularly occurs in the open waters of our study area.

Why do leatherbacks come here? They feed on jellyfish, especially the lion's mane (*Cyanea capillata*, which itself may reach 6 feet, or 1.8 m, in diameter), and on comb jellies, salps, or other jelly organisms that are numerous in our waters during summer. The mouth, throat, and esophagus are lined with numerous spines up to 2 inches (5 cm) long that point inward, presumably aiding in swallowing long, slippery jellyfish.

In our study area, leatherbacks can find jellyfish near the surface or at moderate depth. However, in the oceanic waters they inhabit most of the year, they routinely dive straight down to about 1,600 feet (488 m) to catch jellyfish in the rich band of plankton known as the deep scattering layer (DSL), ascend quickly for a few quick breaths, then dive again. One scientifically instrumented turtle dived to 3,300 feet (1,007 m), at least, and may have reached 4,265 feet (1,300 m). Night dives are shallower, because the DSL migrates upward to a depth of about 650 feet or so (about 200 m). Some of the same adaptations found in marine mammals assist these incessant divers, including large volume of blood, very high abundance of red blood cells, and abundant myoglobin. But these ancient turtles, which evolved tens of millions of years before the earliest cetaceans or pinnipeds, can still outdive almost every mammal in the ocean.

How do leatherbacks survive in these cold waters? Surprisingly, they are warm-blooded. All four flippers contain countercurrent heat-exchange systems. Arteries carrying blood to the flippers are surrounded by veins returning blood to the body. The arterial blood gives up its heat, but not its oxygen or nutrients, to the venous blood. Metabolic heat is thus retained in the massive body, to the extent that leatherbacks in 45°F (7.2°C) water can maintain a body temperature of up to 80°F (27°C). This is exactly the same anatomical adaptation found in cetacean (or pinniped) flippers, flukes, and dorsal fins for heat conservation. A large fat deposit under its shell probably provides energy and insulation but also seems similar to the "brown fat" used by mammals to generate heat. More research is needed to determine whether the fat is thermogenic.

Where do our leatherbacks come from? Western North Atlantic leatherbacks breed from April to November, mainly on a few beaches in Central or South America, although occasional females nest as far north as southern Florida. Leatherbacks apparently wander or migrate farther than any other marine turtle, and their 2,000-mile (3,200 km) swim to eat jellyfish in our study area is not unusual for the species. Females may nest only every other year, during March and April, and may not migrate as far north during breeding years. Perhaps this accounts for the preponderance of males among specimens recorded from our waters.

What is the fate of leatherbacks that visit our study area? Most of the turtles probably go offshore and south again in autumn. Until recently, leatherbacks were often shot or harpooned, mainly out of curiosity. Since the meat is not edible and there is no shell, there has never been any other reason to kill a leatherback. Fortunately, this interesting turtle is now protected by the Endangered Species Act of 1973. Some of the turtles get into difficulty of their own accord, however, for about one-third of all specimens recorded from our waters

Dorsal view of leatherback turtle caught in lobster gear near Corea, Maine. The turtle was released alive.

KATHERINE HEIDINGER

Leatherback turtle, caught accidentally in lobster fishing gear near Round Pond, Maine, August 1, 1979. This turtle was nearly 7 feet (213 cm) long and weighed about 1,500 pounds (680 kg). Ventral view, showing long flippers.

EVERETT BOUTILIER

were found entangled in lobster fishing gear. One intriguing theory proposes that a turtle might occasionally mistake a lobster pot buoy floating at the surface for a jellyfish. If the turtle swooped up to eat it, its long flippers might get caught in the line running to the trap. If the lobsterman finds the turtle in time, it can be released unharmed; however, the animal's struggles may entangle it so tightly or the efforts of dragging the traps around may exhaust it so much that it drowns before being found.

Eating marine debris also threatens leatherbacks and other sea turtles. The turtles can choke or die from blockage of the gastro-intestinal tract after swallowing plastic bags and other floating plastic objects, having mistaken them for prey. In one study, about half of the turtle carcasses examined contained plastic objects in the stomach or intestines.

Marine turtles and marine mammals are eons apart in their evolutionary history, yet the leatherback shares many characteristics with a big whale such as a humpback. Both are large, long-distance travelers of the world's oceans, with long lifetimes, regular migration cycles, and similar adaptations for staying warm in cold water. Both reproduce in specific breeding locations, and both are now on the Endangered Species List. Perhaps the most critical factor shared by leatherbacks (and all marine turtles) and marine mammals is their dependence on human respect and restraint for their future survival. Sightings contributed by readers of this guide will add to knowledge about this endangered species and ultimately aid its survival.

PART 3

SEALS

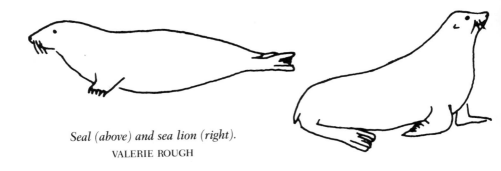

Seal (above) and sea lion (right).
VALERIE ROUGH

Gray seal pup and female, Sable Island, Nova Scotia.
GEOFF BECK

Gray seal (left) and harbor seal (right) showing great size difference. Little Duck Island, Maine.
BOB BOWMAN

Introduction

Besides cetaceans, the only other marine mammals found in our part of the North Atlantic Ocean are seals. We are too far south for polar bears, too far north for manatees, and sea otters never colonized the Atlantic. Although salt water may be a temporary habitat for certain other mammals of our region—for example, white-tailed deer (*Odocoileus virginianus*), moose (*Alces alces*), and beaver (*Castor canadensis*)—they take to near-shore waters only when swimming to an island or when pursued by predators or hunters. Island-dwelling otters (*Lutra canadensis*) and minks (*Mustela vison*) regularly forage for fish or other prey in salt water during some seasons. The maritime habit was even better developed in the extinct sea mink (*Mustela macrodon*), a fat, reddish-brown furbearer that ranged in size from about 20 to 33 inches (51–84 cm), nose to tip of tail, and lived along the rocky shores of Maine and the Bay of Fundy. Sea minks were extirpated by overhunting before their behavior was recorded, but anecdotal accounts suggest they were solitary, nocturnal, and spent much time in the ocean. The last known specimen was taken at Campobello Island, New Brunswick, in 1894, nine years before the sea mink was formally described by a scientist and recognized as a distinct species (see Campbell, 1988, for further details).

Seals and humans are mutually curious about each other. Seals often surface near boats, stare with inquisitive globular eyes, and then suddenly dive with a loud slap of their flippers. For humans, however, seals have not been merely an object of study for the inquisitive naturalist or scientist. For thousands of years seals were hunted in the Arctic to provide life's essentials for natives and their dogs: meat; oil for light and heat; hides for boots, clothing, and skin boat covering; and strong rawhide thongs for harnesses, lashings, and tools. Then the insatiable desire of American and European markets for furs made sealskins an important trading item. Small-scale commercial sealing of the immense herds in the Canadian Arctic began in the seventeenth century. By the early nineteenth century, seal harvesting had become a lucrative industry compensating for the declining bowhead whale and sperm whale fisheries. Subsequently, intense hunting of harp, hooded, bearded, and ringed seals and walruses severely reduced stocks and led us to realize that survival of these species depends on good management and protection efforts. Public awareness has stimulated population studies and scientific investigations to learn more about all aspects of seal biology.

All fur seals, sea lions, walruses, and true seals belong to the order of mammals called Pinnipedia (from the Latin meaning wing- or feather-footed). The pinnipeds evolved from carnivorous terrestrial ancestors about 30 million years ago, which apparently entered the ocean to exploit new food resources created as climatic change cooled northern oceans, increasing upwelling and marine production. Within the Pinnipedia, fur seals and sea lions belong to the family Otariidae and true seals to the family Phocidae. Whether the two families evolved from a single common ancestor (monophyletic origin), as molecular evidence suggests, or from two different ancestors (biphyletic origin), as fossil and anatomical evidence indicates, is a matter of some controversy. In any event, these two families developed separately and show differences in their anatomy and adaptation to terrestrial and aquatic locomotion. The walruses (family Odobenidae) are unique but display similarities to both otariid and phocid groups; debate continues as to which of the two family lines they may have evolved from.

The three families can be summarized as follows. The fur seals and sea lions (Otariidae) are characterized by visible external ear flaps (pinnae) and long, sinuous necks; long, almost hairless foreflippers, with the first digit much longer and stronger than the other four, thin webbing between digits, and rudimentary claws set back from their tips; and long, webbed, almost hairless hindflippers, which turn forward for movement on land. The hindflipper claws are reduced on the outer two digits but well developed on the middle three. Otariids have four teats. The testes are contained in a scrotum, and the tail is distinct and free from the hindflippers. Propulsion in the water is

Young harbor seal at Mt. Desert Rock, Maine, showing V-shaped nostrils. The long vibrissae of the eyebrows and mustache are visible.
BEVERLY AGLER

Harbor seals on a half-tide ledge. Flanders Bay, Maine, July 1982.
STEVEN KATONA

accomplished by simultaneous penguinlike strokes of the foreflippers, while movement on land is achieved by running or walking with the body supported on all four limbs. According to the biphyletic view, otariids probably had a bearlike ancestor.

The true seals (also called "hair seals" or "earless seals") are all classified in the family Phocidae. The phocid family is further divided into two subfamilies: the southern phocids, or Monachinae, including the elephant, monk, and Antarctic seals; and the northern phocids, or Phocinae, which includes the true seals of the North Atlantic (containing our study area) and North Pacific oceans. In the Phocidae, ear pinnae are lacking and there is no clearly defined neck region. The foreflippers are haired, and in northern phocids are short, with digits connected in thick tissue. In northern phocids digits decrease slightly in length from the first to the fifth, each terminating in a prominent claw. (Some southern phocids, such as the Antarctic Ross and leopard seals, have elongated foreflippers, similar in shape to those of otariids.) Phocid hindflippers are of intermediate length, haired, with extensive webbing, and claws on all five digits. Northern phocids have larger claws than southern ones. Phocid hindflippers are directed backward and cannot be turned forward. There are two or four teats. Testes are internal, and the tail is distinct and separate from the hindflippers.

Phocids swim by moving the posterior part of the body side-to-side, sculling with the webbed hindflippers. Usually the foreflippers lie flat against the body, except when maneuvering at slow speed or turning. Movement on land is clumsy even though it can be fast. The chest and front flippers are hitched forward, then the body is humped to advance hindquarters. Seals can also slither quickly over ice and snow using a side-to-side swimming motion. In the biphyletic view, seals probably evolved from an otterlike ancestor. The drawings below will help the reader visualize differences between seals and sea lions.

The walruses (Odobenidae) have no ear pinnae; the ear canal is covered by a fold of skin. They have a thick, robust, nearly hairless body. The foreflippers, similar to those of sea lions but relatively shorter and more square, are sparsely haired, with five tiny claws. The hindflippers, too, resemble those of sea lions. They are sparsely haired, webbed, and can turn forward; claws are very small on the outer two digits but well developed on the middle three. There are four teats. Testes are internal, and the tail is enclosed in a web of skin. Walruses have a highly specialized tooth arrangement with very long upper canines. They swim with sea-lionlike foreflipper strokes and seal-like sweeps of the hindflippers. On land they walk or run on all four limbs, like sea lions, but with a lunging gait to clear the body from the ground.

The North Atlantic is unique among the world's oceans in having no otariid pinnipeds, although California sea lions (*Zalophus californianus*), which have escaped from captivity, occasionally appear off the East Coast of North America. One was killed in Newfoundland in 1965.

Seals have a streamlined, torpedolike form, with reduced forelimbs that can flatten against the body and hindlimbs modified for swimming. Genitalia and mammaries lie beneath the body's smooth surface. The skin consists of a waterproof epidermis and thick dermis rich with blood vessels. Covering the epidermis are flattened guard hairs and wavy strands of underfur in follicles well supplied with oil glands. Underneath the dermis and closely connected to it lies a layer of blubber, which provides insulation against cold, a source of reserve energy, buoyancy, and padding to enhance the streamlined body shape.

Seals breathe air like other mammals, yet can submerge for periods lasting from 5 to 40 minutes. Many species routinely dive to 657 feet (200 meters). The champions are the Antarctic Weddell seals, which can dive for as long as 73 minutes and to a depth of 1,970 feet (600 meters), though not in the same dive; and the northern elephant seal, which can go down for 77 minutes to an astounding 5,020 feet (1,529 meters). To withstand pressures at depth, the seal exhales before diving and depends on oxygen stored by the hemoglobin of the blood and the myoglobin of the muscles. Most of the seal's body is incompressible underwater, and air spaces are limited to reinforced structures in the ear and respiratory system. During a dive, circulation to most of the body is drastically curtailed, except to the brain and vital organs. In addition, heartbeat slows to as low as one-tenth the normal rate, and noncore body temperature and metabolic rate are reduced to conserve oxygen. A seal may attain swimming speeds of 6 to 16 miles (10 to 26 km) per hour, but the bulky, less-streamlined walrus is slower, except under chase, when it may briefly reach 18 miles (30 km) per hour.

Pinnipeds are carnivores. Their diet consists primarily of fish and invertebrates but can include birds or mammals. The Antarctic leopard seal, for example, is partial to penguins and crabeater seal pups, and our local gray seal occasionally supplements its fish regimen with ducks or black guillemots. Unlike many terrestrial carnivores, whose teeth are adapted for tearing and grinding flesh, seals have pointed teeth suited for gripping slippery prey, which may be swallowed whole. The small, relatively uniform cheek teeth have a cusp pattern distinctive in each species, as shown in the illustration at right. Walrus cheek teeth are roughly conical to start but soon become worn by sand and gravel ingested with the food.

Like other carnivorous mammals, pinnipeds are intelligent, with well-developed senses. Seals have large eyes in relation to body size and good underwater vision, adaptable to the darkness of ocean depths. They also see well in air except in dim light, when they become nearsighted. Only the walrus has relatively small eyes, and it does not need the sharp vision of other pinnipeds for capturing its meals of shellfish on the bottom. Still, sight is not essential for survival, as shown by numerous reports of blind but otherwise healthy seals in the wild.

Although our knowledge of a seal's sensory world is imperfect, some generalizations can be made. Hearing is good in air and excellent in water. The seal's ear, a short distance behind the eye, appears externally as a small oval hole that is open in air and closed during dives. The internal ear bones are massive compared with those of terrestrial mammals. With their vocal cords, seals produce diverse species-specific vocalizations in air and water, and certain clicking sounds have been detected that seem suitable for echolocation. Nevertheless, years of research have thus far failed to produce convincing evidence for pinniped echolocation. The tactile sense is important. Vibrissae, or whiskers, are coarse, continuously growing, nerve-equipped hairs located above the eyes and on lateral pads of the upper lips. The latter are called mystacial vibrissae (from the Greek *mystax*, meaning mustache). The mystacial vibrissae are sensitive to vibration and touch and apparently play a role in capturing food at short range. The seal may also use the vibrissae to determine swimming speed, to locate holes in ice at night, and to explore the sea bottom. The vibrissae can be drawn back, held sideways or stiffly forward, positions that may reflect or communicate the seal's attentive or emotional state.

The olfactory sense operates in air—as when a cow seal identifies her hauled-out pup by its smell—and possibly underwater via the rhinarium, which surrounds the nostrils and may, like a dog's wet nose, pick up stimuli from dissolved molecules. As with the ear,

Young harbor seal at Mt. Desert Rock, Maine. As in all true seals (Phocidae) the ear opening has no pinna (external ear flap).
KIM ROBERTSON

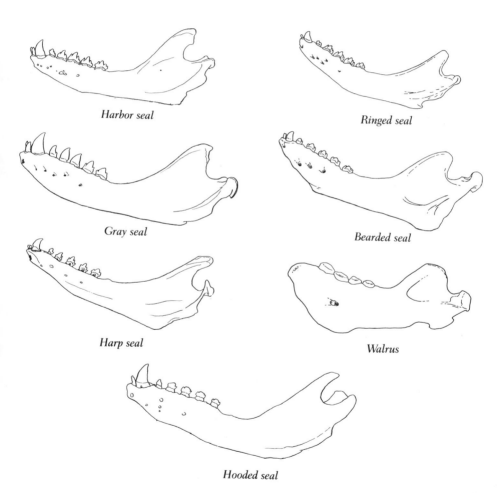

Harbor seal

Ringed seal

Gray seal

Bearded seal

Harp seal

Walrus

Hooded seal

Lower jaws of seal species and walrus from study area.
ARTHUR MANSFIELD, ARCTIC BIOLOGICAL STATION, DEPARTMENT OF
FISHERIES AND OCEANS, CANADA

nostrils are normally closed and opened by voluntary muscles only when the head is above water.

Little is known of feeding and other behavior at sea. Seals are most conspicuous when hauled out to rest, breed, or molt, on rocks, sand, or ice, usually where an adjacent channel or other steep dropoff provides rapid access to the water. Many species are highly gregarious, and haulouts of hundreds or even thousands of individuals occur, particularly at molting time. Seals on shore are wary and easily frightened into the sea so it is important to avoid disturbing them. Kayaks and other small craft should stay well away from haulout sites. (In the United States, federal law prohibits harassment of marine mammals.) Naturalist cruises offer excellent opportunities for viewing seals from the water. On land, a cautious approach terminating several hundred feet from a haulout site will permit satisfactory viewing with binoculars or telescope. Bear in mind that seals which haul out on land (i.e., gray and harbor seals) generally do so during low-tide hours, except on salt marsh banks, where high-tide haulout may occur. Seal watching can stimulate the curious naturalist to ask many questions, some of which have probably not yet been answered. There are other benefits, too, for a quiet session of observation, punctuated only by the cries of gulls and the muffled barking of seals across the water, can restore one's sense of time, patience, and well-being.

Though seals in the water are often less visible than they are on land, they can occasionally be seen resting or sleeping (often in the "bottling" position—hanging vertically at the surface, with just the face and nostrils exposed to the air); feeding; and even leaping, rolling, and splashing. In their watery element seals (especially the young) may boldly approach boats or shorelines, to stare inquisitively at humans and their dogs. Sudden movements may frighten the seals—they may loudly smack a flipper on the water surface and rush away to a safe distance before reappearing.

Reproductive details are given in the specific accounts. Nearly all seals have single pups; twinning is rare. Adoption of a pup may occur but is also rare. In most seals, whelping (giving birth) takes place on land or ice, followed within a few days or weeks by mating. The new embryo does not grow for several months, a phenomenon known as delayed implantation. The start of fetal development is timed so that gestation takes almost one year. This important adaptation causes pups to be born at the same time each year, in the most favorable season. It also synchronizes breeding behavior of adults.

Seal watchers in our study area are fortunate that the region is frequented or visited by all six true seals found in the North Atlantic. Coastal islands, sandbars, and ledges from Cape Cod to Labrador are inhabited seasonally or all year by thousands of harbor and gray seals. Sea ice in the Gulf of St. Lawrence and offshore from Newfoundland is used for pupping and mating by many thousands of harp and hooded seals. These energetic predators, each of which may consume about 5 percent of its body weight in fish per day, play an important part in the ecology of our waters. Two abundant and ecologically important Arctic species, the ringed seal and bearded seal, are uncommon visitors to our study area. Finally, the walrus, now rare south of northern Labrador and Greenland, once occupied the Gulf of St. Lawrence and Sable Island.

In addition to their roles in natural ecosystems, pinnipeds play an important part in human economies wherever they occur abundantly. Shallow Arctic seas can produce enormous stocks of fish and invertebrate foods for walrus and several species of seals, if humans do not deplete the fisheries or pollute the ocean. Walrus and all Arctic seals are still important to subsistence of local natives, who hunt them for food, oil, fur, and hides. Canadian landsmen still hunt harp seals for food and pelts in the Gulf of St. Lawrence in winter and off Newfoundland and Labrador in spring. New tourist industries have arisen at the Magdalen Islands and at Charlottetown, Prince Edward Island, with the inauguration of excursions to view breeding harp seals on the ice.

Gray and harbor seals have little direct commercial value despite their substantial numbers. They have been bountied in both the Gulf of Maine and eastern Canada at various times because of suspected competition with fishermen, damage to fishing gear, and involvement in the life cycles of parasites infecting commercially important fishes. In U.S. waters all pinnipeds are protected by the Marine Mammal Protection Act of 1972.

Wherever they occur, pinnipeds are clearly of interest and importance to humans, but our knowledge of them is limited, despite many scientific studies completed or in progress. The amateur observer can make valuable contributions to our understanding of seals by keeping careful records. A sample sighting data form is provided on page 246. Be on the lookout for brands and hindflipper tags, as seals of some species have been individually marked so their movements can be tracked. Please report all tags and brands seen, and any

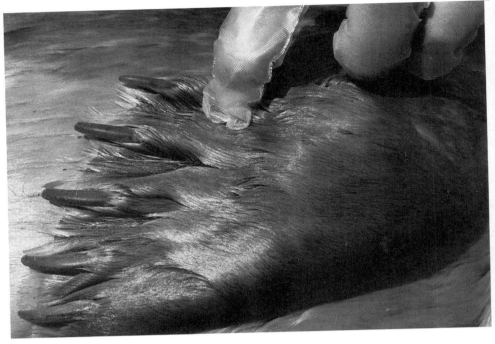

Each digit of the foreflipper has a strong claw in seals of the family Phocidae, as in this photo of a harbor seal.
STEVEN KATONA

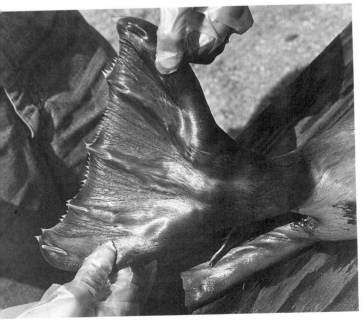

Hindflipper of harbor seal stretched to show webbing between digits. As in all members of the family Phocidae, each digit ends in a stout claw.
STEVEN KATONA

walruses south of northern Labrador, to Brian Beck (address on page 246) if seen in eastern Canada, and to Allied Whale at College of the Atlantic, Bar Harbor, Maine, if seen in the eastern United States. In the northeastern United States, all stranded seals, sick or dead, should be reported immediately to the New England Aquarium in Boston, at 617-973-5247, or to one of the other organizations listed in the next section. We look forward to your reports. Several commercial natural history cruises that provide opportunities to observe seals are listed in Appendix II, and references on seals of our study area are in the Bibliography.

SEAL STRANDINGS

Each year dozens of seals of various species individually strand or beach themselves on our New England shores, and some, but not all, require veterinary care. The New England Aquarium (NEA) in Boston (617-973-5247) is the primary institution in the U.S. portion of our study region responsible for rescue and rehabilitation of stranded marine mammals and should be notified of such occurrences in New England, whether the seal is alive or dead. Do not attempt to touch a living seal. They bite. Wounds may become infected and difficult to heal.

Before approaching a live seal, it is important to establish whether it is healthy or sick. For example, harbor seal pups, which frequently strand in late spring, may appear abandoned, but this is not always the case. The mother may still be in the vicinity, and your approach may drive her away. Therefore, you should monitor the situation from a safe distance, through a complete tide cycle and for up to 24 hours, but no longer. Meanwhile, you should communicate with NEA. If the seal is still present after the observation period, NEA staff will arrange to collect it for rehabilitation.

Gray, harp, hooded, and ringed seals also strand singly at various times of year. Individuals of those species will not flee, as harbor seals do, when approached by people. The ice seals (harp, hooded, and ringed) can be recognized by their ice-adapted locomotion when on land—they walk on their nails and drag their hindquarters along as though sledding. The observation and notification procedures outlined above should be followed. Be certain that orphaned and sick seals receive care, but also that seals merely seeking rest are left undisturbed. Dogs should be kept off the beach, away from the stranded seal, during the observation period.

If you are unable to reach NEA, contact a local office of the National Marine Fisheries Service (NOAA Fisheries), or local police. In Connecticut or Rhode Island you may contact Mystic Marinelife Aquarium in Mystic, Connecticut (203-536-9631); in New York contact Okeanos Ocean Research Foundation in Hampton Bays (516-728-8013), and in New Jersey the Marine Mammal Stranding Center in Brigantine (609-266-0538). In Canada contact the Prince Edward Island Stranding Network in Charlottetown (902-569-4803), the Nova Scotia Stranding Network in Dartmouth (902-469-2420), or the Department of Fisheries and Oceans in St. John's, Newfoundland (709-772-5430; after hours and weekends 709-772-2033).

Species Accounts

HARBOR SEAL
(*Phoca vitulina concolor*)

I n New England this is by far the most common and frequently reported seal; it is also familiar in eastern Canada. These two regions lie in the center of the species' northwest Atlantic distribution.

Harbor seals bask and sleep on coastal islands, ledges, and sandbars, usually during low tide, and forage during high tide, although high tide haulout may occur on salt marsh banks. Where sites are available at all tides the haulout may last through daylight hours. Harbor seals also haul out on near-shore ice in winter but do not maintain breathing holes through ice. Harbor seals often lie with head and rear flippers elevated, in a characteristic crescent.

The scientific name (Gr. *phoca*, seal, + L. *vitulus*, calf) means "sea calf" or, more loosely, "sea dog." Indeed, the harbor seal head viewed in profile reveals a short, concave muzzle like that of a cocker spaniel, with the tip slightly upturned. The eye is roughly equidistant from tip of nose to ear opening, and in a frontal view the nostrils form a broad V, almost meeting at the bottom. The pelage (coat) color has a bluish-gray background overlaid dorsally with profuse small dark spots or mottling; a whitish network develops around the spots in older seals. Spotting is more scattered on the belly. The overall color effect varies from light gray or tan to brown, dark gray, almost black, or even reddish. A complete spectrum of pelages can often be observed

Harbor seal cow nursing pup,
with typical seal ledge in background.
Size range: up to 6 feet.

D. D. TYLER

within a group of several dozen basking seals. Dry pelage usually appears lighter than wet pelage.

Adult males average 5 feet (153 cm) and 200 pounds (91 kg) and may attain 5 feet 6 inches (168 cm) and 250 pounds (114 kg). Adult females average 4 feet 8 inches (143 cm) and 154 pounds (70 kg) and may reach 5 feet 6 inches (168 cm) and 200 pounds (91 kg). Males mature at 5 to 6 years of age and females at 3 to 4 years. The sexes are similar, not only in size but also in pelage color and pattern and in head features. They are difficult to tell apart in the wild except when the bellies are seen. The configurations shown on page 206 apply to all North Atlantic pinnipeds except bearded seals and walruses.

The harbor seal can be found in near-shore waters of all northern oceans and their adjoining seas above about 30 degrees north latitude. Bays, estuaries, and even some accessible lakes are occupied if islets, reefs, shoals, and sheltered inlets are present and if humans do not disturb the seals. The present breeding range in the northwestern Atlantic extends from ice-free waters of the Arctic to New Hampshire. Breeding occurred as far south as Cape Cod Bay in the first half of the twentieth century. Harbor seals regularly winter south to Long Island, New York, and occasionally to the Carolinas, rarely appearing in Florida.

In the last century, harbor seals inhabited Lake Ontario and Lake Champlain, having gained entry via the St. Lawrence River, but today they can swim only as far as Montreal. A subspecies, *Phoca vitulina mellonae*, inhabits certain freshwater lakes in northern Quebec. In eastern Canada the seals occur in the St. Lawrence estuary and Northumberland Strait; at Anticosti, the Magdalen Islands, and Newfoundland; and in greatest numbers along the shores of Nova Scotia, including Sable Island. They are also found near Grand Manan Island in the Bay of Fundy. In 1990 the eastern Canada population (south of Labrador) was about 34,500 and expanding.

Harbor seals exist throughout eastern Canada in a series of more or less isolated groups, most of which have not been studied in detail. For example, seals marked as pups at Sable Island usually return there to breed each year, yet tagged pups and juveniles also disperse widely, with resightings in mainland Nova Scotia, New England, and New Jersey, showing the potential for exchange between groups, particularly as the overall population is expanding.

More information is available for the New England population, which from spring through autumn spreads along the Maine and New

HARBOR SEAL
D. D. TYLER

fur pattern

side view

front view

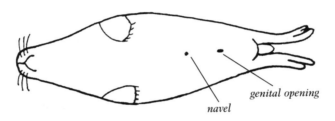

genital opening

navel

MALE

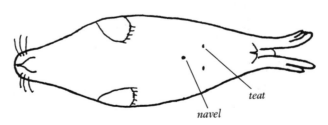

teat

navel

FEMALE

Sketch of ventral side of male and female harbor seals.
Length in all species is measured in a straight line from nose to tip of tail.
VALERIE ROUGH

Harbor seal resting at Mt. Desert Rock, Maine,
*showing **V**-shaped nostrils and five long nails on each foreflipper.*
BOB McKENZIE

Neck of harbor seal cut by monofilament mesh of gill net.
Mt. Desert Rock, Maine, August 29, 1989.
KIM ROBERTSON

Female harbor seal nursing her pup. Shown here is Snow Woman with a five-day-old pup. Snow Woman is part of a long-term study in midcoast Maine. She has been observed each spring and summer from 1987 through 1991. Snow Woman apparently weans her pups when they are only 11 to 13 days old, one of the shortest nursing periods observed.

BRUCE M. WELLMAN, MAINE SEAL, 167 BEDFORD RD., LINCOLN, MA 01773

Nose-to-nose contact between a mother harbor seal and her pup. Individually distinctive odors help seals recognize each other. Shown here is Helena, nuzzling her two-day-old male pup. First observed in 1982, Helena was seen every year until 1990. Each year Helena nursed her pup for 4 weeks, the longest nursing period seen for any adult female at a long-term study site in midcoast Maine.
LESLIE COWPERTHWAITE, MAINE SEAL, 167 BEDFORD RD., LINCOLN, MA 01773

Hampshire coast in several hundred colonies, the largest ones containing from 150 to 800 seals. The greatest concentration of seals is located in Machias and Penobscot bays, off Jonesport, and off Mt. Desert and Swans islands. Aerial surveys over the past 20 years show that the Maine population increased from 5,800 in 1973 to about 14,500 in 1986. Although some harbor seals overwinter in northern New England, by the end of November Maine populations have diminished. Concurrently, thousands of seals, including young of the year and juveniles, start to appear around Cape Cod and associated islands, with a few hundred going south to Long Island. A similar autumn migration may occur from the Bay of Fundy coast of New Brunswick into New England. The autumn migration evidently reverses in the following spring, and by early May Maine's seal herds are almost back to normal size, while counts in southern New England dwindle, approaching zero by early July.

In late spring, pregnant females move to upper reaches of bays and estuaries seeking out protected areas on reefs or islands, somewhat apart from males and juveniles. Pups are born from mid-April to mid-June, weighing 22 pounds (10 kg) and measuring 2.5 feet (76 cm) on average. Usually the pup's coat at birth (natal coat) is similar to the adult's, but up to 25 percent of the pups at some colonies are born with long white fur called lanugo (from Latin for downy). This fur is always shed by two weeks of age and replaced with the adult coat. Pups can and do swim shortly after birth, usually with their mothers, who are solicitous and playful with their young. Nursing usually takes place ashore, but can occur in the water, and lasts for 25 to 30 days, by which time the pup has grown to about 35 inches (90 cm) and 55 pounds (25 kg). After weaning, the pup starts to feed on small crustaceans such as amphipods and shrimp.

The first-year mortality rate is about 28 percent; some of the causes are storms, abandonment by the mother, disease, parasites, entanglement in fishing gear, sharks, and possibly killer whales. Annual mortality in subsequent years is about 17.5 percent. Harbor seals have lived to 35 years in captivity, but natural longevity may be slightly lower. Mortality can increase substantially as a population becomes more abundant because increased contact between animals provides more efficient transmission of pathogens and parasites. An epidemic of influenza killed several hundred harbor seals in New England in 1979–1980. An even more deadly epidemic killed more than 17,000 harbor seals around Europe's North Sea in 1988. The infectious agent, a previously unknown virus now called phocine distemper virus, or PDV, is similar to the species that causes distemper in dogs. Scientists are still evaluating the possibility that pollutants like organochlorines or heavy metals could increase mortality in such epidemics by debilitating the immune system's ability to fight infection.

Mating occurs about 4 weeks after the pup is born, from early May to late July, invariably in the water. This aspect of behavior is poorly understood. Seals may chase each other, rolling and splashing in pairs or trios during the mating season, but they also do so in most other months. The appearance of cuts and scars on some mature males during this season suggests that there is competition for females.

Molting takes place in July and August. Just before the molt, the hair, when dry, becomes dull brown and the pattern indistinct. The new coat usually appears pale and silvery when dry. In late summer some harbor seals move offshore to deeper water, presumably to feed.

Harbor seals eat fish and invertebrates as available; the most common food items are herring, squid, alewife, flounder, hake, sand lance, and mackerel.

During the late 1800s, Maine and Massachusetts offered a one-dollar bounty on harbor seals to reduce the population and perhaps increase the quantity of fish caught by humans. By the early 1900s Maine's harbor seals were nearly exterminated in certain localities, with no noticeable effect on fish catches. The seals made a good comeback after the Maine bounty was lifted in 1905. Massachusetts retained the bounty until 1962, and this may have led to the extirpation of breeding in Cape Cod Bay. Only occasional pups are born in Massachusetts waters today, but the number may increase as the population grows.

Increased use of the coast in eastern Canada in the 1960s and 1970s disturbed harbor seals and drove them to occupy more exposed breeding sites, with greater danger to their pups. This and bounty hunting may have contributed to population decline in that region up to 1976, when the bounty ended. Now the trend is reversed, and eastern Canadian stocks are increasing rapidly, according to one Canadian scientist.

Harbor seals produce a variety of airborne sounds: flipper smacking and bubble blowing in the water, as well as vocal snorts, snarls, and belching sounds both in water and on land. One individual named Hoover, a male orphaned as a pup in Maine and taken to New England

Aquarium, learned to mimic human speech. Hoover delighted visitors with his guttural "Hello there," "Get out of here," and drunken peals of laughter, always delivered from the water.

Of all the seals in our area, harbor seals are the most highly adapted to water. Their visible surface behavior ranges from dozing to inquisitiveness to playful leaping and porpoising, but the details of their underwater activities remain unknown. Despite the commonness of this seal in our study area, many questions remain, and a satisfactory understanding of this attractive and appealing animal will require further observation and research.

GRAY SEAL
(Halichoerus grypus)

This is a large, imposing seal of remote, exposed islands, reefs, and shoals. The distinctive roman nose and gaping nostrils become more pronounced with age, particularly in males, whence the name "horsehead." The scientific name (Gr. *halios*, marine, + *choiros*, pig, and Gr. *gropos*, hooknosed) means "hooknosed pig of the sea."

Males, or bulls, grow to 8 feet (244 cm) and 990 pounds (450 kg) and the smaller females, or cows, to 7 feet (213 cm) and 594 pounds (270 kg). The donkeylike snout is longer, broader, and more arched in males than in equal-aged females, although an old cow may have a convex profile. The massive appearance of a mature bull is enhanced by thick folds of leathery, scarred skin around the neck and shoulders. Males live to about 35 years and females to 45.

Immature gray seals may be confused with harbor seals of similar size, but the gray seal's eye is closer to the ear than to the nose, and the nostrils are well separated so that when viewed frontally they are more or less parallel, resembling a W, rather than V-shaped as in harbor seals.

Coat color pattern in gray seals is generally bolder with larger, more irregular spots than in harbor seals. The male pelage usually is dark brown, gray, or nearly black, with small lighter marks on the neck and flanks. The female coat has a light background, gray or tan dorsally, and yellowish white on the throat, belly, and flanks, with overlying dark spots and blotches. Some females appear mostly dark. In yearlings of both sexes the pattern may be somewhat indistinct. The heads of gray seals often look brown when dry and dark gray

Young harbor seal, showing concave, spaniel-like head profile.
CHRISTOPHER PACKARD

*Gray seal head, showing long, straight nose and **W** shape of nostrils.*
CHRISTOPHER PACKARD

Gray seals on ledge (females with light coats and males with dark coats). The head of a swimming female gray seal is in the background. Size range: males, up to 8 feet; females, up to 7 feet.
D. D. TYLER

when wet, but since other seals also look gray when wet, the common name is not particularly helpful.

Gray seals are found on both sides of the North Atlantic, with three major populations: in eastern Canada; northwestern Europe from Iceland to Norway and around Great Britain; and the Baltic Sea. These stocks do not mix. The western Atlantic stock centers in the Gulf of St. Lawrence, with ice breeding in Northumberland Strait and George Bay and land breeding at Deadman Island near the Magdalen Islands and at Amet Island in Northumberland Strait. Outside the gulf the seals breed on land, primarily in Nova Scotia at the Basque Islands and Sable Island, and also in small numbers on the east coast of Nova Scotia and near Grand Manan Island in the Bay of Fundy. Gray seals occur as far north as Cape Chidley in northern Labrador, and the southernmost regular location of the species is Nantucket Sound, Massachusetts. Recently there have been sightings in Long Island Sound. Strays are reported as far south as Virginia. A female pupped at Assateague Island, Virginia, in 1986, and the same or another pupped there in 1989.

The world population is in the range of 180,000 to 200,000, about half of which live in the British Isles. Some 80,000 to 100,000 inhabit the Canadian Maritimes, and that stock is expanding. About 400 live in the Grand Manan archipelago, and probably as many along the Maine coast, with most sightings off Mt. Desert and Swans islands and in lower Penobscot Bay. Gray seals select exposed haulout and breeding sites, usually where rough seas and riptides make boating hazardous; for this reason "horseheads" are seen infrequently except by fishermen. Some individuals come ashore during the ice breeding season in the Gulf of St. Lawrence at places such as Prince Edward Island.

In eastern Canada pups are born between mid-December and early February on rocky islands, sandy islands, or land-fast ice or ice floes. The newborn pup, averaging 3 feet (91 cm) and 35 pounds (16 kg), has a coat of long creamy-white hair (lanugo). It nurses for about 16 days, on the land or ice, and may gain 4 to 6 pounds a day on its mother's high-fat milk, thus rapidly acquiring the vital layer of insulating blubber. In 2 to 3 weeks after birth the white coat begins to shed and is replaced by a shorter coat similar to that of adults; the color pattern is silver with scattered dark spots in females and dark gray to black with lighter spots in males. After weaning, pups may

Gray seal (front) and harbor seals (rear). The gray seal is larger, with bolder pelage markings and a longer muzzle. Little Duck Island, Maine.
BOB BOWMAN

Gray seal swimming at Flanders Bay, Maine, July 26, 1982. "Horsey" head contrasts with the spaniel-like profile of harbor seals swimming nearby.
STEVEN KATONA

side view, male   *front view, male*   *side view, female*

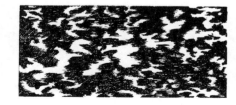

fur pattern, male   **GRAY SEAL**   *fur pattern, female*

D. D. TYLER

Gray seals at Sable Island, Nova Scotia. Left to right: pup, cow, bull.
GEOFF BECK

Gray seal bull, showing "horsehead." Sable Island, Nova Scotia.
GEOFF BECK

Young gray seal, probably male, near harbor seals. Note larger size and elongated profile of gray seal. Little Duck Island, Maine, September 1987.
BOB BOWMAN

remain at the breeding ground for several more days or weeks until molting is complete.

The adults mate, on land or in the water, around the time of weaning. Sexually mature males (at least 3 to 5 years old) may compete for females (mature at 3 to 4 years). Where breeding occurs on rocky or ledgy shores, a few large, vigorous bulls, probably over 8 years old, may be able to drive other bulls away and monopolize 4 to 6 cows apiece, but on sand or ice, cows are more spread out and each bull mates with only one. Competition among males probably contributes to their shorter life span. Once molted, the pup enters the water if it has not done so previously and learns to capture food on its own. Some pups wander far from their birthplaces, such as one, tagged at Sable Island, which traveled 930 miles (1,500 km) to Virginia. The first 4 years are spent mostly at sea. Natural mortality from sharks and other causes is high in young seals; 30 to 55 percent may die during their first year.

The annual molt of seals one year and older takes place between March and June, followed by dispersal for summer feeding. Gray seals consume fish and invertebrates as available. The most common food items in eastern Canada are herring, cod, flounder, skate, squid, mackerel, capelin, lumpfish, silver hake and sand lance.

The expanding gray seal population in Canada's Maritimes has caused problems for fisheries. Seals damage nets and traps set inshore; also, the gray seal is the primary host for codworm (now called seal-worm), a parasite whose adult stage infests cod and flatfish, necessitating inspection of fillets and removal of worms before the fish can be sold. Hoping to reduce the impact on fisheries, the Canadian government placed a bounty on gray seals in 1976, operative from March 15 to December 15 each year. The seals may not be taken during the breeding season.

As Canadian stocks have grown, sightings in New England have become more common. Sable Island–marked individuals are frequently seen. About a dozen Sable-tagged pups strand each year in the United States, and many are rehabilitated and released. At least three Canadian-marked gray seals have pupped in New England, and probably others have taken up residency in U.S. waters.

Harp seals, adult and pup.
Approximate adult length: 6 feet.
JOHN R. QUINN

HARP SEAL
(*Phoca groenlandica*)

The beautiful harp seal, named for the dark harp- or saddle-shaped pattern on its back and flanks, is the most numerous seal in eastern Canada, yet it visits the Gulf of Maine infrequently.

Harp seals resemble harbor seals in body and head form but are larger, averaging 5 feet 7 inches (169 cm) and 286 pounds (130 kg) in both sexes, and proportionately stockier in the thoracic region. Fully mature males and females are white or off-white, silver, cream, or tan, with the head dark gray or black to just behind the eyes and a series of dark blotches on the back forming the harp or saddle. These markings are most dramatically developed in males. Some females have irregular dark spots on the back and no well-defined harp. Like other "ice seals," harps have large claws for making and maintaining breathing holes in the ice.

The pup from birth to 2½ weeks has a fine white fur (yellowish in the first 2 days), which it molts at about 3 weeks for a gray coat with dark spots known as the "beater coat." Immatures of 14 months and older, whose spots have grown larger, are known as "bedlamers" (from the French, *bêtes de la mer*). In females the bedlamer stage lasts into early maturity and is followed by development of a pale saddle that progressively darkens in a few more years. The spotted pattern may coexist with the faint outline of the emerging harp ("spotted harp"). Some females, however, remain spotted and never develop a complete black harp. In contrast, males acquire a dark saddle within 2 years of adulthood. A few males are very dark, with no harp pattern, and are called "smutty" seals.

Females usually mature at age 4 to 6 years; males mature at the same age as females or a year or two later. Life expectancy is about 35 years.

Harp seals are found in the North Atlantic, in three main groups: a western group in eastern Canada and western Greenland (territory of Denmark); a central group associated with eastern Greenland, Spitzbergen, and Jan Mayen; and an eastern group in the White Sea.

The northwest Atlantic harp seals have a complex annual cycle of migration and reproduction. They winter and breed on pack ice in the Gulf of St. Lawrence and off Labrador. In late spring they follow the retreating ice northward, arriving at Baffin Island and south-western Greenland by early summer. Later in summer the seals reach Ellesmere Island and some also enter Hudson Bay to the west. Their close relationship to the ice was commemorated in the species' former name, *Pagophilus*, from the Greek *pagos*, ice, and *philos*, loving. The current species name, *Phoca*, reflects the close relationship of harp seals to harbor seals, ringed seals, and others in the genus *Phoca*.

After a summer of feeding in the far north, nearly all adults and some immatures swim southward ahead of the advancing ice, feeding as they go. (Many young and a few nonbreeding adults stay north all year.) The migrating seals reach Cape Chidley, the northern tip of Labrador, by mid-October, and the Strait of Belle Isle, separating Labrador from Newfoundland, in December. At the peak of the southward migration along the Atlantic coast of Labrador, shore viewers may see a continuous procession of swimming seals, sometimes energetically breasting the water ("porpoising"), a sight that 200 years ago was a vast spectacle, filling the sea to the horizon.

At the Strait of Belle Isle the migrating stream divides, one-third of the seals entering the Gulf of St. Lawrence to feed and the rest continuing south to feed near the Grand Bank. By mid-February well-nourished females seek out large areas of pack ice suitable for pupping, either in the Gulf of St. Lawrence near the Magdalen Islands or at the "Front" off eastern Labrador and northern Newfoundland, where the largest herds are found. Harp seals are highly gregarious, and their density in the breeding "patches" on the ice may be as high as 5,945 females per square mile (2,000 females per square kilometer).

Pups averaging 35 inches (90 cm) and 22–24 pounds (10–11 kg) are born from late February to mid-March, those in the Gulf about 5 days earlier than those at the Front. The whitecoat pup about quadruples its birth weight of 22 pounds (10 kg) after 12 or 13 days of nursing. From 2½ to 3½ weeks, as the white hair is falling out and the "beater" coat is growing in, the pup is called a "ragged jacket." Weaning occurs at about 1½ weeks, and the female then mates, usually in the water, with one or more males in the vicinity. Male courtship includes vocalization and bubble blowing underwater and chasing females on the ice.

At 4 weeks the newly molted pup, or beater, starts to swim and feed. In April and May older seals haul out in great herds on the Front ice to molt over a period of several weeks. Finally, all the seals embark on the long northward migration of early summer. Individual

Harp seal. Adult markings, dorsal view.
D. D. TYLER

Harp seals on the Gulf of St. Lawrence ice pack
during March pupping season. Two adult females are in the foreground,
and a "whitecoat" pup is at the rear.
FRED BRUEMMER

Harp seal pup in beater coat at Beach Point, Truro, Massachusetts, April 25, 1989.
ROBERT PRESCOTT, JR.

harp seals may stray south of the normal range, to the Gulf of Maine and as far south as Virginia. Such occurrences were rare before 1985, but since that year at least 15 have stranded between the Bay of Fundy and New Jersey. The strandings occur between early February and late May and involve animals of both sexes and various ages, from pup and yearling to adult. A healthy harp seal juvenile was seen several times in Boston Harbor during the summer of 1990. Harp seal remains recovered from archaeological sites in New Brunswick, Maine, and Massachusetts, dated 1,000 to 4,000 years before present, suggest that harp seals may have been more abundant in the past, while recent strandings and sightings may be due to population increase in eastern Canada.

Strandings may also occur within the seals' normal range. In one unusual event about 100 pups came ashore at Prince Edward Island, in the winter of 1981, because of premature ice breakup. In general, first-year mortality is 20 to 30 percent and that of older seals is about 10 percent annually. Predators include polar bears, Greenland sharks, killer whales, and man.

Adult harp seals, which routinely dive to 330 feet (100 meters), feed mainly on capelin, polar cod, herring, crustaceans such as krill, amphipods, and shrimp, and to a lesser extent on cod, redfish, plaice, and Greenland halibut. The diet of immatures consists largely of krill and other shrimplike crustaceans.

Populations of harp seals are difficult to estimate. There is little doubt that several million lived in the northwestern Atlantic before 1800, but overexploitation by hunting after that date drastically reduced the stocks. Until 1950 population data were inadequate to define trends; it is known, however, that the population declined from 2.5 to 3 million in 1950 to about 1.5 million in 1970. These figures do not include pups. Restrictions on the harp seal hunt had been introduced in the 1960s, including closing dates and prohibitions on the taking of breeding adults, but more effective management came in 1971 with the imposition of quotas on the annual take, primarily of whitecoat and beater pups. The seal pelts were sold mainly to European markets; in 1983, however, responding to public outcry, the European Economic Community placed a ban on importation of products made from whitecoat harp and blueback hooded seal pups. By 1987 this boycott had brought an end to the large-scale commercial hunt.

The Canadian government, in turn, has banned the harvest of

whitecoat harp seal pups, except that landsmen from the Magdalen Islands and elsewhere may take them for local consumption. Under a quota system, Newfoundlanders take less than 90,000 beaters and bedlamers on ice off the east coast each spring. Arctic Eskimos and Greenland natives may take fewer than 12,000 animals of various ages during the harp seals' northern sojourn.

Estimates of pup production are the basis for determination of population size and management of the stock. Data from surveys conducted in 1990 indicate a population then of about 3 million and surveys in 1983–84 indicate a population then of 2 to 2.5 million and probably increasing. Careful management will ensure the species' continued survival. The value of harp seals lies not only in pelts and meat but also in aesthetic appeal and the species' role in the ecosystem. There are now popular tours in late winter at Prince Edward Island and the Magdalen Islands. Visitors see the islands, sample local culture, and, as weather permits, travel out onto the ice pack to view and photograph the seals.

HOODED SEAL
(*Cystophora cristata*)

Hooded seals share much of the harp seals' range but feed on larger prey in deeper water and breed on older, heavier ice seaward of harp seal herds at the Front off Labrador and northeastern Newfoundland. Some also breed on ice in the Gulf of St. Lawrence. Compared with harp seals, hooded seals are uncommon, and their biology and ecology are not well understood.

The hooded seal is large and distinctive in appearance. Males grow to 8.5 feet (260 cm) and 800 pounds (364 kg); females are somewhat smaller, to 7 feet 3 inches (220 cm) and 500 pounds (227 kg). Females mature at 3 to 6 years and males at 5 to 7 years. Longevity is 30 to 35 years.

Coat pattern is identical in both sexes: the background is bluish gray, overlaid with irregular black patches several inches square, and with smaller spots on the belly. The face is black. The head is relatively larger than the harbor seal's, with a heavier, broader, and more flattened muzzle. The claws are substantial.

The species' most remarkable feature is the male's nose, which is one of the most peculiar organs for visual display possessed by any

Hooded seals, pup (foreground), female (middle), male (rear).
Approximate length: male, 8.5 feet; female, 7.25 feet.
ARTHUR MANSFIELD, ARCTIC BIOLOGICAL STATION,
DEPARTMENT OF FISHERIES AND OCEANS, CANADA

HOODED SEAL

D. D. TYLER

side view, male

side view, female

fur pattern

crest inflated, male

nasal sac inflated, male

mammal. Part of the nasal cavity is enlarged to form a distensible hood running from the crown to the upper lip, which it overhangs, like a proboscis, in older animals. When the seal is angered, this structure can be inflated into a crest almost twice the size of a football. In addition, there is an inflatable nasal membrane that can be blown through one nostril as a red, balloonlike sac; the balloon, when shaken, makes a pinging sound. The species' scientific and common names refer to these structures: the scientific name (Gr. *kostis*, bladder, + *phoros*, to carry, and L. *crista*, crest) translates as "bladder-carrying seal with a crest." This apparatus functions as display and warning during the breeding season. The crest begins developing at 4 years and increases with the male's size and age, reaching a maximum at about 13 years.

Breeding hooded seals are found on drifting, heavy pack ice throughout the northernmost Atlantic, with three major concentrations. The largest is north of Iceland, at the so-called West Ice. Another group breeds on seaward pack ice at the Front off Labrador and northeastern Newfoundland and in the Gulf of St. Lawrence. A third group, in Davis Strait near the Arctic Circle, was rediscovered in 1974.

Pups are born with a well-developed blubber layer, from mid-March to early April, and suckling lasts only 4 days, the shortest nursing period known for any mammal. The newborn pup, called a "blueback," is about 3 feet 5 inches (105 cm) long and weighs about 44 pounds (20 kg). Males are larger than females. The exceptionally beautiful natal fur is slate blue on the back and light gray on the belly. The head appears flattened, and the face is black to just behind the eyes. In nursing for 4 days on its mother's milk, which is more than 50 percent fat, the pup more than doubles its birth weight, much of the gain being blubber.

Mating occurs in the water when the pup is weaned. Females and pups on the ice may cluster loosely or spread out over vast areas. Numbers at the Front reach the highest levels in years when cold and ice conditions are most severe. Males compete on the ice and in the water for proximity to females with pups; from 1 to 7 males may be seen near each female-pup pair. Where females are slightly clustered near the center of the breeding herd, a male may mate with more than one; where females are widely scattered the male may only have a chance to breed once.

After the breeding season the Canadian hooded seals (except the pups) migrate northwest, reaching southwestern Greenland by early May. Within a few weeks many turn and go southward again, later joining large molting groups east of Greenland in June, July, and possibly August. After the molt the seals disperse again, some continuing north and east, while others head to the southern tip of Greenland, then northwest as far as Thule. The pups eventually enter the water and head north; they may be found in April near groups of molting harp seals at the edge of the pack ice.

Young hooded seals molt the blueback coat at 14 months. The second coat is similar to the blueback, but with small, dark spots and blotches. This coat appears silvery when dry.

Hooded seals tend to wander out of range. They have been reported in the St. Lawrence River west to Montreal and infrequently among the islands of the eastern Canadian Arctic. It has been said that a few may have traversed the Northwest Passage to the Beaufort Sea. Stragglers often reach New England. A female and newborn pup were recorded at North Harpswell, Maine, in 1928; another such pair was seen at South Brooksville, Maine, in April 1974; and a third turned up at Wiscasset, Maine, in March 1982. In Canada, disoriented seals occasionally wander inland if pack ice fails during the breeding season. Individual hooded seals have been reported from Cape Cod to as far south as Florida. Since 1984 the number of blueback strandings has increased from New England south to New Jersey. Many have occurred between December and March and involve animals approaching their first birthday. Oddly, a few of these seals had no hair.

Blueback hooded seal pups were hunted along with harp seals at the Front, in the large commercial harvest that ended during the 1980s, but Canadian law now prohibits the taking of bluebacks. An annual quota of 3,500 older seals is set for the landsmen hunt off Newfoundland's east coast in the spring, but hooded seals are completely protected in the Gulf of St. Lawrence. A few are still taken at various times of year by natives of Greenland. There is no harvest of the Davis Strait herd; however, Norway still harvests both hooded and harp seals at the West Ice. Hooded seals are even more difficult to census than harp seals. The northwest Atlantic stock size (including those that breed in Davis Strait) is estimated at about 400,000.

Hooded seals feed in deep water, diving to 660 feet (200 meters), and dining on redfish, Greenland halibut, octopus, squid, herring, capelin, cod, shrimp, and mussels. Predators of the hooded seal in-

Hooded seal male, close-up of crest (left), crest expanded (right).
GEOFF BECK

Hooded seal female and pup on the ice.
GEOFF BECK

Hooded seal female in threat posture. This female and her newborn pup were photographed at South Brooksville, Maine, April 10, 1974.
R. RUSSELL

clude humans, polar bears, Greenland sharks, and possibly killer whales. As with harp seals, wise management is essential for the species' survival.

RINGED SEAL
(Phoca hispida)

This is the most common Arctic seal and a mainstay of the Eskimo subsistence economy. Ringed seals are found wherever there is stable land-fast ice in winter and spring, usually in fjords and bays but also in some lakes and estuaries. The distribution is circumpolar, encompassing all of the Eurasian and Canadian Arctic and extending southward to Japan, Hudson Bay, Labrador, and occasionally northeast Newfoundland and the Gulf of St. Lawrence. There is also a group in the Baltic Sea. Ringed seals have been sighted in the St. Lawrence River up to Quebec City, and there is evidence suggesting an isolated population lived in the Saguenay River about 40 years ago. Until recently ringed seals were not known to occur in the United States; since 1987, however, at least 8 have stranded from New England to New Jersey.

The ringed seal somewhat resembles a small harbor seal. Coat color is variable, generally consisting of a gray background with numerous dark spots, particularly on the back. Many of the spots are surrounded by light areas, forming the typical ringed pattern. The belly is silver. The ringed seal head looks similar to that of the harbor seal but is shorter and narrower and tapers to a more pointed nose. Vibrissae are more profuse and tend to curve down more than in the harbor seal. The claws are large and strong, for making and maintaining breathing holes in the ice and excavating lairs in snowdrifts. A ringed seal on land, such as one that is stranded, may use the claws to pull itself along, a trait not seen in harbor seals.

Size varies according to location and stability of the ice conditions during the pupping season. Average adults range from 4 to 4.5 feet (122–137 cm) in length and from 110 to 150 pounds (50–68 kg) in weight. Females are slightly smaller than males though otherwise similar. Under optimal conditions an adult male may attain a maximum size of 5 feet 5 inches (165 cm) and 250 pounds (113 kg).

During late fall and winter, mature seals live under the ice by maintaining breathing holes, often with snow-covered lairs over them,

Ringed seal mother and pup.
Inset shows typical birth den in the ice.
SARAH LANDRY

while younger individuals stay at the edge of the ice. Pups are born from mid-March to late April in lairs over breathing holes. The female excavates the birth lair out of a snowdrift or may use a space between rafted and uplifted ice blocks. She will defend the breathing hole entrance against other females. The newborn pup has a long white lanugo coat, measures about 26 inches (66 cm), and weighs about 10 pounds (4.5 kg). Nursing may last for 6 to 8 weeks, and the pup may gain up to 30 pounds (14 kg) if the ice is sufficiently stable. If early ice breakup terminates suckling, the stunted pup may not reach maximum size as an adult. Mating probably takes place from March to late May and may occur within two weeks of the female's giving birth. During the breeding season the male's face darkens and the glands of the face give off a strong, offensive odor. The odor is referred to by an outmoded scientific name, *Pusa (Phoca) foetida.*

The ringed seal pup starts to shed the white lanugo at about 2 weeks and by 3 to 4 weeks has developed a coat which is silver on the belly and dark gray on the back with traces of the adult ringed pattern. Such newly molted young are known as "silver jars," and they yielded prime pelts for the now-defunct Eskimo fur trade. In mid-May to mid-July the older seals molt and fast, hauling out to bask near breathing holes or at the ice edge. The hair coats of older seals were worth less in the fur trade than those of the silver jars. The present species name, from the Latin *hispidus,* meaning rough and bristly, refers to the coarse hair texture. The breakup of the fast ice in July terminates the molting haulout, and summer feeding commences. Ringed seals dive at least 300 feet (91 m) to eat, feeding primarily on small polar cod, amphipods, krill, and other shrimplike crustaceans.

Ringed seals, in their turn along the food chain, are killed by men, polar bears, killer whales, arctic foxes, and occasionally walruses. The birth lair provides the pup with vital shelter from such predation. With luck, a ringed seal may live to 40 years, but a shorter life span may be more usual. Females mature at 5 to 6 years and males at 7 years.

No estimates of total population size are available. On the basis of aerial surveys in 1966–69, nearly 166,000 were estimated to occupy three bays in Baffin Island, a very small part of the total range. Density may vary from 3 to 9 seals per square mile (1 to 3 per square kilometer) in largely different areas in the Canadian Arctic, but no extrapolations are possible over such a vast region.

Ringed seal. Note long whiskers and large eyes.
THOMAS G. SMITH, DEPARTMENT OF FISHERIES AND OCEANS, CANADA

Ringed seal, side view.
THOMAS G. SMITH, DEPARTMENT OF FISHERIES AND OCEANS, CANADA

Young adult ringed seal on the coast
of northern Baffin Island, arctic Canada.
Males and females are nearly identical.
FRED BRUEMMER

BEARDED SEAL
(*Erignathus barbatus*)

This distinctive seal inhabits sub-Arctic and Arctic seas to about 85°N and is circumpolar in distribution. It is associated with moving pack ice floes near shallow banks where its diet of shellfish and other bottom organisms may be found.

The bearded is the largest "ice seal" in the Northern Hemisphere and perhaps the most unusual of the northern phocids. The body appears long and heavy and the head disproportionately small. Noticeable on the head are prominent brow ridges; large, dark ear openings; and abundant long, white whiskers, or vibrissae, for which the seal is named. In water the seal can be recognized at a distance by the glistening whiskers, which may form spirals at their tips when dry. The nostrils are angled back toward the top of the snout rather than set vertically at its front. The species' scientific name (Gr. *eri*, an intensive prefix, + *gnathus*, jaw, and L. *barba*, beard) translates loosely as "bearded with a deep jaw." A more common name in the Arctic is "squareflipper," referring to another diagnostic feature of the species. Whereas in the other seals of our study area the foreflipper digits gradually decrease in length from first to last, in this seal the middle digit is slightly longer than the others, giving the flipper a wide, square shape. Each digit terminates in a stout claw.

Unique among northern phocids, the bearded seal is similar to certain southern phocids, the monk seals, in two respects: the vibrissae are smooth, and there are four teats. All other northern phocids have wavy or beaded vibrissae and two teats.

Adults grow to about 7 feet 5 inches (226 cm) and from 425 to 550 pounds (193–250 kg) on average, but they may reach 8 feet 8 inches (264 cm) and 930 pounds (423 kg). Females are the same size as males or slightly heavier. Coat color is the same in both sexes. It varies from light to dark gray, darkest on the back and lighter on the belly. Spotting is uncommon. Females mature at 5 to 6 years, males at 6 to 7 years, and longevity is usually 25 years, although a few may reach 30.

Widely separated females give birth on ice floes around the first of May in the Canadian Arctic. The newborn pups, measuring 4 feet to 4 feet 4 inches (122–132 cm) and weighing about 70 pounds (32

Bearded seal. Size range: up to 8.7 feet.
ARTHUR MANSFIELD, ARCTIC BIOLOGICAL STATION,
DEPARTMENT OF FISHERIES AND OCEANS, CANADA

Bearded seal. Note stiff whiskers and "square" foreflipper gripping snow.
THOMAS G. SMITH, DEPARTMENT OF FISHERIES AND OCEANS, CANADA

Bearded seal, side view.
THOMAS G. SMITH, DEPARTMENT OF FISHERIES AND OCEANS, CANADA

kg), have a long coat of fine, dark brown hair, with light patches on the head, the shoulder, and the mid-dorsal region. Pups can and do swim shortly after birth, an adaptation allowing escape from predation by polar bears, which share the same habitat. Nursing lasts for 12 to 18 days, but pups may start to feed on shrimp before the end of this period. At weaning the pup averages 4 feet 10 inches (147 cm) and 200 pounds (91 kg). The first coat is shed by about 3 weeks and replaced with one similar to that of adults.

The adults mate in May, around the time of weaning, in the water. During the breeding season males become very vocal underwater, emitting a long, descending warble that can be heard through the ice in air. Females also may sing in some areas. Populations of bearded seals in different areas have been found to have distinct vocal repertoires, or dialects, indicating that the seals may be sedentary and the populations discrete.

Although bearded seals have been reported in water over 1,642 feet (500 m) deep, and may dive to considerable depths, they are thought to feed in relatively shallow water. The diet includes clams, whelks, hermit crabs, sea cucumbers, shrimp, worms, and polar cod. Like the walrus, the seal probably uses its sensitive vibrissae to obtain food items on the bottom and in the sediment. The teeth become very worn with age from abrasion by grit. Predators of the bearded seal are polar bears, men, walruses, and killer whales.

In summer the normally rather solitary squareflipper will haul out with others on sandbars or gravel beaches. Then, as at other seasons, the close association with pack ice is maintained; the seals follow it north in the summer and south in the fall. They prefer floes that are not too heavy and are adjacent to open water. If caught under land-fast ice, the seals can make breathing holes by bashing with the head if the ice is not too thick, or by scratching through ice up to 6½ feet (2 meters) thick with the claws of the foreflippers. Bearded seals generally avoid land, but some young individuals may enter river mouths in the fall.

In the northeastern Atlantic the bearded seal's range extends from the Arctic southward to Norway and occasionally as far as Portugal, while in the northwestern Atlantic the range is south to northeast Newfoundland and, uncommonly, into the Gulf of St. Lawrence and the St. Lawrence estuary. No precise population estimates are available for this poorly known species. Bearded seals are patchy in distribution and most abundant within their range near wide coastal shelves.

The bearded seal was once highly valued by Eskimos for the tough, pliant skin, which was made into boot soles, dog harnesses, harpoon lines, and covering for the large skin boat or umiak; today the squareflipper is still taken occasionally for food, and the skin is used mainly for boot soles.

ATLANTIC WALRUS
(*Odobenus rosmarus rosmarus*)

The walrus is a rare visitor to eastern Canada south of Labrador today. Its scarcity is a result of overexploitation by early European settlers and seafarers, for walruses were abundant farther south in early historic times. Until the eighteenth century, several thousand inhabited the Gulf of St. Lawrence, notably the Magdalen Islands, and Nova Scotia as far south as Sable Island. Now there are about 20,000 in the eastern Canadian Arctic, ranging from Hudson Strait, Hudson Bay, and Foxe Basin north to Ellesmere Island, and west to Bathurst Island, and in western Greenland. This northwest Atlantic stock is the stronghold of the Atlantic walrus subspecies; there may be only a few thousand in the rest of its range, from eastern Greenland, and Spitzbergen, to the Barents and Kara seas. The Pacific walrus subspecies, *Odobenus rosmarus divergens*, however, has flourished in the Alaskan and Siberian Arctic, where between 200,000 and 250,000 remain. Pacific walruses are slightly bigger than Atlantic walruses.

The walrus is the largest North Atlantic pinniped and should not be mistaken for any other species. (However, large bull gray seals have occasionally been reported to us as "walrus" by inexperienced seal watchers.) Characteristic features are great size; somewhat square-shaped head; small, often bloodshot eyes; large mustache pads bristling with hundreds of stout sensory whiskers; and, of course, long, ever-growing tusks. The skin is brown, sparsely covered by reddish-brown hair. Young animals are much darker brown or slate gray, while some old males may be pale, almost like albinos. A walrus in cold water may appear very pale because blood flow to the skin is restricted, while walruses hauled out in warm air may look sunburned as the skin is suffused with blood to dissipate heat.

Adult males may reach 10 feet (3 m) and 2,640 pounds (1,200

Walruses.
Approximate length: male, 10 feet; female, 8 feet.
JOHN R. QUINN

Two adult male Atlantic walruses on Coats Island, in northern Hudson Bay. Male on right has a broken tusk.
FRED BRUEMMER

Skull of young walrus recovered from Chandler River, Machias, Maine, by Darrel Richards, June 1976.
DAVID RICHARDSON

kg). The massiveness of the bull's neck and shoulders is accentuated by thick, lumpy skin. Females are smaller, reach a length of 8 feet 3 inches (2.5 m) and a weight of 1,760 pounds (800 kg), and have a relatively smaller head with tusks more slender than the male's. There are four teats.

Tusks, which are elongated upper canine teeth, first form at 4 months of age and reach 1 inch (2.5 cm) at 1 year, 4 inches (10 cm) at 2 years, and 11 inches (28 cm) at 5 years. Adult tusks of up to 40 inches (100 cm) and 12 pounds (5.4 kg) have been recorded. The genus name (Gr. *odous*, tooth, + *baino*, I walk) suggests that the tusks help the walrus to walk. In fact, walruses do use their tusks to pull themselves up onto ice floes. Tusks are also employed by males in dominance and threat displays and by both sexes in aggressive encounters, for defense against predators, and to keep ice holes open. The species name is from Norwegian *rossmaal* or *rossmar* and earlier Scandinavian words meaning "whale horse." One can imagine early Viking explorers attempting to describe this bizarre animal and meeting some success with "whale horse."

Another unique feature is a pair of pouches, part of the elastic pharynx, which extend back laterally between the neck muscles. If a walrus in the water is sleeping or wounded, the pouches may be inflated to act as buoys. In males, the pouches also produce a remarkable bell-like sound, heard most often during periods of sexual activity. One selection on the recording *Callings*, listed in the Bibliography, features that sound. Pacific walruses use the bell-like sound to start or end long, complex vocal displays comparable to the songs of humpback whales. The songs include a stereotyped, but individually distinctive, pattern of knocks, taps, and bell sounds produced underwater and lasting about 7 minutes, interspersed with shorter periods of knocks produced at the surface between breaths. As in humpbacks, songs are produced only by males. A dominant male sings continuously while accompanying a small herd of females and attempting to monopolize sexual access to them. One male called continuously for 55 hours. The sounds travel for 5 to 10 miles underwater.

Calves, weighing 120 pounds (55 kg) and measuring almost 4 feet (122 cm), are born from April to June. The calf's skin is dark brown or slate gray and visible under its natal coat of sparse gray hair, which is shed shortly after birth. The period of maternal care lasts about 2 years. Mothers are very attentive to calves and protect them fiercely. The calf is often carried clinging to her back, or may be sheltered between her foreflippers.

Females first breed at 4 to 7 years of age and bear young every 2 years at first, while older females tend to give birth at intervals of 3 years or longer. Males may mature at 7 years but usually do so at 9 or 10. Longevity ranges from 16 to 30 years.

The highly gregarious walrus favors a habitat of sea ice floating above shallow shellfish beds. The affinity for pack ice adjacent to temporary patches of open water persists year-round in extreme northern areas, but where ice breaks up in summer, walruses may haul out at traditional island sites that Eskimos call *uglit*. For most of the year, adult males herd separately from females and immatures. Mating occurs from January to March, in the water, and dominant males may secure access to several females. Molting takes place from June until early fall.

The walrus apparently feeds by standing almost on its head and furrowing the bottom with the front and sides of the tusks as it moves forward, while the sensitive vibrissae contact shellfish and other animals in the sediment. Clams and cockles are the principal food; the meat is sucked or torn from the shell before being swallowed. Other dietary items include whelks, sea cucumbers, worms, crustaceans, and small polar cod. A few walruses, probably males, eat ringed and bearded seals, which they attack with their tusks. Narwhals and belugas are also eaten occasionally, perhaps as carrion. Recently some walruses have been reported to feed on seabirds such as eider ducks.

Killer whales, polar bears, and men prey on walrus. The ferocious and aggressive adult walruses often deter killer whales and polar bears and may even kill humans by turning over a small boat. Polar bear predation is probably significant, however, particularly on younger animals in areas where both bears and walruses are numerous, for example, at Southhampton Island in Hudson Bay, and where climate is cold enough that walruses may be "frozen out" and unable to escape to water, as in the Canadian High Arctic.

Traditionally, Eskimos have hunted walrus for meat and ivory, and this native hunting continues for subsistence purposes under a licensed quota system. The loss of carcasses that sink before they can be hauled in adds to hunting mortality, an important consideration because the species is slow to reproduce. Oil and gas exploration in the Canadian Arctic portends further threats to walruses as well as other organisms.

Sightings of walruses south of northern Labrador are of great interest. About one a year may reach Newfoundland or the Gulf of St. Lawrence, but they are much rarer farther south. One was seen at Bear Cove, Nova Scotia, in the Bay of Fundy in 1937, another at Cape Sable, Nova Scotia, in 1976, and a third, an immature, lingered on the east shore of Nova Scotia in the summer of 1989. The southernmost record of a live walrus in historic times is that of an immature taken at Plymouth, Massachusetts, in 1734. Fossil bones, some dating back to the last ice age, have been found in New England and as far south as Georgia. Other bones recovered in New England may be those of individuals that strayed south of the normal range in more recent times.

FIELD IDENTIFICATION SUMMARY FOR SEALS, CAPE COD TO NEWFOUNDLAND

Common name Species	Length, nose to tail, Male, Female	Maximum adult weight	Coat, Fur	Head
Harbor seal (*Phoca vitulina concolor*)	M 5–5.5 ft. 153–168 cm F 4.7–5.5 ft. 143–168 cm	M 250 lb. 114 kg F 200 lb. 91 kg	Variable; light gray, tan, brown, dark gray, almost black, or reddish, with profuse dark spots dorsally, scattered spots ventrally. Pup coats similar, except occasional individuals born with embryonal white fur ("whitecoat").	Short snout; profile concave (spaniel-like). Eye about equidistant from tip of nose and ear. Nostrils form a broad **V** almost meeting at bottom.
Gray seal (*Halichoerus grypus*)	M 8 ft. 244 cm F 7 ft. 213 cm	M 990 lb. 450 kg F 594 lb. 270 kg	Variable; general rule is females light gray, tan, or cream-colored background with dark spots and blotches. Males dark brown, gray, or nearly black with small light markings. Pups born with embryonal white fur ("whitecoat").	Long snout with profile straight or convex ("Roman nose"). Head donkey-shaped ("horsehead"). Eye closer to ear than nose. Nostril openings form a **W** when viewed frontally. Female has a smaller head than male.
Harp seal (*Phoca groenlandica*)	M 5.6 ft. 169 cm F same as male	M 400 lb. 182 kg F same as male	Pups born in "whitecoat"; juvenile coat spotted on silver, cream, or tan; adults may have distinct harp or horseshoe pattern on back and flanks.	Streamlined doglike muzzle similar to harbor seal. Head and face dark in contrast to neck and chest.

Common name Species	Length, nose to tail, Male, Female	Maximum adult weight	Coat, Fur	Head
Hooded seal (*Cystophora cristata*)	M 8.5 ft. 260 cm F 7.25 ft. 220 cm	M 800 lb. 364 kg F 500 lb. 227 kg	"Blueback" pups have silver-bluish-gray back with light gray belly; adults gray with distinct black patches of irregular shape; black muzzle and face.	Larger and heavier muzzle than harbor seal, with broader, more flattened snout when viewed frontally. Crest of hood on top of head and muzzle of mature male. Inflatable nasal sac in male.
Ringed seal (*Phoca hispida*)	M 4–5.4 ft. 122–165 cm F slightly smaller	M 150–250 lb. 68–113 kg F slightly smaller	Variable; generally a gray background with numerous dark spots surrounded by light areas, forming ringed pattern. Pups born in "whitecoat."	Similar to harbor seal head but smaller, with more pointed snout.
Bearded seal (*Erignathus barbatus*)	M 7.4–8.7 ft. 226–264 cm F same as male	M 550–930 lb. 250–423 kg F same as male or slightly heavier	Light to dark gray in both sexes; darkest on the back.	Head appears disproportionately small. Prominent brow ridges and ear openings. Abundant long, white whiskers or vibrissae.
Atlantic Walrus (*Odobenus rosmarus rosmarus*)	M 10 ft. 3 m F 8.25 ft. 2.5 m	M 2,640 lb. 1,200 kg F 1,760 lb. 800 kg	Rough, wrinkled brown skin with very sparse reddish brown hair.	Short, squarish head with small eyes, and large white tusks and stiff whiskers (both sexes). Pharyngeal pouches in neck area.

SAMPLE SEAL SIGHTING DATA FORM

Seals may be censused at any time of the year in clear weather; in rocky areas harbor and gray seals should be censused at low tide. We encourage you, when possible, to identify individual seals by natural markings (pigmentation and scars), using photographs for documentation; and/or by tags and brands. A series of sightings or counts, when recorded, can form the basis of an ongoing study. A suggested format for reporting sightings and counts is given below.

DATE	TIME	LOCATION	NO. HAULED OUT	NO. IN WATER	STATE OF TIDE	WEATHER*	COMMENTS**

* Air temperature, visibility, sun, wind speed and direction, sea condition and sea surface temperature.
**Group composition (size, sex); behavior, special markings, tags or brands; etc.

PLEASE REPORT ALL TAGS AND BRANDS SEEN,
AND ANY WALRUSES SOUTH OF NORTHERN LABRADOR, TO:

If seen in Canada

Brian Beck, Marine Fish Division
Bedford Institute of Oceanography
P.O. Box 1006
Dartmouth, Nova Scotia
B2Y 4A2 CANADA

If seen in United States

Allied Whale
College of the Atlantic
Bar Harbor, ME 04609
U.S.A.

APPENDICES

Important Prey Species of Whales, Porpoises, and Seals

A list of every animal that occurs in the diet of whales, porpoises, or seals within our study area would include dozens of species. Nearly all these animals will feed on whatever fishes or invertebrates are abundant that they can catch. Staple foods for various marine mammals in our study area include copepods (especially *Calanus finmarchicus*), krill (*Meganyctiphanes norvegica* and several species of *Thysanoessa*), capelin (*Mallotus villosus*), herring (*Clupea harengus*), sand lance (*Ammodytes americanus*), mackerel (*Scomber scombrus*), and short-finned squid (*Illex illecebrosus*). Brief life histories of these important species may help the reader to understand the feeding ecology of the whales and seals that eat them.

Calanus finmarchicus, found throughout the temperate waters of the Northern Hemisphere, is the most abundant herbivorous copepod in the North Atlantic Ocean and perhaps the most abundant animal on earth. An adult *Calanus* is about one-fifth inch (5 mm) long, and about 200,000 of them would weigh 1 pound (454 gm). During a day each adult could filter tiny planktonic plant cells (phytoplankton) from about half a cup of water. The life cycle includes twelve developmental stages, and several generations may be produced each year under favorable circumstances. During early spring, immature males and females that have spent the winter in the eleventh developmental stage (Stage V copepodite) at depths of about 328 feet (100 meters) or more become active again and migrate to the surface to feed on the new growth of phytoplankton. They mature and mate, and the females lay fertilized eggs in the surface layers. After the eggs hatch, the resulting teardrop-shaped nauplius larva molts six times, eventually becoming a miniature adult that grows during six more molts to full size. Total development time from egg to ripe female adult lasts about two and a half months during spring and summer in the Gulf of Maine. This species is the principal food of right whales and basking sharks and is also important in the diet of sei whales. Even finback whales and minke whales may take *Calanus* on occasion. Certain seabirds, notably Wilson's petrel, Leach's petrel, and the northern and red phalaropes, feed on *Calanus*. The sight of these birds busily dipping their bills into the water is a good clue that copepods are present near the surface.

Calanus is frequently abundant enough to dominate a plankton net haul taken in coastal waters, filling the sample bottle with a nearly solid mass of copepods. They taste like a shrimp paté. Attempts have been made to harvest *Calanus* for human consumption by anchoring large plankton nets in Norwegian fjords, straining the copepods as the tide moves in and out, but yields were not sufficient for commercial operations.

The life cycles of two of the krill species important in our study area, *Meganyctiphanes norvegica* and *Thysanoessa inermis*, are similar. Mating occurs in late spring, peaking in June. Eggs are released in early July, and larvae molt and grow through September. Little growth occurs in winter, but further growth and sexual maturation take place in spring as planktonic plants (phytoplankton) become abundant. Both sexes can survive to mate a second time the following summer. Both species attain maximum adult lengths of about 1.5 inches (38 mm) and fresh weights of perhaps 600 to a pound (750 mg each).

Swarms of krill can color the sea pink during summer where upwelling or converging currents occur, but these swarms do not achieve the extraordinary abundance of Antarctic species. Little is known about the absolute abundance of krill in our study area because they are very difficult to catch in nets. Their compound eyes can easily see an approaching net, especially if any luminescent organisms (including the krill themselves) have been caught, for then the net is readily visible. The krill can swim fast enough to get out of the way of most nets. Furthermore, adults usually spend daylight hours on or very close to the bottom, which presents additional sampling problems for towed nets. We do not know how the baleen whales, all of which feed on krill to some extent, manage to catch them more efficiently than we can. Other creatures whose diet depends heavily on krill at times include cod, herring, capelin, mackerel, seals, and seabirds. We have dipped krill from surface swarms in Passamaquoddy Bay, eaten them raw, and found them to have a delicious crablike flavor.

Herring is one of the most important bait fishes in the southern half of our study area, especially in the Gulf of Maine, along the Nova Scotia coast, and in the Gulf of St. Lawrence. Herring feed predominantly on zooplankton, especially *Calanus* and other copepods, plus the krill species. The western North Atlantic population is apparently broken into many local spawning stocks, whose location and size may be determined largely by the existence of current patterns that retain the larvae in the spawning areas. Major spawning areas include Georges Bank, the southeast coast of Nova Scotia, shoals southwest of Grand Manan Island, and several locations on the south shore of the Gulf of St. Lawrence. Adult herring, usually over 4 years old and 10 inches (25 cm) long, spawn during late August and September in the Gulf of Maine. A female lays about 30,000 eggs on average. The sticky eggs sink and remain in place on the bottom close to the coast. The eggs hatch in about 2 weeks into larvae the size of a large *Calanus*. By Christmas they are 1 or 2 inches (25–50 mm) long; by June, 2 to 2.5 inches (50–63 mm) long. At age 1 year the 3- to 5-inch (76–127 mm) fish are called brit, and at this size they become choice food for whales, porpoises, seals, and seabirds. During summer and autumn, schools of brit and older herring feed in coastal waters, often close to shore, rising to the surface near dawn and dusk to catch plankton. The fish continue to grow to 9 or 10 inches (23–25 cm) by 3 years, and reach approximately 1 foot (30 cm) at age 7. Herring can live to be 20 years old, 17 inches (43 cm) long, and about 1.5 pounds (680 gm) in weight, though most will be eaten much earlier. Although herring populations rise and fall with variable success of spawning, an indication of the extraordinary potential abundance is given by the total catch for the Gulf of Maine in 1928, when over 250 million pounds, representing probably 5 or 6 billion fish, were harvested.

The capelin is the chief bait fish of Arctic and sub-Arctic portions of the North Atlantic Ocean. Smaller and slimmer than a herring, it grows to only 6.5 or 7.5 inches (16–19 cm) and runs perhaps 22 to

A sand lance trying to escape from the tip of
this humpback whale's lower jaw shows the relative size
of predator and this important prey species.
Stellwagen Bank, August 1989.
SCOTT MARION (SEAFARERS EXPEDITIONS)

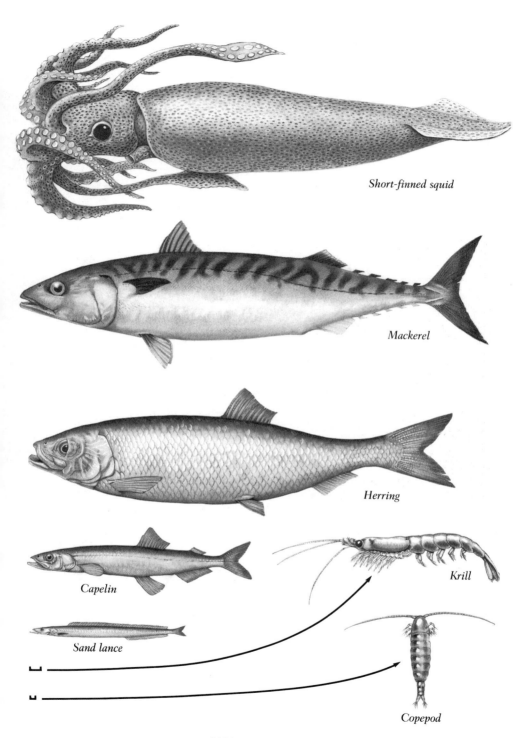

Short-finned squid

Mackerel

Herring

Capelin

Krill

Sand lance

Copepod

SARAH LANDRY

the pound (about 20 gm each). Capelin spend most of the year at sea but form vast schools that come inshore to spawn, usually at night, when water temperature is from 40°F to 47°F (4.4°–8.3°C). Spawning starts in June along the Newfoundland coast and in July or August in Labrador. Most spawn on gravel beaches just below the wave line, but some spawn along the coast in water up to 165 feet (50 meters) deep. Females lay up to 50,000 small (.04 inch, or 1 mm) red eggs that stick to the bottom and hatch in 2 to 3 weeks, depending on temperature.

After spawning, the spent adults form large but listless inshore schools that fall easy prey to humpback, finback, and minke whales, as well as seals, seabirds, and fish such as cod. Some capelin survive to mate a second or third time. A capelin will be about 3.5 inches (9 cm) long at 1 year of age and will begin to spawn at age 3 or 4. Throughout its life it will feed mainly on copepods, especially *Calanus*, krill, or other small crustaceans.

During the late 1960s and early 1970s, European fleets began to harvest the offshore population of immature capelin on the Grand Bank for use as human food, dog food, fertilizer, and fish meal. After several years of heavy fishing, the Grand Bank capelin catch fell sharply, perhaps because of overfishing. At about the same time, humpback whales began to appear inshore in increasing numbers during summer along the Newfoundland coast, feeding on still abundant inshore populations of capelin. The whales caused a great deal of damage to coastal fishing gear, and in the process up to several dozen humpbacks per year drowned or were shot after becoming entangled in nets. The Grand Bank capelin fishery was closed, the offshore capelin stock began to recover, but the number of humpback entanglements did not decrease.

Capelin biologists now think that the decline in catch during the period from about 1974 to 1980 was not caused by overfishing but by meteorologic and hydrologic factors. New research by William Leggett and colleagues (e.g., Leggett and Frank, 1990) shows that newly hatched capelin larvae enter the water column only when an onshore wind blows warm surface water onto the beach. This response to warm temperature ensures that larvae enter water containing small plankton animals that they can eat. The cooler subsurface water contains larger plankton animals that the larvae cannot eat, as well as jellyfish and other predators that will eat the tiny fishes. Each larva is provisioned with enough food in its yolk sac to survive in the gravel for up to about 6 days. If an onshore wind does not come within that time, the larvae die. Reproduction of beach-spawning capelin populations fails during years with infrequent onshore winds, as was the case during 1974 to 1980.

The sand lance (also called sand eel) is extraordinarily important in the diet of whales, porpoises, seabirds, and commercial fish such as cod, haddock, mackerel, hake, and others. On shoal banks with sandy bottoms, these little fish (maximum 7 inches, 18 cm) occur in dense schools during spring through autumn, feeding mainly on copepods. They can be recognized in the water by their eel-like undulations while swimming. Sand lance frequently bury themselves 4 to 6 inches (10–15 cm) deep in the sand, perhaps to avoid predators or, in very shallow locations, to avoid desiccation when the tide is out. Sand lance are abundant in the southern part of the Gulf of Maine, on Georges and Browns banks, in the Gulf of St. Lawrence, and along the Newfoundland and Labrador coasts. They spawn in autumn and early winter. Eggs stick to sand grains at depths of about 65 feet (20 meters). The young fish grow to about 3 or 4 inches (7–10 cm) in their first year and may mature during the second. Adults average 4 to 6 inches (10–15 cm) in length, with 6-inch fish running about 25 to the pound (18 gm each). Although they are occasionally found in European fish markets, sand lance are not caught for food in our study area. A few are taken for bait.

Mackerel roam the coastal waters of the southern part of our study area during warmer months, but their abundance and distribution vary more than in the other bait fishes. Enormous numbers of mackerel are present during some summers, with schools of many thousands rippling the surface, but in other years few can be found. Large schools usually appear in the Gulf of Maine from Georges Bank to Cape Cod and Jeffreys Ledge, but abundance declines farther east. The fish again become abundant along the outer Nova Scotia coast and in the southern Gulf of St. Lawrence, tapering off in Newfoundland waters. Wherever they are abundant, mackerel eat most suitably sized planktonic animals, especially crustaceans, or small fishes, notably herring and sand lance. In turn, they become food for bluefish, tuna, sharks, seals, porpoises, some whales, and seabirds such as gannets. During winter 1987, at least 15 humpback whales died in Massachusetts Bay after eating mackerel whose guts contained saxitoxin, a poison produced naturally by planktonic plants called dinoflagellates and subsequently bioaccumulated through the food web.

During winter the mackerel schools apparently migrate to deeper water over the continental shelf offshore from Virginia to Nova Scotia. Reappearance along the coasts occurs rather unpredictably during spring or summer, sometime after surface water warms to over 46°F (7.8°C). After feeding voraciously for several months, mackerel spawn at temperatures from 48°F to 57°F (9–14°C), usually south of our study area. Eggs are broadcast and fertilized externally wherever the fish happen to be. A female weighing 1.5 pounds (680 gm) may release up to 500,000 eggs in batches of about 50,000 over a period of some weeks. The free-floating eggs hatch in about 6 days at 55°F (13°C). The larvae, only 0.125 inch (3 mm) long, usually grow to 8 or 9 inches (20–23 cm) by autumn, when they migrate offshore. They reach 12 to 13 inches (30–33 cm) by the next autumn and 14 to 15 inches (36–38 cm) in their third year. Most mackerel spawn the following summer at age 3 years and every summer thereafter until they die. Life span is at least 8 or 10 years.

The short-finned squid is important in the food web of our study area, both as a predator on herring, capelin, and mackerel and as food for pilot whales, other odontocetes, seals, and seabirds, especially fulmars and shearwaters. As is typical for squid, this species grows very quickly, breeding and then dying at the end of 1 year. Within that single year, a typical male will grow to a mantle length, tentacles excluded, of 1 foot (30 cm) and a weight of 12 ounces (340 gm). A female will reach 14 inches (36 cm) and 18 ounces (510 gm). A herring would take 4 years to reach the same size. From Newfoundland and southern Labrador to Massachusetts, this squid comes inshore during late spring to feed on schooling fish. From May to November the weight of a typical individual will increase up to tenfold in coastal waters. During late autumn, the mature squid apparently swim offshore to spawn in deep water at the edge of the continental shelf, and most of them probably die shortly thereafter. Small squid feed on zooplankton, especially krill, as they grow and come inshore. Hundreds of tons of short-finned squid are caught along the Newfoundland and Nova Scotia coasts for use as bait in the long-line fishery for cod and other ground fish, and for food, especially in the Chinese, Portuguese, and Italian markets. The squid are caught with jigs, either by hand or with large mechanized reels. In the southern part of the Gulf of Maine, the longfin squid (*Loligo pealii*) is also eaten by marine mammals and caught for human consumption.

APPENDIX II

PUBLISHER'S NOTE: These excursion listings provided by the authors are printed for the convenience of the reader and do not constitute recommendation or endorsement by the Smithsonian Institution or any of its offices, including the Smithsonian Institution Press.

Excursions are listed geographically, from south to north. Further information on some of these excursions and on trips available throughout North America can be found in *Where the Whales Are,* by Patricia Corrigan, 1991.

Part 1.

Whale-Watching Excursions

MASSACHUSETTS

Nantucket Whale Watch Straight Wharf Nantucket, MA 02554 (508) 283-0313 1-800-322-0013 in New England	Full-day naturalist-led trips, mid-July through mid- September, Tuesday– Thursday on the M/V *Yankee Clipper* and M/V *Yankee Spirit*.
Whale Watcher Cruises P.O. Box 254 Barnstable Harbor Barnstable, MA 02630 (508) 775-1622 or 362-6088 1-800-942-0920 MA only	Naturalist-led day trips aboard the M/V *Whale Watcher*, food/ beverage service.

Capt. Al Avellar The Dolphin Fleet Macmillan Wharf P.O. Box 162 Eastham, MA 02642 (508) 255-3857 1-800-826-9300	Four-hour trips, nine times daily, spring through autumn to Stellwagen Bank, naturalists supplied by the Provincetown Center for Coastal Studies.
Portuguese Princess P.O. Box 1469 Provincetown, MA 02657 (508) 487-2651 1-800-442-3188 in New 　　England	Three half-day (3.5 hour) trips daily to Stellwagen Bank, mid-April to late October. Naturalist-led trips, hands-on childrens' programs, Portuguese food available on board, Whale Watching General Store.
Cape Cod Cruises, Inc. Fisherman's Wharf Provincetown, MA 02657 (508) 747-2400	Morning and afternoon trips, April through October, on M/V *Cape Cod Clipper* with naturalists from Plymouth Marine Mammal Research Center.
Provincetown Whale Watch M/V *Ranger V* 29 Standish Street Provincetown, MA 02657 (508) 487-1582	Three trips daily, spring through mid-November, food and beverages, naturalist provided.
Capt. Tim Brady & Sons M/V *Mary Elizabeth* 254 Sandwich Street Plymouth, MA 02360 (508) 746-4809 or -3920	Leaving daily from the town wharf, April through November, marine biologist on board.
Captain John Boats Inc. Town Wharf 117 Standish Avenue Plymouth, MA 02360 (508) 746-2643	Morning and afternoon trips, April through October, on M/V *Capt. John and Sons* with naturalists from Plymouth Marine Mammal Research Center.

A.C. Cruise Lines 28 Northern Avenue Boston, MA 02210 (617) 426-8419 1-800-422-8419	Weekends, April through early July, daily until Labor Day. Naturalist-led full-day trips aboard the M/V *Cape Ann* and the M/V *Virginia Sea II* to Stellwagen Bank or Jeffreys Ledge.
New England Aquarium Central Wharf Boston, MA 02110 (617) 973-5277	Day trips, April through October, accompanied by marine naturalists.
Cape Ann Whale Watch Main Street, Rose's Wharf P.O. Box 345 Gloucester, MA 01930 (508) 283-5110 1-800-339-1990 for (508) and (617) area only	Half-day trips, twice daily, May through October, accompanied by naturalists from the Cetacean Research Unit.
Captain Bill & Sons Whale Watch 9 Traverse Street Gloucester, MA 01930 (508) 281-6995	Two half-day trips daily, May through October, and extra evening trips on Saturday and Sunday in July and August. Naturalists from the Cetacean Research Unit.
Gloucester Whalewatch (The Yankee Fleet) 75 Essex Avenue, Rt. 133 Gloucester, MA 01930 1-800-WHALING	Half-day trips, twice daily, spring through autumn.
Seven Seas Whale Watch Seven Seas Wharf, Rt. 127 Gloucester, MA 01930 (508) 283-1776 1-800-331-6228 in New England	Naturalist-led trips on the M/V *Privateer* and the M/V *Privateer II* daily, mid-May through the first week of October. Reservations suggested.

Newburyport Whale Watch 54 Merrimac Street Newburyport, MA 01950 (508) 465-9885 1-800-848-1111	Naturalist-led trips to Stellwagen Bank or Jeffreys Ledge on the M/V *Captain Red*, daily, May through September.

NEW HAMPSHIRE

New England Whale Watch Box 825 Hampton, NH 03842 (508) 465-7165	Day trips from Newburyport, Massachusetts, April through October, accompanied by naturalist Scott Mercer.
Gauron Fisheries, Inc. 1 Ocean Boulevard Hampton Beach, NH 03842 (603) 926-2469	Charters on the M/V *Northern Star* and school groups on the M/V *Starfish*, M/V *White Star*, and M/V *Thumper*. Trips run May through September from the state pier.
N.H. Seacoast Cruises P.O. Box 232 Rye, NH 03870 (603) 964-5545 or 382-6743	Six-hour, naturalist-led whale- watch expeditions on the M/V *Granite State*, May through October.
Isles of Shoals Steamship Barker Wharf 315 Market Street P.O. Box 311 Portsmouth, NH 03801 1-800-441-4620 or (603) 431-5500	Weekends mid-April to mid- June, daily through Labor Day, weekends after Labor Day to mid-October.

MAINE

Cape Arundel Cruises P.O. Box 2777 Kennebunkport, ME 04046 (207) 967-0707	Whale-watch trips daily, June through September, weekends May and October. Five- to six- hour, naturalist-led trips on board the M/V *Nautilus*.

Indian Whale Watch P.O. Box 2672 Kennebunkport, ME 04046 (207) 967-5912	Daily whale-watching trips, June through October, on the M/V *Indian*.
Ugly Anne P.O. Box 863, 9 King's Lane Ongunquit, ME 03907 (207) 646-7202	Two trips daily, May through October, on the M/V *Ugly Anne*.
The Olde Port Mariner Fleet P.O. Box 1084 Long Wharf Portland, ME 04104 (207) 642-3270 or 775-0727	Day trips and sunset cruises aboard the M/V *Odyssey* to view whales, seals, and seabirds.
M/V *Scotia Prince* Prince of Fundy Cruises International Terminal Portland, ME 04101 (207) 775-5616 (Portland) (902) 742-6460 (Yarmouth) USA 1-800-341-7540	Service between Portland and Yarmouth, Nova Scotia. Trip lasts about 11 hours, with up to 8 hours of daylight on the Yarmouth-Portland leg.
The Argo Pier Six Boothbay Harbor, ME 04538 (207) 633-4925 or -5090	Whale watching aboard the M/V *Argo III*, hour-and-a-half- long trips to seal rocks, special whale- and puffin-watching cruises in season.
Captain Bob Campbell P.O. Box 102 62 Commercial Street Boothbay Harbor, ME 04538 (207) 633-2284	The M/V *Balmy Days* departs daily, late May to early October, for Monhegan Island. Whales, seals, and dolphins may be spotted.
Captain Sam Blanchard Northeast Whale Watch P.O. Box 153 Seal Harbor, ME 04675 (207) 276-5803	Full-day cruises from Northeast Harbor, Mt. Desert Island, to observe whales, seals, and seabirds. Naturalist- led cruises daily, June through September.

Acadian Whale Watch Co. 52 West Street Bar Harbor, ME 04609 (207) 288-9776	Whale-watching trips leave Bar Harbor twice per day, June through October 15, on M/V *Acadian Whalewatcher*.
Frenchman Bay Co. Harbor Place 1 West Street Bar Harbor, ME 04609 (207) 288-3322	Whale watching aboard the M/V *Friendship III*. Two trips daily from Bar Harbor, June through October 15.
Butch Huntley M/V *Seafarer* 9 High Street Lubec, ME 04652 (207) 733-5584	Full-day trips and charters from Lubec to Passamaquoddy Bay and lower Bay of Fundy, July through October.
CANADA	
NEW BRUNSWICK	
Ocean Search Marathon Inn North Head Grand Manan Island, NB CANADA E0G 2M0 (506) 662-8144	Trips in the lower Bay of Fundy, with one- and five-day packages during summer and early autumn.
Cline Marine Leonardville Deer Island, NB CANADA E0G 2G0 (506) 529-4188	Cruises into the Bay of Fundy, June through Labor Day, boat picks up at St. Andrews, Deer Island, and Campobello Island.
NOVA SCOTIA	
Pirate's Cove Whale Cruises Tiverton, NS Canada B0V 1G0 (902) 839-2242	Two cruises daily aboard the M/V *Todd & Cherida*, June 15 through end of September.

Brier Island Whale and Seabird Cruises Limited Westport Digby County, NS CANADA B0V IH0 (902) 839-2995	Naturalist-led trips, two to three times daily to the lower Bay of Fundy. Four- to five-hour cruises on the M/V *Cetacean Venture*.
Halifax Whale Watch East Coast Charter Services 1751 Lower Water Street Halifax, NS CANADA B3H 3A6 (902) 422-3608	Half-day trips from Cable Wharf, January through March.

QUEBEC

Linnean Society of Quebec Quebec Aquarium 1675 Avenue du Parc Sainte-Foy, Quebec CANADA G1W 4S3 (418) 653-8186	Day trips in the estuary of St. Lawrence, summer and autumn.
Compagnie de la Baie de Tadoussac 145 Bord-de-l'eau Tadoussac, Quebec CANADA G0T 2A0 (418) 235-4548	Three trips daily on the St. Lawrence River, May 1 through October 15 (June is the best month). Naturalist-led excursions in small, inflatable boats.
Croisieres Du Grand Fleuve 1495 Volt Charlesbourg, Quebec CANADA G2L 1H8 (418) 622-2566	Whale watching on the M/V *Grand Fleuve*, three trips daily on the St. Lawrence, naturalists from the Research and Educational Group on Marine Environment.
Croisieres Navimex, Inc. 25 Place Marche Champlain Suite 101 Quebec City, Quebec CANADA G1R 2C8 (418) 692-4643	Three, three-hour trips on the St. Lawrence, June 1 through October 15, two naturalists on board.

Famille DeFour Hotel Tadoussac 165 Bord-de-l'Eau Tadoussac, Quebec CANADA G0T 2A0 (418) 235-4421 1-800-463-5250	Naturalist-led cruises on the historic 130-foot schooner *Marie-Clarisse*, three three-hour trips daily, May 1 through October 31.
Base Plein Air Sault-au-Mouton Inc. 81, rue Principale Sault-au-Mouton, Quebec CANADA G0T 1Z0 (418) 231-2214	Two three-hour trips by motorboat in the St. Lawrence, April 15 through October 15, to see blue whales.
Compagnie de la Baie des Escoumins 100, rue St. Marcellin Les Escoumins, Quebec CANADA G0T 2A0 (418) 233-3151 or -2835	Three trips daily on the St. Lawrence in small inflatables, May 1 through October 15.
Tan Incorporated 29, rue des Pilotes Les Escoumins, Quebec CANADA G0T 1K0 (418) 233-3488	Nine trips daily, two- to three-hour whale-watch cruises, four-hour trips to watch blue whales, or all-day whale-watch trips in Saguenay Fjord, June through October.
Le Gite du Phare de Pointe des Monts 1684 Joliet Boulevard Baie Comeau, Quebec CANADA G5C 1P8 (418) 589-8408	Two trips daily on weekdays, three daily on weekends, June 1 through September 30.

Mingan Island Cetacean Study Winter: 285, Green Street St-Lambert, Quebec CANADA J4P 1T3 (514) 465-9176 Summer: 106, rue Bord de la Mer Longue-Pointe, Quebec CANADA G0G 1V0 (418) 949-2845	Five- to ten-day programs of day trips around Mingan Islands, Gulf of St. Lawrence, to observe whales and seabirds.

NEWFOUNDLAND

Bontours Norris Point, Newfoundland CANADA A0K 3V0 (709) 458-2256	Two-hour trips, daily, June 1 through September 30.
Pelley Inn P.O. Box 428 Springdale, Newfoundland CANADA A0J 1T0 (709) 673-3931	Week-long programs with daily excursions to view humpback and pilot whales, May 1 through September 30.
Twillingate Island Boat Tours Ltd. P.O. Box 127 Twillingate, Newfoundland CANADA A0G 4M0 (709) 884-2317	Two trips daily into Notre Dame Bay, late May to late September.
Ocean Watch Tours Squid Tickle Burnside, Newfoundland CANADA A0G 1K0 (709) 677-2327	Naturalist-led trips on the M/V *Northern Fulmar*, late June to Labor Day.

Ocean Contact, Ltd. The Village Inn P.O. Box 10 Trinity, Newfoundland CANADA A0C 2S0 (709) 464-3269 Fax (709) 464-3700	Week-long programs with daily trips into Trinity Bay.
Eastern Edge Outfitters Ltd. P.O. Box 13981 Station A St. John's, Newfoundland CANADA A2B 4G8 (709) 368-9720	Sea kayak trips, June 2 through September 30, to see humpback, minke, and pilot whales and other species.
Harbor Charters P.O. Box 5395 St. John's, Newfoundland CANADA A1C 5W2 (709) 754-1672	Four two-hour trips daily by Grand Bank schooner or longliner, May 1 through October 1.
Wildland Tours P.O. Box 383 Station C St. John's, Newfoundland CANADA A1C 5J9 (709) 722-3335	Three-, five- or seven-day whale-watch and seabird tours, early May through mid-August, biologist on board.
Great Island Tours P.O. Box 21 Cape Broyle, Newfoundland CANADA A0A 1P0 (709) 432-2355 1-800-563-2355	Three-hour naturalist-led trips, three times daily, May 15 through October 31, on the M/V *Historic Venture*. Minke, humpback, fin, and sperm whales are seen as well as Atlantic puffins.

Bird Island Charters Bay Bulls, Newfoundland CANADA A0A 1C0 (709) 753-4850	Naturalist-led 2.5- to 3-hour trips, three or four times daily, May through September.
Gatherall's Sanctuary Boat Charters Bay Bulls, Newfoundland CANADA A0A 1C0 (709) 334-2887	Three two-hour trips daily, June and July, to view humpback and minke whales.
ONTARIO	
Canadian Nature Tours Federation of Ontario Naturalists 355 Lesmill Road Don Mills, Ontario CANADA M3B 2W8 (416) 444-8419	Natural history tours include opportunities to see whales, seals, and seabirds. Programs vary annually.
EXTENDED VOYAGES WITHIN STUDY AREA	
Dirigo Cruises 39 Waterside Lane Clinton, CT 06413 (203) 669-7068 1-800-845-5520	Week-long marine mammal and whale study courses each August from Boston, two-week courses for teachers with College of the Atlantic include graduate credits, introduction to marine mammals, advanced whale courses.
Earthwatch The Center for Field Research 680 Mt. Auburn Street Box 403 Watertown, MA 02272 (617) 926-8200	Places volunteers on field research projects throughout the world. Opportunities to help in whale research projects vary annually.

School for Field Studies 16 Broadway Beverly, MA 01915 (508) 927-7777	Three-month environmental research programs (one month in summer), credit-worthy courses in various scientific disciplines, including marine mammal biology and cetacean behavioral ecology for undergraduates and advanced secondary students.
Sea Education Association, Inc. P.O. Box 6 Woods Hole, MA 02543 (508) 540-3954	Undergraduate programs including research cruises in western North Atlantic and Caribbean aboard the M/V *Westward* and the M/V *Corwith Cramer*. Semester-long programs for credit and shorter seminars offered. Data on marine mammal distribution collected while conducting oceanographic research.
Seafarers P.O. Box 691 Bangor, ME 04402-0123 (207) 942-7942	Three- to fourteen-day trips featuring land-based and offshore naturalist-led programs from Arctic to Caribbean, including many trips to the Gulf of Maine and lower Bay of Fundy region.

Part 2.

Seal-Watching Excursions

MASSACHUSETTS	
Nantucket Harbor Cruises Straight Wharf Nantucket, MA 02554 (508) 228-1444	Short cruises to view seals on and near the Jetties, weekends, November to May.
Cape Cod Museum of Natural History Brewster, MA 02631 (508) 896-3867	Cruises to Monomoy National Wildlife Refuge to view harbor and gray seals, late fall to early spring.
Wellfleet Bay Wildlife Sanctuary P.O. Box 236 So. Wellfleet, MA 02663 (508) 349-2615	Seal and sea duck cruises in Cape Cod Bay, October and November. Hikes to view harbor seals in Cape Cod Bay and at Coast Guard Beach, Eastham, January to March. Charter and regular cruises to view harbor and gray seals at Monomoy Natural Wildlife Refuge, January to April.
Massachusetts Audubon Society South Shore Regional Center Marshfield, MA 02050 (617) 837-9400	Introductory talk followed by outing in motor vehicle to sites where harbor seals may be viewed, January and February.

MAINE	
Captain Thomas Ring 25 Main Street Freeport, ME 04078 (207) 865-6112	Three-hour trips, twice daily on the M/V *Atlantic Seal*, Memorial Day through mid-October. Departs from South Freeport town dock to Eagle Island in Casco Bay. Harbor seals are usually seen, harbor porpoise are also often sighted.
The Good Times Excursions Pier 1, Boothbay Harbor P.O. Box 660 Boothbay Harbor, ME 04538 207-633-2626	One- to three-hour cruises from Boothbay Harbor, several times daily, Memorial Day through October. Harbor seals seen on all trips.
Breakaway Cruises, Inc. Royall Road Box 860 East Boothbay, ME 04544 (207) 633-4414	Sunset cruises from end of May through June 14, and Labor Day through October 15, include viewing seal rocks.
Hardy Boat Cruises RR1 Box 530 Shore Road Edgecomb, ME 04556 In season (207) 677-2026 Off season (207) 882-7909	From Shaw's Wharf, New Harbor, short cruises to view harbor seals, twice daily. Harbor and gray seals are also seen on day-long trips to Monhegan Island.
Capt. John Earl M/V *Henrietta* Spruce Head, ME 04859 (207) 594-5826	Harbor seals are frequently seen during daily fishing trips to Matinicus Islands group, mid-May to October 1.
Bass Harbor Cruises Bass Harbor, ME 04653 (207) 244-5365	Bass Harbor Naturalist Cruises emphasize natural history; sightings of harbor seals and gray seals are possible from June through September.

Captain Sam Blanchard Northeast Whale Watch P.O. Box 153 Seal Harbor, ME 04675 (207) 276-5803	Full-day cruises from Northeast Harbor, Mt. Desert Island, to observe whales, harbor seals, gray seals, and seabirds. Naturalist-led cruises daily from June through September.
Sea Princess Cruises Sea Street Northeast Harbor, ME 04662 (207) 276-5352	Two- and three-hour cruises from Northeast Harbor, May through October, emphasizing history and geography, travel up Somes Sound, often opportunities to view harbor seals and seabirds.
Aunt Elsie Acadia Boat Tours and Charters, Inc. Golden Anchor Pier Bar Harbor, ME 04609 (207) 288-9505 (summer) (207) 288-4324 (off season)	Short cruises to view seals on ledges in Frenchman Bay, leaving daily from the Golden Anchor Pier, June through October.
Frenchman's Bay Co. Harbor Place 1 West Street Bar Harbor, ME 04609-0153 (207) 288-3322 (8941 FAX)	Several trips daily, Memorial Day through September, aboard the M/V *Katherine*, harbor seals and porpoises often sighted.
Barna Norton M/V *Chief* Jonesport, ME 04649 (207) 497-5933	Charter trips from Jonesport to Machias Seal Island to view puffins and other birds, harbor seals, and gray seals. Also trips to Petit Manan Island.

CANADA	
Capt. Preston Wilcox Seal Cove Grand Manan, NB CANADA E0G 3B0 (506) 662-8296	Gray seals, harbor seals, and seabirds may be viewed during charter trips to Machias Seal Island.
Atlantic Marine Wildlife 　Tours 227 Wright Street Frederickton, NB CANADA E3B 2E3 (506) 459-7325	Excursions by helicopter from Charlottetown, Prince Edward Island, to view breeding harp seals on icefields in the Gulf of St. Lawrence. Hooded seals may be sighted. February 28 to March 16.
Natural Habitat Wildlife 　Adventures 1 Sussex Station Sussex, NJ 07461 1-800-543-8917 (US only) (201) 702-1525	Air charters from Halifax, Nova Scotia, to the Magdalen Islands, followed by helicopter excursions to view breeding harp seals on ice in the Gulf of St. Lawrence. Hooded seals may be sighted. March 1–18.

BIBLIOGRAPHY

SPECIES GUIDE TO THE BIBLIOGRAPHY ON CETACEANS, "BONUS" SPECIES, AND PREY SPECIES

Finback whale: 1, 2, 47, 56, 95, 116, 132, 135, 156, 159, 185, 192, 218, 219, 229

Minke whale: 11, 25, 37, 38, 69, 74, 114, 143, 159, 189, 238

Humpback whale: 9, 26, 27, 28, 53, 58, 80, 81, 84, 109, 156, 157, 158, 159, 213, 219, 220, 225, 227, 228, 229, 230, 232, 233, 235, 236, 239, 240

Right whale: 31, 50, 60, 90, 91, 92, 93, 110, 123, 138, 148, 172, 219, 242

Blue whale: 10, 184, 226

Sei whale: 73, 138, 141, 219, 221

Gray whale (Atlantic): 174

Harbor porpoise: 48, 51, 76, 102, 163, 164, 166, 167, 168, 169, 201, 203

Pilot whale: 131, 152, 179, 187, 188

White-sided dolphin: 54, 83, 182, 186, 195

White-beaked dolphin: 5, 98

Common dolphin: 186

Striped dolphin: 144, 151

Bottlenose dolphin: 86, 100, 129, 177, 196, 222, 223

Risso's dolphin: 98, 99

Killer whale: 7, 15, 32, 67, 78, 82, 197, 198, 207, 224, 231

Beluga: 12, 19, 21, 57, 120, 171, 193, 194

Sperm whale: 6, 13, 29, 126a, 147, 175, 216, 217, 226, 234

Pygmy sperm whale: 20

Northern bottlenose whale: 67, 128, 139, 142

Blainville's beaked whale: 66, 67, 75a, 127, 145

True's beaked whale: 66, 67, 75, 127, 145

Sowerby's beaked whale: 36, 66, 67, 104, 104a, 127, 145

Narwhal: 45, 206

Basking shark: 14, 34, 105

I. CETACEANS, "BONUS" SPECIES, AND PREY SPECIES

1. Agler, B. A., J. A. Beard, R. S. Bowman, H. D. Corbett, S. E. Frohock, M. P. Hawvermale, S. K. Katona, S. S. Sadove, and I. E. Seipt. 1990. Fin whale (*Balaenoptera physalus*) photographic identification: methodology and preliminary results from the western North Atlantic. *Rep. Int. Whal. Commn* (special issue 12):349–56.

2. Agler, B. A., and S. K. Katona. 1987. Photo-identification of individual finback whales. *Whalewatcher* 21(3):3–6.

3. Ahrens, M. A. 1985. *Mackerel. Underwater World.* Ottawa: Department of Fisheries and Oceans.

4. Allen, G. M. 1916. The whalebone whales of New England. *Mem. Boston Soc. Nat. Hist.* 8(2):1–322.

5. Alling, A. K., and H. P. Whitehead. 1987. A preliminary study of the sta-

tus of white-beaked dolphins, *Lagenorhynchus albirostris*, and other small cetaceans of the coast of Labrador. *Canadian Field-Nat.* 101(2):131–35.

6. Arnbom, T. 1987. Individual identification of sperm whales. *Rep. Int. Whal. Commn* 37:201–4.

7. Balcomb, K. C., III, J. R. Boran, R. W. Osborne, N. J. Haenel, and S. L. Heimlich. 1980. *Killer Whales in Great Puget Sound: A Mini-guide to Whales and Porpoises of the Inland Waters of Washington State.* Friday Harbor, Wash.: Whale Museum.

8. Barstow, R. 1986. Non-consumptive utilization of whales. *Ambio* 15(3):155–63.

9. Beamish, P. 1979. Behavior and significance of entrapped baleen whales. In H. E. Winn and B. L. Olla, eds., *Behavior of Marine Ani-*

mals, vol. 3, *Cetaceans*, pp. 291–309. New York: Plenum Press.

10. Beamish, P., and E. Mitchell. 1971. Ultrasonic sound recorded in the presence of a blue whale, *Balaenoptera musculus*. *Deep-Sea Res.* 18:803–9.

11. Beamish, P., and E. Mitchell. 1973. Short pulse length audio frequency sounds recorded in the presence of a minke whale (*Balaenoptera acutorostrata*). *Deep-Sea Res.* 20:375–86.

12. Beland, P. 1988. Witness for the prosecution. *Nature Canada*, Fall 1988, pp. 28–36.

13. Best, P. 1979. Social organization in sperm whales. In H. E. Winn and B. L. Olla, eds., *Behavior of Marine Animals*, vol. 3, *Cetaceans*, pp. 227–89. New York: Plenum Press.

14. Bigelow, H. B., and W. C. Schroeder. 1953. Fishes of the Gulf of Maine. *Fish. Bull. Fish and Wildlife Service*, vol. 53. Museum of Comparative Zoology, Harvard University, Cambridge, Mass.

15. Bigg, M. A., G. M. Ellis, J. K. B. Ford, and K. C. Balcomb. 1987. *Killer Whales: A Study of Their Identification, Genealogy and Natural History in British Columbia and Washington State.* Nanaimo, British Columbia: Phantom Press and Publishers.

16. Bleakney, J. S. 1965. Reports of marine turtles from New England and Canadian waters. *Canadian Field-Nat.* 79(2):120–28.

17. Breton, M. 1986. *Guide to Watching Whales in Canada.* Ottawa: Department of Fisheries and Oceans.

18. Brodie, P. F. 1975. Cetacean energetics, an overview of intraspecific size variation. *Ecology* 50:152–61.

19. Brodie, P. 1989. The white whale—*Delphinapterus leucas* (Pallas, 1776). In S. H. Ridgway and R. Harrison, eds., *Handbook of Marine Mammals*, vol. 4, *River Dolphins and the Larger Toothed Whales*, pp. 119–44. London: Academic Press.

20. Caldwell, D. K., and M. C. Caldwell. 1989. Pygmy sperm whale—*Kogia breviceps* (de Blainville, 1838); Dwarf sperm whale (*Kogia simus*) Owen, 1866. In S. H. Ridgway and R. Harrison, eds., *Handbook of Marine Mammals*, vol. 4, *River Dolphins and the Larger Toothed Whales*, pp. 235–60. London: Academic Press.

21. Caron, L. M. J., and D. E. Sergeant. 1989. Yearly variation in the frequency of passage of beluga whales at the mouth of the Saguenay River, Quebec, over the past decade. *Naturaliste Can. (Rev. Ecol. Syst.)* 155:111–16.

22. Carr, A. 1984. *So Excellent a Fishe.* New York: Charles Scribner's Sons.

23. Carscadden, J. E. 1981. *Capelin. Underwater World.* Ottawa: Department of Fisheries and Oceans.

24. CETAP. 1982. A characterization of marine mammals and turtles in the mid- and North-Atlantic area of the U.S. outer continental shelf. Final report to the Bureau of Land Management. Springfield, Virginia: NTIS PB83-243289.

25. Christensen, I. 1981. Age determination of minke whales, *Balaenoptera acutorostrata*, from laminated structures in the tympanic bullae. *Rep. Int. Whal. Commn* 31:245–53.

26. Chu, K. 1987. The length of the

song of the humpback whale. *Whale-watcher*, 21(2):7–8.

27. Clapham, P. J., and C. A. Mayo. 1987. Reproduction and recruitment of individually identified humpback whales, *Megaptera novaeaneangliae*, observed in Massachusetts Bay, 1979–1985. *Can. J. Zool.* 65:2853–63.

28. Clapham, P. J., and C. A. Mayo. 1990. Reproduction of humpback whales (*Megaptera novaeangliae*) observed in the Gulf of Maine. *Rep. Int. Whal. Commn* (special issue 12):171–76.

29. Clarke, M. R. 1979. The head of the sperm whale. *Sci. Amer.* 240(1):128–41.

30. Corrigan, P. 1991. *Where the Whales Are*. Chester, Conn.: Globe Pequot Press.

31. Crone, M. J., and S. D. Kraus, eds. 1990. Right whales (*Eubalaena glacialis*) in the western North Atlantic: a catalog of identified individuals. Boston: Edgerton Research Laboratory, New England Aquarium.

32. Dahlheim, M. E. 1981. A review of the biology and exploitation of the killer whale, *Orcinus orca*, with comments on recent sightings from Antarctica. *Rep. Int. Whal. Commn* 31:451–46.

33. Darling, J. D. 1988. Whales: an era of discovery. *National Geographic* 174:872–909.

34. Davis, C. 1983. The awesome basking shark. *Sea Frontiers* 29(2):78–85.

35. Dietz, T. 1982. *Tales of Whales*. Portland, Maine: Guy Gannet.

36. Dix, L., J. Lien, and D. E. Ser-geant. 1986. A North Sea beaked whale, *Mesoplodon bidens*, in Conception Bay, Newfoundland. *Canadian Field-Nat.* 100(3):389–91.

37. Dorsey, E. M. 1983. Exclusive adjoining ranges in individually identified minke whales (*Balaenoptera acutorostrata*) in Washington State. *Can. J. Zool.* 61(1):174–81.

38. Dorsey, E. M., S. J. Stern, A. R. Hoelzel, and J. Jacobsen. 1990. Minke whales (*Balaenoptera acutorostrata*) from the west coast of North America: individual recognition and small-scale site fidelity. *Rep. Int. Whal. Commn* (special issue 12): 357–68.

39. Ellis, R. 1980. *The Book of Whales*. New York: Knopf.

40. Ellis, R. 1982. *Dolphins and Porpoises*. New York: Knopf.

41. Evans, P. G. H. 1987. *The Natural History of Whales and Dolphins*. New York: Facts on File.

42. Evans, W. E., and F. T. Awbrey. 1988. Natural history aspects of marine mammal echolocation: feeding strategies and habitat. In P. E. Nachtigall and P. W. B. Moore, eds., *Animal Sonar*, 521–34. New York: Plenum Press.

43. Finnell, R. B., ed. 1991. Symphony beneath the sea. *Nat. Hist.* March 1991:36–76. (Eleven short articles about marine mammal vocalizations.)

44. Fontaine, P. H. 1988. *Biologie & écologie des baleines de l'Atlantique Nord*. Quebec: Sylvio Thibeault.

45. Ford, J., and D. Ford. 1986. Narwhal: unicorn of the Arctic seas. *National Geographic* 170:354–63.

46. Frair, W., R. E. Ackman, and N.

Mrosovsky. 1972. Body temperature of *Dermochelys coriacea*: warm turtle from cold water. *Science* 177:791–93.

47. Gambell, R. 1985. Fin whale, *Balaenoptera physalus* (Linnaeus, 1758). In S. H. Ridgway and R. Harrison, eds., *Handbook of Marine Mammals*, vol. 3, pp. 171–192. London: Academic Press.

48. Gaskin, D. E. 1977. Harbor porpoise (*Phocoena [L.]*) in the western approaches to the Bay of Fundy, 1969–75. *Rep. Int. Whal. Commn* 27:487–92.

49. Gaskin, D. E. 1982. *The Ecology of Whales and Dolphins.* Exeter, N. H.: Heinemann Educational Books.

50. Gaskin, D. E. 1991. An update on the status of the right whale, *Eubalaena glacialis,* in Canada. *Canadian Field-Nat.* 105(2):198–205.

51. Gaskin, D. E., P. W. Arnold, and B. A. Blair. 1974. *Phocoena phocoena. Mamm. Species* 42:1–8.

52. Geraci, J. R. 1978. The enigma of marine mammal strandings. *Oceanus* 21(2):38–47.

53. Geraci, J. R., D. M. Anderson, R. J. Timperi, D. J. St. Aubin, G. A. Early, J. H. Prescott, and C. A. Mayo. 1989. Humpback whales (*Megaptera novaeangliae*) fatally poisoned by dinoflagellate toxin. *Can. J. Fish. Aquat. Sci.* 46:1895–98.

54. Geraci, J. R., S. A. Testaverde, D. J. St. Aubin, and T. H. Loop. 1976. A mass stranding of the Atlantic white-sided dolphin, *Lagenorhynchus acutus*: a study into pathobiology and life history. Springfield, Va.: NTIS PB-289361.

55. Gibbs, J. M. 1982. *Whales off New England.* Newbury, Mass.: Gibbs and Gibbs.

56. Gunnlaugsson, T., and J. Sigurjonsson. 1989. Analysis of North Atlantic fin whale marking data from 1979–1988 with special reference to Iceland. *Rep. Int. Whal. Commn* 39:383–88.

57. Gurevich, V. S. 1980. Worldwide distribution and migration patterns of the white whale (Beluga), *Delphinapterus leucas. Rep. Int. Whal. Commn* 30:465–80.

58. Hain, J. H. W., G. R. Carter, S. D. Kraus, C. A. Mayo, and H. E. Winn. 1982. Feeding behavior of the humpback whale, *Megaptera novaeangliae,* in the western North Atlantic. *Fish. Bull.* 80:259–68.

59. Hain, J. H. W., M. A. M. Hyman, R. D. Kenney, and H. E. Winn. 1985. The role of cetaceans in the shelf-edge region of the northeastern United States. *Marine Fisheries Rev.* 47(1):12–17.

60. Hamilton, P. K., and C. A. Mayo. 1990. Population characteristics of right whales (*Eubalaena glacialis*) observed in Cape Cod and Massachusetts Bays, 1978–1986. *Rep. Int. Whal. Commn* (special issue 12):203–8.

61. Hammond, P. S., S. A. Mizroch, and G. P. Donovan, eds. 1990. Individual recognition of photo-identification of cetaceans: use of photo-identification and other techniques to estimate population parameters. *Rep. Int. Whal. Commn* (special issue 12):1–440.

62. Harrison, R. G., ed. 1972–77. *The Functional Anatomy of Marine Mammals.* Vol. 1 (1972), vol. 2 (1974), vol. 3 (1977). New York: Academic Press.

63. Harrison, R., and M. M. Bryden, eds. 1988. *Whales, Dolphins and Porpoises*. New York: Facts on File.

64. Herman, L. M., ed. 1980. *Cetacean Behavior: Mechanisms and Functions*. New York: Wiley-Interscience.

65. Heyning, J. E. 1984. Functional morphology involved in intraspecific fighting of the beaked whale, *Mesoplodon carlhubbsi*. *Can. J. Zool.* 62:1645–54.

66. Heyning, J. E. 1989. Comparative facial anatomy of beaked whales (*Ziphiidae*) and a systematic revision among the families of extant odontoceti. *Contributions in Science*, No. 405, pp. 1–64. Los Angeles: Natural History Museum of Los Angeles County.

67. Heyning, J. E., and M. E. Dahlheim. 1988. *Orcinus orca. Mammalian Species* No. 304, pp. 1–9.

68. Heyning, J. E., and J. G. Mead. 1990. Evolution of the nasal anatomy of cetaceans. In J. Thomas and R. Kastelein, eds., *Sensory Abilities of Cetaceans*, pp. 67–79. New York: Plenum Press.

69. Hoelzel, A. R., E. M. Dorsey, and S. J. Stern. 1989. The foraging specializations of individual minke whales. *Anim. Behav.* 38:786–94.

70. Holland, D. L., J. Davenport, and J. East. 1990. The fatty acid composition of the leatherback turtle *Dermochelys coriacea* and its jellyfish prey. *J. mar. biol. Ass. U.K.* 70: 761–70.

71. Hollingshead, K. W., and S. Corey. 1974. Aspects of the life history of *Meganyctiphanes norvegica* (M. Sars), Crustacea (Euphausiacea), in Passamaquoddy Bay. *Can. J. Zool.* 52:495–505.

72. Holt, S., and N. Young. 1991. *Guide to the Review of the Management of Whaling*. Washington, D.C.: Center for Marine Conservation.

73. Horwood, J. W. 1987. *The Sei Whale: Population Biology, Ecology and Management*. New York: Routledge, Chapman and Hall.

74. Horwood, J. 1989. *Biology and Exploitation of the Minke Whale*. Boca Raton, Fla.: CRC Press.

75. Houston, J. 1990a. Status of True's beaked whale, *Mesoplodon mirus*, in Canada. *Canadian Field-Nat.* 104(1): 135–37.

75a. Houston, J. 1990b. Status of Blainville's beaked whale, *Mesoplodon densirostris*, in Canada. *Canadian Field-Nat.* 104(1):117–20.

76. Hoyt, E. 1989. Harried harbor porpoise. *Defenders*, January–February 89, pp. 10–17.

77. Hoyt, E. 1990a. *Seasons of the Whale*. Post Mills, Vt.: Chelsea Green.

78. Hoyt, E. 1990b. *The Whale Called Killer*. Rev. ed. Camden East, Ontario: Camden House.

79. Hoyt, E. 1991. *Meeting the Whales*. Camden East, Ontario: Camden House.

80. Jurasz, C., and V. Jurasz. 1979. Feeding modes of the humpback whale, *Megaptera novaeangliae*, in Southeast Alaska. *Sci. Rep. Whales Res. Inst.* 31:67–81.

81. Katona, S. K., and J. A. Beard. 1990. Population size, migrations and feeding aggregations of the humpback whale (*Megaptera no-*

vaeangliae) in the western North Atlantic Ocean. *Rep. Int. Whal. Commn* (special issue 12):295–305.

82. Katona, S. K., J. A. Beard, P. E. Girton, and F. Wenzel. 1988. Killer whales (*Orcinus orca*) from the Bay of Fundy to the equator, including the Gulf of Mexico. *Rit. Fiskideildar* 11:205–24.

83. Katona, S. K., S. A. Testaverde, and B. Barr. 1978. Observations on a white-sided dolphin, *Lagenorhynchus acutus*, probably killed in gill nets in the Gulf of Maine. *Fish. Bull.* 76(2):475–76.

84. Katona, S. K., and H. P. Whitehead. 1981. Identifying humpback whales using their natural markings. *Polar Record* 20:439–44.

85. Katona, S. K., and H. P. Whitehead. 1988. Are cetacea ecologically important? *Oceanogr. Mar. Biol. Ann. Rev.* 26:553–68.

86. Kenney, R. D. 1990. Bottlenose dolphins off the northeastern United States. In S. Leatherwood and R. R. Reeves, eds., *The Bottlenose Dolphin*, pp. 369–86. New York: Academic Press.

87. Kenney, R. D., M. A. M. Hyman, R. E. Owen, and H. E. Winn. 1986. Estimation of prey densities required by western North Atlantic right whales. *Mar. Mamm. Sci.* 2(1):1–13.

88. Kenney, R. D., M. A. M. Hyman, and H. E. Winn. 1985. Calculation of standing stocks and energetic requirements of the cetaceans of the northeast United States outer continental shelf. NOAA Tech. Mem. NMFS-F/NEC-41. Woods Hole, Mass.: Northeast Fisheries Center.

89. Kenney, R. D., and H. E. Winn. 1986. Cetacean high-use habitats of the northeastern continental shelf. *Fish. Bull.* 84(2):345–57.

90. Kraus, S. D. 1987. A move to the right: A collaborative effort for the rarest whale. *Whalewatcher* 21(3): 14–15.

91. Kraus, S. D. 1990. Rates and potential causes of mortality in North Atlantic right whales (*Eubalaena glacialis*). *Mar. Mamm. Sci.* 6(4):278–91.

92. Kraus, S. D., K. E. Moore, C. A. Price, M. J. Crone, W. A. Watkins, H. E. Winn, and J. H. Prescott. 1987. The use of photographs to identify individual north Atlantic right whales (*Eubalaena glacialis*). *Rep. Int. Whal. Commn* (special issue 10):145–52.

93. Kraus, S. D., J. H. Prescott, A. R. Knowlton, and G. S. Stone. 1987. Migration and calving of right whales (*Eubalaena glacialis*) in the western North Atlantic. *Rep. Int. Whal. Commn* (special issue 10): 139–44.

94. Kulka, D. W., and S. Corey. 1978. The life history of *Thysanoessa inermis* (Kroyer) in the Bay of Fundy. *Can. J. Zool.* 56:492–506.

95. Larsen, F. 1991. Review of information on west Greenland fin whales. Special meeting on North Atlantic Fin Whales, Reykjavik, Iceland, February 25–March 1. SC/F91/F29. Unpublished manuscript. 9 pp.

96. Lazell, J. D., Jr. 1976. *This Broken Archipelago*. New York: Quadrangle Press, Harper & Row.

97. Lazell, J. D., Jr. 1980. New England waters: critical habitat for marine turtles. *Copeia* 1980(2):290–95.

98. Leatherwood, S., D. K. Caldwell, and H. E. Winn. 1976. *Whales, Dolphins and Porpoises of the Western North Atlantic: A Guide to Their Identification.* NOAA Tech. Rept. NMFS Circ. 396, Washington, D.C.: U.S. Government Printing Office.

99. Leatherwood, S., and R. Reeves. 1983. *Whales and Dolphins.* San Francisco: Sierra Club Books.

100. Leatherwood, S., and R. R. Reeves, eds. 1990. *The Bottlenose Dolphin.* New York: Academic Press.

101. Leggett, W. C., and K. T. Frank. 1990. The spawning of the capelin. *Sci. Amer.* 262(5):102–7.

102. Leighton, A. H. 1937. The twilight of the Indian porpoise hunters. *Nat. Hist.*, June, pp. 410–16, 458–60.

103. Leim, A. H., and W. B. Scott. 1966. *Fishes of the Atlantic Coast of Canada.* Fish. Res. Bd. Canada Bull. No. 155. Ottawa: Queen's Printer.

104. Lien, J., and Barry, F. 1990. Status of Sowerby's Beaked Whale, *Mesoplodon bidens*, in Canada. *Canadian Field-Nat.* 104(1):125–30.

104a. Lien, J., F. Barry, K. Breeck, and U. Zuschlag. 1990. Multiple strandings of Sowerby's beaked whales, *Mesoplodon bidens*, in Newfoundland. *Canadian Field-Nat.* 104:414–20.

105. Lien, J., and L. Fawcett. 1986. Distribution of basking sharks, *Cetorhinus maximus*, incidentally caught in inshore fishing gear in Newfoundland. *Canadian Field-Nat.* 100(2):246–52.

106. Lien, J., L. Fawcett, and S. Staniforth. 1985. *Wet and Fat: Whales and Seals of Newfoundland and Labrador.* St. John's, Newfoundland: Breakwater Books.

107. Lien, J., J. Huntington, W. Ledwell, and T. Huntsman. 1990. Whale entrapments in inshore fishing gear and a summary of the entrapment assistance program in Newfoundland and Labrador during 1990. Preliminary Report, Fisheries Development Branch, Department of Fisheries and Oceans and Newfoundland and Labrador Department of Fisheries.

108. Lien, J., and S. Katona. 1990. *A Guide to the Photographic Identification of Whales Based on Their Natural and Acquired Markings.* San Pedro, Calif.: American Cetacean Society.

109. Lien, J., and B. Merdsoy. 1979. The humpback is not over the hump. *Nat. Hist.* 88(6):46–49.

110. Lien, J., R. Sears, G. B. Stenson, P. W. Jones, and I. H. Ni. 1989. Right whale, *Eubalaena glacialis*, sightings in waters off Newfoundland and Labrador and the Gulf of St. Lawrence, 1978–1987. *Canadian Field-Nat.* 103(1):91–93.

111. Lien, J., G. B. Stenson, and I. H. Ni. 1990. A review of incidental entrapment of seabirds, seals and whales in inshore fishing gear in Newfoundland and Labrador: a problem for fishermen and fishing gear designers. In *Proceedings of World Symposium on Fishing Gear and Fishing Vessel Design*, pp. 67–71. St. John's, Newfoundland: Marine Institute.

112. Lien, J., S. Todd, and J. Guigne. 1990. Inferences about perception in large cetaceans, especially humpback whales, from incidental catches in fixed fishing gear, enhancement of nets by "alarm" devices, and the acoustics of fishing gear. In J. Thomas and R. Kastelein, eds., *Sensory Abilities of Cetaceans*, pp. 347–62. New York: Plenum Press.

113. Little, E. A., and J. C. Andrews. 1982. Drift whales at Nantucket: the kindness of Moshup. *Man in the Northeast* 23:17–38.

114. Lockyer, C. 1981. Estimation of the energy costs of growth, maintenance, and reproduction in the female minke whale (*Balaenoptera acutorostrata*) from the Southern Hemisphere. *Rep. Int. Whal. Commn* 31:337–44.

115. Lockyer, C. 1986. Review of baleen whale (Mysticeti) reproduction and implications for management. *Rep. Int. Whal. Commn* (special issue 6):27–49.

116. Lockyer, C., and J. Sigurjonsson. 1991. The Icelandic fin whale (*Balaenoptera physalus*): biological parameters and their trends over time. Special meeting on North Atlantic Fin Whales, Reykjavik, Iceland, February 25–March 1. SC/F91/F8. Unpublished manuscript. 36 pp. + appendices.

117. Marine Mammal Commission. 1990. *Annual report of the Marine Mammal Commission, Calendar Year 1990*. Washington, D.C.: Marine Mammal Commission.

118. Martin, A. R. 1990. *Whales and Dolphins*. London: Bedford Editions.

119. Martin, K. R. 1975. *Whalemen and Whaleships of Maine*. Brunswick, Maine: Harpswell Press.

120. Martineau, D., P. Beland, C. Desjardins, and C. Lagace. 1987. Levels of organochlorine chemicals in tissues of beluga whales, *Delphinapterus leucas*, 1985. *Can. Vet. J.* 26:297–302.

121. May, J., ed. 1990. *The Greenpeace Book of Dolphins*. New York: Sterling Publishing Co.

122. Mayo, C. A. 1982. *Observations of Cetaceans: Cape Cod Bay and Southern Stellwagen Bank, Massachusetts, 1975–1979*. Springfield, Va.: NTIS PB-82-186263.

123. Mayo, C. A. and M. K. Marx. 1990. Surface foraging behaviour of the North Atlantic right whale, *Eubalaena glacialis*, and associated zooplankton characteristics. *Can. J. Zool.* 68:2214–20.

124. Mackay, R. S., and H. M. Liaw. 1981. Dolphin vocalization mechanisms. *Science* 212:676–77.

125. Mackay, R. S., and J. Pegg. 1988. Debilitation of prey by intense sounds. *Mar. Mamm. Sci.* 4:356–59.

126. Mate, B. 1989. Satellite-monitored radio tracking as a method for studying cetacean movements and behavior. *Rep. Int. Whal. Commn* 39:389–91.

126a. McAlpine, D. F. 1985. First records of the sperm whale (*Physeter macrocephalus*) from New Brunswick and the Bay of Fundy. *Naturaliste Can. (Rev. Ecol. Syst.)* 112:433–34.

127. Mead, J. G. 1989a. Beaked whales of the genus *Mesoplodon*. In S. H. Ridgway and R. Harrison, eds., *Handbook of Marine Mammals*, vol. 4, *River Dolphins and the Larger*

Toothed Whales, pp. 349–430. Lonmdon: Academic Press.

128. Mead, J. G. 1989b. Bottlenose whales—*Hyperoodon ampullatus* (Forster, 1770) and *Hyperoodon planifrons* Flower, 1882. In S. H. Ridgway and R. Harrison, eds., *Handbook of Marine Mammals*, vol. 4, *River Dolphins and the Larger Toothed Whales*, pp. 321–48. London: Academic Press.

129. Mead, J. G., and C. W. Potter. 1990. Natural history of bottlenose dolphins along the central Atlantic coast of the United States. In S. Leatherwood and R. R. Reeves, eds., *The Bottlenose Dolphin*, pp. 165–95. New York: Academic Press.

130. Mercer, M. C. 1973. Observations on distribution and intraspecific variation in pigmentation patterns of odontocete cetacea in the western North Atlantic. *J. Fish. Res. Bd. Canada* 30:1111–30.

131. Mercer, M. C. 1975. Modified Leslie–De Lury population models of the long-finned pilot whale (*Globicephala melaena*) and annual production of the short-finned squid (*Illex illecebrocus*) based upon their interaction at Newfoundland. *J. Fish. Bd. Canada* 32(7):1145–1154.

132. Meredith, G. N., and R. R. Campbell. 1988. Status of the fin whale, *Balaenoptera physalus*, in Canada. *Canadian Field-Nat.* 102(2):351–68.

133. Meyer, T. L., R. A. Cooper, and R. W. Langton. 1979. Relative abundance, behavior, and food habits of the American sand lance, *Ammodytes americanus*, from the Gulf of Maine. *Fish. Bull.* 77(1):243–53.

134. Minasian, S. M., K. C. Balcomb, and L. Foster. 1984. *The World's Whales*. Washington, D.C.: Smithsonian Books.

135. Mitchell, E. 1974. Present status of northwest Atlantic fin and other whale stocks. In W. E. Schevill, ed., *The Whale Problem—A Status Report*, pp. 108–69. Cambridge, Mass.: Harvard University Press.

136. Mitchell, E. 1975a. *Porpoise, Dolphin, and Small Whale Fisheries of the World: Status and Problems*. IUCN Monograph No. 3, Int. Morges, Switzerland: Union for Conservation of Nature and Natural Resources.

137. Mitchell, E., ed. 1975b. Report of the meeting on smaller cetaceans, Montreal, April 1–11, 1974. *J. Fish. Res. Bd. Canada* 32(7):891–945.

138. Mitchell, E. 1975c. Trophic relationships and competition for food in northwest Atlantic Whales. In M. D. B. Burt, ed., *Proceedings of the Annual Meeting of the Canadian Society of Zoology, June 2–5, 1974*. Abstract. Frederickton, N. B.: University of New Brunswick.

139. Mitchell, E. 1977. Evidence that the northern bottlenose whale is depleted. *Rep. Int. Whal. Commn* 27:195–203.

140. Mitchell, E. 1989. A new cetacean from the Late Eocene La Meseta formation, Seymour Island, Antarctic Peninsula. *Can. J. Fish. Aquat. Sci.* 46:2219–35.

141. Mitchell, E., and D. G. Chapman. 1975. Preliminary assessment of stocks of northwest Atlantic sei whales (*Balaenoptera borealis*). *Rep. Int. Whal. Commn* (special issue 1):117–20.

142. Mitchell, E., and V. M. Kozicki. 1975a. Autumn stranding of a northern bottlenose whale (*Hyperoodon ampullatus*) in the Bay of Fundy, Nova Scotia. *J. Fish. Res. Bd. Canada* 32(7):1019–40.

143. Mitchell, E., and V. M. Kozicki. 1975b. Supplementary information on minke whale (*Balaenoptera acutorostrata*) from Newfoundland Fishery. *J. Fish. Res. Bd. Canada* 32(7):985–94.

144. Miyazaki, N. 1977. School structure of *Stenella coeruleoalba*. *Rep. Int. Whal. Commn* 27:498–99.

145. Moore, J. C. 1966. Diagnoses and distributions of beaked whales of the genus *Mesoplodon* known from North American waters. In K. Norris, ed., *Whales, Dolphins and Porpoises*, pp. 32–61. Berkeley: University of California Press.

146. Moulton, J. M. 1963. The capture of a marked leatherback turtle in Casco Bay, Maine. *Copeia* 1963(2): 434–35.

147. Mullins, J., H. Whitehead, and L. S. Weilgart. 1988. Behaviour and vocalizations of two single sperm whales, *Physeter macrocephalus*, off Nova Scotia. *Can. J. Fish. Aquat. Sci.* 45:1736–43.

148. Murison, L. D., and D. E. Gaskin. 1989. The distribution of right whales and zooplankton in the Bay of Fundy, Canada. *Can. J. Zool.* 67(6):1411–20.

149. Nagasaki, F. 1990. The case for scientific whaling. *Nature* 344 (March 15, 1990):189–90.

150. Nemoto, T. 1970. Feeding pattern of baleen whales in the ocean. In J. H. Steele, ed., *Marine Food Chains*, pp. 241–52. Berkeley: University of California Press.

151. Nishiwaki, M. 1975. Ecological aspects of smaller cetaceans, with emphasis on the striped dolphin, *Stenella coeruleoalba*. *J. Fish. Res. Bd. Canada* 32(7):1069–72.

152. Nores, C., and C. Perez. 1988. Overlapping range between *Globicephala macrorhynchus* and *Globicephala melaena* in the northeastern Atlantic. *Mammalia* 52:51–55.

153. Norris, K. S., ed. 1966. *Whales, Dolphins and Porpoises*. Berkeley: University of California Press.

154. Norris, K. S. 1974. *The Porpoise Watcher*. New York: Norton.

155. *Oceanus*. Vol 32(1) for Spring 1989; and Vol. 21(2) for Spring 1978, were devoted to marine mammals. Back issues may be ordered from Oceanus, 93 Water St., Woods Hole, Massachusetts.

156. Overholtz, W. J., and J. R. Nicolas. 1979. Apparent feeding by the fin whale, *Balaenoptera physalus*, and humpback whale, *Megaptera novaeangliae*, on the American sand lance, *Ammodytes americanus*, in the northwest Atlantic. *Fish. Bull.* 77(1):285–87.

157. Payne, P. M., D. N. Wiley, S. B. Young, S. Pittman, P. Clapham, and J. Jossi. 1990. Recent fluctuations in the abundance of baleen whales in the southern Gulf of Maine in relation to changes in selected prey. *Fish. Bull.* 88:687–96.

157a. Payne, P. M., D. W. Heinemann, and L. A. Selzer. 1991. A distributional assessment of cetaceans in shelf/shelf-edge and adjacent slope waters of the northeastern

United States based on aerial and shipboard surveys, 1978–1988. Report to National Marine Fisheries Service, Northeast Fisheries Center, Woods Hole, Mass. 108 pp. + tab. Unpublished manuscript.

158. Perkins, J. S., and P. C. Beamish. 1979. Net entanglements of baleen whales in the inshore fishery of Newfoundland. *J. Fish. Res. Bd. Canada* 36:521–28.

159. Perkins, J., and H. Whitehead. 1977. Observations on three species of baleen whales off Newfoundland waters. *J. Fish. Res. Bd. Canada* 34:1436–40.

160. Perrin, W. F., and S. B. Reilly. 1986. Reproductive parameters of dolphins and small whales of the Family Delphinidae. *Rep. Int. Whal. Commn* (special issue 6):97–132.

161. Pivorunas, A. 1979. The feeding mechanisms of baleen whales. *Amer. Sci.* 67(4):432–40.

162. Powers, K. D., P. M. Payne, and S. J. Fitch. 1982. *Marine Observer Program. Distributions of Cetaceans, Seabirds and Turtles, Cape Hatteras to Nova Scotia, June 1980–December 1981.* Final Report for NOAA/NMFS Contract No. NA-81-FA-C-00023. Manomet, Mass.: Manomet Bird Observatory.

163. Prescott, J. H., and P. M. Fiorelli. 1980. *Review* of the *Harbor Porpoise* (Phocoena phocoena) *in the Northwest Atlantic.* Final Report for Marine Mammal Commission Contract MM8ACO16. Springfield, Va.: NTIS PB80-176 928.

164. Prescott, J. H., S. D., Kraus, P. Fiorelli, and D. E. Gaskin. 1981. Harbor porpoise (*Phocoena phocoena*)

distribution, abundance, survey methodology and preliminary notes on habitat use and threats. Final Report to National Marine Fisheries Service, Northeast Fisheries Laboratory, Woods Hole, Mass. Unpublished manuscript.

165. Prior, K., and K. S. Norris, eds. 1991. *Dolphin Societies.* Berkeley: University of California Press.

166. Read, A. 1990a. Reproductive seasonality in harbour porpoises, *Phocoena phocoena,* from the Bay of Fundy. *Can. J. Zool.* 68:284–88.

167. Read, A. 1990b. Age at sexual maturity and pregnancy rates of harbour porpoises *Phocoena phocoena* from the Bay of Fundy, *Can. J. Fish. Aquat. Sci.* 47:561–65.

168. Read, A., and D. E. Gaskin. 1988. Incidental catch of harbor porpoises by gill nets. *J. Wildlife Management* 52:517–23.

169. Recchia, C. A., and A. J. Read. 1989. Stomach contents of harbor porpoises, *Phocoena phocoena* (L.), from the Bay of Fundy. *Can. J. Zool.* 67(9):2140–46.

170. Reeves, R. R., and M. F. Barto. 1985. Whaling in the Bay of Fundy. *Whalewatcher* 19(4):14–18.

171. Reeves, R. R., and S. K. Katona. 1980. Extralimital records of white whales (*Delphinapterus leucas*) in eastern North American waters. *Canadian Field-Nat.* 94(3)239–47.

172. Reeves, R. R., J. G. Mead, and S. K. Katona, 1977. The right whale, *Eubalaena glacialis,* in the western North Atlantic. *Rep. Int. Whal. Commn* 28:303–12.

173. Reeves, R. R., and E. Mitchell. 1987. *Cetaceans of Canada.* Under-

water World Factsheet 59. Minister of Supply and Services, Canada, Fs 4/59-1987E. 27 pp. This publication is also available in French.

174. Reeves, R. R., and E. Mitchell. 1988. Current status of the gray whale, *Eschrichtius robustus*. *Canadian Field-Nat.* 102(2):369–90.

175. Rice, D. W. 1989. Sperm whale —*Physeter macrocephalus Linnaeus*, 1758. In S. H. Ridgway and R. Harrison, eds., *Handbook of Marine Mammals*, vol. 4, *River Dolphins and the Larger Toothed Whales*, pp. 177–233. London: Academic Press.

176. Ridgway, S. H, ed. 1972. *Mammals of the Sea: Biology and Medicine.* Springfield, Ill.: Charles C. Thomas.

177. Rigley, L. 1983. Dolphins feeding in a South Carolina salt marsh. *Whalewatcher* 17(2):3–5.

178. Rowell, T. W. 1986. *Squid. Underwater World.* Ottawa: Department of Fisheries and Oceans.

179. Rumage, T. 1983. Pilot whales of Trinity Bay, Newfoundland. *Whalewatcher* 20(4):9–11.

180. Sanderson, S. L., and R. Wassersug. 1990. Suspension feeding vertebrates. *Sci. Amer.* 262(3):96–101.

181. Scattergood, L. W., and C. Packard. 1960. Records of marine turtles in Maine. *Maine Field Naturalist* 16 (3):46–50.

182. Schevill, W. E. 1956. *Lagenorhynchus acutus* off Cape Cod. *J. Mamm.* 37:128–29.

183. Schevill, W. E., ed. 1974. *The Whale Problem: A Status Report.* Cambridge, Mass.: Harvard University Press.

184. Sears, R., J. M., Williamson, F. W., Wenzel, M. Berube, D. Gendron, and P. Jones. 1990. Photographic identification of the blue whale (*Balaenoptera musculus*) in the Gulf of St. Lawrence, Canada. *Rep. Int. Whal. Commn* (special issue 12):335–42.

185. Seipt, I. E., P. J., Clapham, C. A. Mayo, and M. P. Hawwermale. 1990. Population characteristics of individually identified fin whales *Balaenoptera physalus* in Massachusetts Bay. *Fish. Bull.* 88:271–78.

186. Selzer, L. A., and P. M. Payne. 1988. The distribution of white-sided (*Lagenorhynchus acutus*) and common dolphins (*Delphinus delphis*) vs. environmental features of the continental shelf of the United States. *Mar. Mamm. Sci.* 4 (2): 141–53.

187. Sergeant, D. E. 1962a. The biology of the pilot or pothead whale *Globicephala melaena* (Traill) in Newfoundland Waters. *Fish. Res. Bd. Canada Bull.* 132. 34 pp.

188. Sergeant, D. E. 1962b. On the external characters of the blackfish or pilot whales (genus *Globicephala*). *J. Mammal.* 43:395–413.

189. Sergeant, D. E. 1963. Minke whales, *Balaenoptera acutorostrata Lacepede*, of the Western North Atlantic. *J. Fish. Res. Bd. Canada* 20:1490–1504.

190. Sergeant, D. E. 1966. *Populations of Large Whale Species in the Western North Atlantic with Special Reference to the Fin Whale.* Fisheries Research Board of Canada, Arctic Biological Station Circular No. 9.

191. Sergeant, D. E. 1969. Feeding

rates of cetacea. *Fisk. Dir. Skr. Ser. HavUnders.* 15:246–58.

192. Sergeant, D. E. 1977. Stocks of fin whales *Balaenoptera physalus* L. in the North Atlantic Ocean. *Rep. Int. Whal. Commn* 27:460–73.

193. Sergeant, D. E., and P. F. Brodie. 1975. Identity, abundance, and present status of populations of white whale, *Delphinapterus leucas*, in North America. *J. Fish. Res. Bd. Canada* 32 (7):1047–54.

194. Sergeant, D. E., and W. Hoek. 1988. An update of the status of white whales, *Delphinapterus leucas*, in the St. Lawrence Estuary, Canada. *Biological Conservation* 45:287–302.

195. Sergeant, D. E., D. J. St. Aubin, and J. R. Geraci. 1980. Life history and northwest Atlantic status of the Atlantic white-sided dolphin, *Lagenorhynchus acutus. Cetology*, No. 37. 12 pp.

196. Shane, S. 1988. *The Bottlenose Dolphin in the Wild.* San Carlos, Calif.: Hatcher Trade Press.

197. Sigurjonsson, J., and S. Leatherwood, eds. 1988. North Atlantic Killer Whales *Rit. Fiskideildar* 11:1–316.

198. Silber, G. K., M. W. Newcomber, and H. Perez-Cortes M. 1990. Killer whales (*Orcinus orca*) attack and kill a Bryde's whale (*Balaenoptera edeni*). *Can. J. Zool.* 68:1603–6.

199. Sinclair, M., and T. D. Iles. 1985. Atlantic herring (*Clupea harengus*) distributions in the Gulf of Maine—Scotian Shelf area in relation to oceanographic features. *Can. J. Fish. Aquat. Sci.* 42:880–87.

200. Slijper, E. J. 1979. *Whales.* Ithaca, N.Y.: Cornell University Press.

201. Smith, G. J. D., and D. E. Gaskin. 1974. The diet of harbor porpoises (*Phocoena phocoena* [L]) in coastal waters of eastern Canada, with special reference to the Bay of Fundy. *Can. J. Zool.* 52:777–82.

202. Snow, D. 1974. The changing prey of Maine's early hunters. *Nat. Hist.* 83(11):15–24.

203. Spotte, S., J. L. Dunn, L. E. Kezer, and F. M. Heard. 1978. Notes on the care of a beach stranded harbor porpoise (*Phocoena phocoena*). *Cetology* 32:1–5.

204. Squires, H. J. 1957. Squid, *Illex illecebrosus* (Le Sueur) in the Newfoundland Fishing Area. *J. Fish. Res. Bd. Canada* 14:693–728.

205. Squires, H. J. 1967. Growth and hypothetical age of the Newfoundland bait squid *Illex illecebrosus. J. Fish. Res. Bd. Canada* 24:1209–17.

206. Strong, J. T. 1988. Status of the narwhal, *Monodon monoceros*, in Canada. *Canadian Field-Nat.* 102(2):391–98.

207. Tarpy, C. 1979. Killer whale attack. *Nat. Geogr.* 155:542–45.

208. Thomas, J., and R. Kastelein, eds. 1990. *Sensory Abilities of Cetaceans.* New York: Plenum Press.

209. Thurston, H. 1983. The little fish that feeds the North Atlantic. *Audubon,* January, pp. 52–71.

210. Tomilin, A. G. 1957. *Mammals of the U.S.S.R. and Adjacent Countries*, vol. 9, *Cetacea.* Springfield, Va.: NTIS.

211. True, F. W. 1904. The whalebone whales of the western North Atlantic compared with those occur-

ring in European waters with some observations on the species in the North Pacific. *Smithsonian Contrib. Knowl.* 33 (1414):1–332.

212. Tuck, J. A., and R. Grenier. 1981. Sixteenth century basque whaling station in Labrador. *Sci. Amer.* 245(5):180–90.

213. Tyack, P. 1981. Why do whales sing? *The Sciences* (New York Academy of Sciences), September, pp. 22–25.

214. Warhol, P. 1982. Can odontocetes stun prey with sound? The "Big Bang" theory. An interview with Ken Norris. *Whalewatcher* 16(2): 6–8, 23.

215. Waring, G. T., P. Gerrior, P. M. Payne, B. L. Parry, and J. R. Nicholas. 1990. Incidental take of marine mammals in foreign fishery activities off the northeast USA, 1977–1988. *Fish. Bull.* 88:347–60.

216. Watkins, W. A. 1977. Acoustic behavior of sperm whales. *Oceanus* 20:50–58.

217. Watkins, W. A. 1980. Acoustics and the behavior of sperm whales, In R. G. Busnel and J. F. Fish, eds., *Animal Sonar Systems*, pp. 283–90. New York: Plenum.

218. Watkins, W. A. 1981. Activities and underwater sounds of fin whales. *Sci. Rep. Whales Res. Inst.* 33:83–118.

219. Watkins, W. A., and W. E. Schevill. 1979. Aerial observation of feeding behavior in four baleen whales: *Eubalaena glacialas, Balaenoptera borealis, Megaptera novaeangliae*, and *Balaenoptera physalus*. *J. Mammal.* 60:155–63.

220. Weinrich, M. T. 1991. Stable social associations among humpback whales (*Megaptera novaeangliae*) in the southern Gulf of Maine. *Can. J. Zool.* 69:3012–3019.

221. Weinrich, M. T., C. R. Belt, M. R. Schilling, and M. Marcy. 1987. Behavior of sei whales in the southern Gulf of Maine, Summer 1986. *Whalewatcher* 20(4):4–7.

222. Wells, R. 1985. Bottlenose dolphin social behavior: longterm research in a natural laboratory. *Whalewatcher* 19(4):3–6.

223. Wells, R. S. 1991. Bringing up baby. *Nat. Hist.* 8/91: 56–62.

224. Wenzel, F., and R. Sears. 1988. A note on killer whales in the Gulf of St. Lawrence, including an account of an attack on a minke whale. *Rit. Fiskideildar* 11:202–4.

225. Whitehead, H. 1982. Populations of humpback whales in the northwest Atlantic. *Rep. Int. Whal. Commn* 32:345–53.

226. Whitehead, H. 1984. Rare look at sperm and blue whales, the unknown giants. *Nat. Geogr.* 166:774–89.

227. Whitehead, H. 1985. Why whales leap. *Sci. Amer.* 252(3):84–93.

228. Whitehead, H. 1987. Updated status of the humpback whale, *Megaptera novaeangliae*, in Canada. *Canadian Field-Nat.* 101(2):284–94.

229. Whitehead, H., and C. Carlson. 1988. Social behaviour of feeding finback whales off Newfoundland: comparisons with the sympatric humpback whale. *Can. J. Zool.* 66:217–21.

230. Whitehead, H., and J. E. Carscadden. 1985. Predicting inshore

whale abundance—whales and capelin off the Newfoundland coast. *Can. J. Fish. Aquat. Sci.* 42:976–81.

231. Whitehead, H., and C. Glass. 1985a. Orcas (killer whales) attack humpback whales. *J. Mamm.* 66(1):183–85.

232. Whitehead, H., and C. Glass. 1985b. The significance of the southeast shoal of the Grand Bank to humpback whales and other cetacean species. *Can. J. Zool.* 63:2617–25.

233. Whitehead, H., R. Silver, and P. Harcourt. 1982. The migration of humpback whales along the northeast coast of Newfoundland. *Can J. Zool.* 60(9):2173–79.

234. Whitehead, H., and S. Waters. 1990. Social organization and population structure of sperm whales off the Galapagos Islands, Ecuador (1985 and 1987). *Rep. Int. Whal. Commn* (special issue 12):249–58.

235. Williamson, J. M. 1985. Humpback whale research in the Gulf of St. Lawrence. *Whalewatcher* 19(3): 9–11.

236. Winn, H. E., R. K. Edel, and A. G. Taruski. 1975. Population estimate of the humpback whale (*Megaptera novaeangliae*) in the West Indies by visual and acoustic techniques. *J. Fish. Res. Bd. Canada* 32:499–506.

237. Winn, H. E., J. H. W. Hain, M. A. M. Hyman, and G. P. Scott. 1987. Whales, dolphins and porpoises. In R. H. Backus, ed., *Georges Bank*, pp. 375–82. Cambridge, Mass.: MIT Press.

238. Winn, H. E., and P. J. Perkins. 1976. Distribution and sounds of the minke whale, with a review of mysticete sounds. *Cetology* 19:1–12.

239. Winn, H. E., and L. K. Winn. 1978. The song of the humpback whale, *Megaptera novaeangliae*, in the West Indies. *Mar. Biol.* 47:97–114.

240. Winn, L. K., and H. E. Winn 1985. *Wings in the Sea: The Humpback Whale.* Hanover, N.H.: University Press of New England.

241. Winslade, P. 1975. Behavioral studies on the lesser sand eel *Ammodytes marinus* (Raitt):III. The effect of temperature on activity and the environmental control of the annual cycle of activity. *J. Fish. Biol.* 6(5):587–99.

242. Wishner, K., E. Durbin, A. Durbin, M. Macaulay, H. Winn, and R. Kenney. 1988. Copepod patches and right whales in the Great South Channel off New England. *Bull Mar. Sci.* 43:825–44.

243. Wursig, B. 1979. Dolphins. *Sci. Amer.* 240(3):136–48.

244. Wursig, B. 1989. Cetaceans. *Science* 244:1550–57.

SPECIES GUIDE TO THE BIBLIOGRAPHY ON SEALS

Titles most suitable for young readers or laymen are set in **boldface**. Many of the other titles can be profitably read by nonscientists.

General: 1, 7, 8, **9,** 10, 21, 22, 24, **33,** 51, 55, 76, 77, 78, 82, 83, 84, 85, 87, 91, 96, 98, 99, 102, 104, 108, **115, 120,** 124, 125, 135, **144,** 147, 152, 155, 157, 161, 162, 163, 166, 167, 169, 173, 174, 175, **176, 177,** 178, 189, 199, 202, 213, 214, 220, 221, 225, 229, 230

Harbor seal: 2, 3, 12, 13, 14, 19, 23, 29, 39, 48, 50, 54, 57, 69, 70, **72,** 79, 80, 94, **107,** 116, **117,** 131, 139, 140, 143, 153, 154, 160, 170, 180, 181, 208, 209, 212, **215,** 222, 226, 227

Gray seal: 3, 4, 5, 6, 8, 11, 15, 16, 18, 19, 20, 24, 31, 32, 40, 41, **44,** 47, 49, 50, 52, 53, 63, 66, 75, 80, 81, 97, 105, **106, 107,** 110, **114, 117,** 118, 130, 142, 160, 206, 207, 210, 219, 226, 228, 232

Harp seal: 26, 30, **34, 35,** 38, 46, 65,

92, **100,** 101, 111, 121, 127, 132, 136, 138, 164, 165, 168, **171,** 182, 183, 184, 185, 186, 188, 200, 211, 216, 217, 218, 223, 224

Hooded seal: 17, 25, 27, 28, **36,** 38, 42, 67, 93, 95, **100,** 111, 134, 136, 151, 159, 183, 187, 188

Ringed seal: 50, 64, 68, 88, 89, 122, **192,** 193, 194, **195,** 196, 197, 198, 201, 203, 205

Bearded seal: 37, 45, 89, 123, 146, 148, 196, 203, 204

Walrus: 58, 59, 60, 61, 62, 71, 73, 86, 109, 112, **113,** 119, 126, 128, 129, 133, 137, **141,** 145, 149, 150, 156, 158, 172, 179, 190, **191**

Elephant seals: 56, 103
Weddell seals: 90, 231
California sea lion: 74, 156
Sea mink: 43

II. SEALS

1. Allen, J. A. 1880. *History of North American Pinnipeds.* U.S. Geogr. Surv. Terr., Misc. Publ. 12.
2. Allen, S. G. 1985. Mating behavior in the harbor seal. *Mar. Mamm. Sci.* 1:84–87.
3. Anderson, S. S. 1981. Seals in Shetland waters. *Proc. Roy. Soc. Edinburgh* 80B:181–88.
4. Anderson, S. S., R. W. Burton, and C. F. Summers. 1975. Behavior of grey seals, Halichoerus grypus, during a breeding season at North Rona. *J. Zool.* (London) 177:179–95.
5. Anderson, S. S., and M. A. Fedak. 1985. Grey seal males: energetic and behavioral links between size and sexual success. *Anim. Behav.* 33:829–38.
6. Andrews, J. C., and P. R. Mott. 1967. Gray seals at Nantucket, Massachusetts. *J. Mamm.* 48(4):657–58.

7. Arnason, U., and B. Widegren. 1986. Pinniped phylogeny enlightened by molecular hybridizations using highly repetitive DNA. *Mol. Biol. and Evol.* 3:356–65.

8. Backhouse, K. M. 1961. Locomotion of seals with particular reference to the forelimb. *Symp. Zool. Soc. Lond.* No. 5:59–75.

9. Backhouse, K. M. 1969. *Seals.* New York: Golden Press.

10. Beddington, J. R., R. J. H. Beverton, and D. M. Lavigne, eds. 1985. *Marine Mammals and Fisheries.* London: George Allen & Unwin.

11. Benoit, D., and W. D. Bowen. 1990. Seasonal and geographic variation in the diet of grey seals, *Halichoerus grypus*, in eastern Canada. *Can. Bull. Fish. Aquat. Sci.* 222:215–26.

12. Bigg, M. A. 1969. Clines in the pupping season of the harbour seal, *Phoca vitulina. J. Fish. Res. Board Can.* 26:449–55.

13. Bigg, M. A. 1981. Harbour seal, *Phoca vitulina* and *P. largha.* In S. H. Ridgway and R. J. Harrison, eds., *Handbook of marine mammals*, vol. 2, Seals, pp. 1–27. London: Academic Press.

14. Bigg, M. A., and H. D. Fisher. 1975. Effect of photoperiod on annual reproduction in female harbor seals. *Rapp. P.-v. Reun Cons. Int. Explor. Mer* 169:141–44.

15. Boness, D. J. 1979. The social system of the grey seal, *Halichoerus grypus*, on Sable Island, Nova Scotia. Ph.D. dissertation, Dalhousie University, Halifax, Nova Scotia.

16. Boness, D. J., S. S. Anderson, and C. R. Cox. 1982. Functions of female aggression during the pupping and mating season of grey seals, *Halichoerus grypus* Fabricus. *Can. J. Zool.* 60:2270–78.

17. Boness, D. J., W. D. Bowen, and O. T. Oftedal. 1988. Evidence of polygyny from spatial patterns of hooded seals, *Cystophora cristata. Can. J. Zool.* 66:703–6.

18. Boness, D. J., and H. James. 1979. Reproductive behavior of the grey seal, *Halichoerus grypus*, on Sable Island, Nova Scotia. *J. Zool.* (London) 188:477–500.

19. Bonner, W. N. 1972. The grey seal and common seal in European waters. *Oceanogr. Mar. Biol. Ann. Rev.* 10:461–507.

20. Bonner, W. N. 1981. Grey seal, *Halichoerus grypus.* In S. H. Ridgway and R. J. Harrison, eds., *Handbook of Marine Mammals*, vol. 2, Seals, pp. 111–144. London: Academic Press.

21. Bonner, W. N. 1982. *Seals and Man: A Study of Interactions.* Washington Sea Grant Publication. Seattle: University of Washington Press.

22. Bonner, W. N. 1986. Seals in the human environment. *Ambio* 15(3): 173–76.

23. Boulva, J., and I. A. McLaren. 1979. Biology of the harbor seal, *Phoca vitulina*, in eastern Canada. *Bull. Fish. Res. Board Canada.* No. 200.

24. Bowen, W. D., ed. 1990. Population biology of sealworm (*Pseudoterranova decipiens*) in relation to its intermediate and seal hosts. *Can. Bull. Fish. Aquat. Sci.* 222: 1–306.

25. Bowen, W. D., D. J. Boness, and

O. T. Oftedal. 1987. Mass transfer from mother to pup and subsequent mass loss by the weaned pup in the hooded seal, *Cystophora cristata*. *Can. J. Zool.* 65:1–8.

26. Bowen, W. D., C. K. Capstick, and D. E. Sergeant. 1981. Temporal changes in the reproductive potential of female harp seals, *Pagophilus groenlandicus*. *Can. J. Fish. Aquat. Sci.* 38:495–503.

27. Bowen, W. D., R. A. Myers, and K. Hay. 1987. Abundance estimation of a dispersed, dynamic population: hooded seals, *Cystophora cristata*, in the Northwest Atlantic. *Can. J. Fish. Aquat. Sci.* 44:282–95.

28. Bowen, W. D., O. T. Oftedal, and D. J. Boness. 1985. Birth to weaning in four days: remarkable growth in the hooded seal, *Cystophora cristata*. *Can. J. Zool.* 63:2841–46.

29. Bowen, W. D., O. T. Oftedal, and D. J. Boness. 1989. Variation in efficiency of mass transfer in harbour seals, *Phoca vitulina*, over the course of lactation. *Proceedings of the 8th Biennial Conference on the Biology of Marine Mammals*, December 7–11, Pacific Grove, Calif. Abstract.

30. Bowen, W. D., and D. E. Sergeant. 1983. Mark-recapture estimates of harp seal pup, *Phoca groenlandica*, production in the Northwest Atlantic. *Can. J. Fish. Aquat. Sci.* 40:728–42.

31. Boyd, I. L. 1984. The relationship between body condition and the timing of implantation in pregnant grey seals, *Halichoerus grypus*. *J. Zool.* (London) 203:113–23.

32. Brodie, P., and B. Beck. 1983. Pre-dation by sharks on the grey seal, *Halichoerus grypus*, in eastern Canada. *Can. J. Fish. Aquat. Sci.* 40:267–71.

33. Bruemmer, F. 1972. *Encounters with Arctic Animals.* Toronto and New York: McGraw-Hill, Ryerson.

34. Bruemmer, F. 1975. A year in the life of a harp seal. *Nat. Hist.* 84(4):42–49.

35. Bruemmer, F. 1977. *The Life of the Harp Seal.* New York: Times Book Co.

36. Bruemmer, F. 1990. Survival of the fattest. *Nat. Hist.* 7:26–33.

37. Burns, J. J. 1981. Bearded seal, *Erignathus barbatus*. In S. H. Ridgway and R. J. Harrison, eds. *Handbook of Marine Mammals*, vol. 2, Seals, pp. 145–70. London: Academic Press.

38. Busch, B. C. 1985. *The War against the Seals: A History of the North American Seal Fishery.* Montreal, Quebec, and Kingston, Ontario: McGill-Queen's University Press.

39. Caldwell, D. K., and M. C. Caldwell. 1969. The harbor seal, *Phoca vitulina*, in Florida. *J. Mamm.* 50(2):379–80.

40. Cameron, A. W. 1967. Breeding behavior in a colony of western Atlantic gray seals. *Can. J. Zool.* 45:161–73.

41. Cameron, A. W. 1970. Seasonal movements and diurnal activity rhythms of the gray seal, *Halichoerus grypus*. *J. Zool.* (London) 161:15–23.

42. Campbell, R. R. 1987. Status of the hooded seal, *Cystophora cristata*, in Canada. *Canadian Field-Nat.* 101(2):253–65.

43. Campbell, R. R. 1988. Status of

the Sea Mink, *Mustela macrodon*, in Canada. *Canadian Field-Nat.* 102(2): 304–306.

44. Clarkson, C. 1970. *Halic: The Story of a Gray Seal*. New York: Dutton.

45. Cleator, H. J., I. Stirling, and T. G. Smith. 1989. Underwater vocalizations of the bearded seal, *Erignathus barbatus*. *Can. J. Zool.* 67:1900–1910.

46. Cook, H. W., and B. E. Baker. 1969. Seal milk. I. Harp seal (*Pagophilus groenlandicus*) milk, composition and pesticide residue content. *Can. J. Zool.* 47(6):1129–32.

47. Coulson, J. C., and G. Hickling. 1964. The breeding biology of the grey seal, *Halichoerus grypus*, (Fab.), on the Farne Islands, Northumberland. *J. Animal Ecol.* 33:485–512.

48. Cowperthwaite, L. 1987. Parent offspring conflict in harbor seals. *Proceedings of the 7th Biennial Conference on the Biology of Marine Mammals*, December 5–9, Miami, Fla. Abstract.

49. Curry-Lindahl, K. 1970. Breeding biology of the Baltic grey seal, *Halichoerus grypus*. *Der Zoologische Garten* (Leipzig) 38:16–29.

50. Curry-Lindahl, K. 1975. Ecology and conservation of grey seal, *Halichoerus grypus*, common seal, *Phoca vitulina* and ringed seal, *Pusa hispida*, in the Baltic Sea. *Rapp. P.-v. Reun. Cons. Int. Explor. Mer* 169:527–32.

51. Dailey, M. D. 1975. The distribution and intraspecific variation of helminth parasites in pinnipeds. *Rapp. P.-v. Cons. Int. Explor. Mer* 169:338–52.

52. Davies, J. L. 1957. The geography of the gray seal. *J. Mammal.* 38:297–310.

53. Davis, J. E., and S. S. Anderson. 1976. Effects of oil pollution on breeding grey seals. *Mar. Pollut. Bull.* 7(6):115–18.

54. Davis, M. B., and D. Renouf. 1987. Social behavior of harbor seals, *Phoca vitulina*, on haulout grounds at Miquelon. *Canadian Field-Nat.* 101(1):1–5.

55. deJong, W. W. 1982. Eye lens proteins and vertebrate phylogeny. In M. Goodman, ed., *Macromolecular Sequences in Systematic and Evolutionary Biology*, pp. 75–114. New York: Plenum.

56. DeLong, R. L., and B. S. Stewart. 1989. Diving patterns of northern elephant seal bulls. *Proceedings of the 8th Biennial Conference on the Biology of Marine Mammals*, December 7–11, Pacific Grove, Calif. Abstract.

57. Dickson, D. 1988. Canine distemper may be killing North Sea seals: harbor seals. *Science* 241:1284.

58. Fay, F. H. 1960. Structure and function of the pharyngeal pouches of the walrus, *Odobenus rosmarus* Linnaeus. *Mammalia* (Paris) 24: 361–71.

59. Fay, F. H. 1981. Walrus, *Odobenus rosmarus*. In S. H. Ridgway and R. J. Harrison, eds., *Handbook of Marine Mammals*, vol. 1, *The Walrus, Sea Lions, Fur Seals, and Sea Otters*, pp. 1–23. London: Academic Press.

60. Fay, F. H. 1982. *Ecology and Biology of the Pacific Walrus*, Odobenus rosmarus divergens *Illiger*. Washington, D. C.: U.S. Department of the

Interior, Fish and Wildlife Service. North American Fauna, No. 74.

61. Fay, F. H., B. P. Kelley, and J. L. Sease. 1989. Managing the exploitation of Pacific walruses: a tragedy of delayed response and poor communication. *Mar. Mamm. Sci.* 5:1–16.

62. Fay, F. H., and C. Ray. 1968. Influence of climate on the distribution of walruses, *Odobenus rosmarus* Linnaeus, part 1: evidence from thermoregulatory behavior. *Zoologica* 53:1–18.

63. Fedak, M. A., and S. S. Anderson. 1982. The energetics of lactation: accurate measurements from a large wild mammal, the grey seal, *Halichoerus grypus*. *J. Zool.* (London) 198:473–79.

64. Fedoseev, G. A. 1975. Ecotypes of the ringed seal, *Pusa hispida* Schreber, and their reproductive capabilities. *Rapp. P.-v. Reun. Cons. Int. Explor. Mer* 169:156–60.

65. Finley, K. J., M. S. W. Bradstreet, and G. W. Miller. 1990. Summer feeding ecology of harp seals, *Phoca groenlandica*, in relation to arctic cod, *Boreogadus saida*, in the Canadian High Arctic. *Polar. Biol.* 10:609–18.

66. Fogden, S. C. L. 1971. Mother-young behavior at grey seal breeding beaches. *J. Zool.* (London) 164:61–92.

67. Frank, R. J., and K. Ronald. 1982. Some underwater observations of hooded seal, *Cystophora cristata* Erxleben, behavior. *Aquat. Mamm.* 9:67–68.

68. Frost, K. J., and L. F. Lowry. 1981. Ringed, Baikal and Caspian seals. In S. H. Ridgway and R. J. Harrison, eds., *Handbook of Marine Mammals*, vol. 2, *Seals*, pp. 29–53 London: Academic Press.

69. Geraci, J. R., D. J. St. Aubin, I. K. Barker, R. G. Webster, V. S. Hinshaw, W. J. Bean, H. L. Ruhnke, J. H. Prescott, G. Early, A. S. Baker, S. Madoff, and R. T. Schooley. 1981. Mass mortality of harbor seals: pneumonia associated with influenza A virus. *Science* 215:1129–31.

70. Gilbert, J. R., and K. M. Wynne. 1984. *Harbor Seal Populations and Marine Mammal-Fisheries Interactions (1983)*. Annual report. Contract No. NA-80-FAC-0029. Woods Hole, Mass.: National Marine Fisheries Service, Northeast Fisheries Center.

71. Gjertz, I. 1990. Walrus predation of seabirds. *Polar Rec.* 26(159):317.

72. Goodridge, H., and L. Dietz. 1975. *A Seal Called Andre*. Camden, Maine: Downeast Books.

73. Gordon, K. R. 1981. Locomotor behavior of the walrus, *Odobenus*. *J. Zool.* (London) 195:349–67.

74. Gunter, G. 1968. The status of seals in the Gulf of Mexico. *Gulf Res. Rept.* 2(3):301–8.

75. Hammond, P. S., and J. H. Prime. 1990. The diet of British grey seals, *Halichoerus grypus*. *Can. Bull. Fish. Aquat. Sci.* 222:243–54.

76. Harrison, R. J. 1972, 1974, 1977. *Functional Anatomy of Marine Mammals*. Vols. 1, 2, 3. London: Academic Press.

77. Harrison, R. J., R. C. Hubbard,

R. S. Peterson, C. E. Rice, and R. J. Schusterman. 1968. *The Behavior and Physiology of Pinnipeds.* New York: Appleton-Century-Crofts.

78. Harrison, R. J., and J. E. King. 1980. *Marine Mammals.* 2d ed. London: Century Hutchinson.

79. Harwood, J. 1990. The 1988 seal epizootic. *J. Zool.* (London) 222:349–51.

80. Hewer, H. R. 1974. *British Seals.* London: Collins.

81. Hickling, G. 1962. *Grey Seals and the Farne Islands.* London: Routledge & Kegan Paul.

82. Hofman, R. J., and W. N. Bonner. 1985. Conservation and protection of marine mammals: past, present and future. *Mar. Mamm. Sci.* 1:109–27.

83. Holden, A. V. 1978. Pollutants and seals: a review. *Mammal Rev.* 8(1 and 2):53–66.

84. Irving, L., and J. S. Hart. 1957. The metabolism and insulation of seals as bare-skinned mammals in cold water. *Can. J. Zool.* 35:497–511.

85. Jamieson, G. S., and H. D. Fisher. 1972. The pinniped eye: a review. In R. J. Harrison, ed., *Functional Anatomy of Marine Mammals*, vol. 1, pp. 245–261. London: Academic Press.

86. Kiliaan, H. P., and I. Stirling. 1978. Observations on overwintering walruses in the eastern Canadian high arctic. *J. Mamm.* 59(1):197–200.

87. King, J. E. 1983. *Seals of the World.* 2d ed. London: British Museum of Natural History and Ithaca, N.Y.: Cornell University Press.

88. Kingsley, M. C. S. 1990. Status of the ringed seal, *Phoca hispida*, in Canada. *Canadian Field-Nat.* 104(1): 138–45.

89. Kingsley, M. C. S., I. Stirling, and W. Calvert. 1985. The distribution and abundance of seals in the Canadian High Arctic. *Can. J. Fish. Aquat. Sci.* 42:1189–1210.

90. Kooyman, G. L. 1981. *Weddell Seal: Consummate Diver.* Cambridge: Cambridge University Press.

91. Kooyman, G. L., M. A. Castellini, and R. W. Davis. 1981. Physiology of diving in marine mammals. *Ann. Rev. Physiol.* 43:343–56.

92. Kovacs, K. M. 1987. Maternal behavior and early behavioral ontogeny of harp seals, Phoca groenlandica. *Anim. Behav.* 35:844–55.

93. Kovacs, K. M. 1990. Mating strategies in male hooded seals, *Cystophora cristata. Can. J. Zool.* 68: 2499–2502.

94. Kovacs, K. M., K. M. Jonas, and S. E. Welke. 1990. Sex and age segregation by *Phoca vitulina concolor* at haul-out sites during the breeding season in the Passamaquoddy Bay region, New Brunswick. *Mar. Mamm. Sci.* 6(3):204–14.

95. Kovacs, K. M., and D. M. Lavigne. 1986a. *Cystophora cristata. Mamm. Species* 258:1–9.

96. Kovacs, K. M., and D. M. Lavigne. 1986b. Maternal investment and neonatal growth in phocid seals. *J. Applied Ecology* 55:1035–51.

97. Kovacs, K. M., and D. M. Lavigne. 1986c. Growth of grey seal, *Halichoerus grypus*, neonates: differential maternal investment in the sexes. *Can. J. Zool.* 64:1937–43.

98. Lavigne, D. M., C. D. Bernholz,

and K. Ronald. 1977. Functional aspects of pinniped vision. In R. J. Harrison, ed., *Functional Anatomy of Marine Mammals*, vol. 3, pp. 135–73. London: Academic Press.

99. Lavigne, D. M., S. Innes, G. A. Worthy, K. M. Kovacs, O. J. Schmitz, and J. P. Hickie. 1986. Metabolic rates of seals and whales. *Can. J. Zool.* 64:279–84.

100. Lavigne, D. M., and K. M. Kovacs. 1988. *Harps and Hoods: Ice-Breeding Seals of the Northwest Atlantic.* Ontario: University of Waterloo Press.

101. Lavigne, D. M., and K. Ronald. 1972. The harp seal, *Pagophilus groenlandicus* (Erxleben, 1777): Spectral sensitivity. *Can. J. Zool.* 50:1197–1206.

102. Le Boeuf, B. J. 1986. Sexual strategies of seals and walruses. *New Sci.* 1491:36–39.

103. Le Boeuf, B. J., Y. Naito, A. C. Huntley, and T. Asaga. 1989. Prolonged, continuous, deep diving by northern elephant seals. *Can. J. Zool.* 67:2514–19.

104. Ling, J. K. 1970. Pelage and molting in wild mammals with special reference to aquatic forms. *Quart. Rev. Biol.* 45:16–54.

105. Ling, J. K., and C. E. Button. 1975. The skin and pelage of grey seal pups, *Halichoerus grypus* Fabricus: with a comparative study of foetal and neonatal moulting in the Pinnipedia. *Rapp. P.-v. Reun. Cons. Int. Explor. Mer* 169:112–32.

106. Lockley, R. M. 1955. *The Saga of the Grey Seal.* New York: Devin-Adair.

107. Lockley, R. M. 1966. Gray Seal, *Common Seal: An Account of the Life Histories of British Seals.* London: Deutsch.

108. Lowenstein, J. M. 1986. The pinniped family tree puzzle. *Oceans* 19:72.

109. Lowry, L. F., and F. H. Fay. 1984. Seal eating by walruses in the Bering and Chukchi seas. *Polar Biol.* 3:11–18.

110. Lucas, Z., and I. A. McLaren. 1988. Apparent predation by grey seals, *Halichoerus grypus*, on seabirds around Sable Island, Nova Scotia. *Canadian Field-Nat.* 102(4):675–78.

111. Malouf, A. 1986. *Seals and Sealing in Canada: Report of the Royal Commission.* 3 vols. Ottawa: Supply and Services Canada.

112. Mansfield, A. W. 1958. *The Biology of the Atlantic Walrus, Odobenus rosmarus rosmarus (Linnaeus) in the Eastern Canadian Arctic.* Fisheries Research Board of Canada, Manuscript Report Series (Biology) 653.

113. Mansfield, A. W. 1966a. The walrus in Canada's Arctic. *Canad. Geogr. J.* 72(3):88–95.

114. Mansfield, A. W. 1966b. The grey seal in eastern Canadian waters. *Can. Audubon Mag.* November–December, pp. 160–66.

115. Mansfield, A. W. 1967a. *Seals of Arctic and Eastern Canada.* 2d ed. Fisheries Research Board of Canada Bulletin 137.

116. Mansfield, A. W. 1967b. Distribution of the harbor seal, *Phoca vitulina* Linnaeus, in Canadian arctic waters. *J. Mamm.* 48(2):249–57.

117. Mansfield, A. W. 1967c. The mammals of Sable Island. *Canadian Field-Nat.* 81:40–49.

118. Mansfield, A. W., and B. Beck. 1977. *The Grey Seal in Eastern Canada*. Fisheries and Marine Service Technical Report No. 704.

119. Manville, R. H., and P. G. Favour, Jr. 1960. Southern distribution of the Atlantic walrus. *J. Mamm.* 41(4):499–503.

120. Maxwell, G. 1967. *Seals of the World*. World Wildlife Series 2. Boston: Houghton Mifflin.

121. McAlpine, D. F., and R. H. Walker. 1990. Extralimital records of the harp seal, *Phoca groenlandica*, from the western North Atlantic: a review. *Mar. Mamm. Sci.* 6(3):248–52.

122. McLaren, I. A. 1958a. *The Biology of the Ringed Seal, Phoca hispida Schreber, in the Eastern Canadian Arctic*. Bulletin of the Fisheries Research Board of Canada. No. 118.

123. McLaren, I. A. 1958b. Some aspects of growth and reproduction of the bearded seal, *Erignathus barbatus* (Erxleben). *J. Fish. Res. Bd. Canada* 15(2):219–27.

124. McLaren, I. A. 1960. Are the pinnipeds biphyletic? *Systematic Zoo.* 9:18–28.

125. McLaren, I. A., and T. G. Smith. 1985. Population ecology of seals: retrospective and prospective views. *Mar. Mamm. Sci.* 1:54–83.

126. Mercer, M. C. 1967. Records of the Atlantic walrus, *J. Odobenus rosmarus rosmarus*, from Newfoundland. *J. Fish. Res. Bd. Can.* 24(12):2631–35.

127. Merdsoy, B. R., W. R. Curtsinger, and D. Renouf. 1978. Preliminary underwater observations of the breeding behavior of the harp seal, *Pagophilus groenlandicus*. *J. Mamm.* 59(1):181–85.

128. Miller, E. H. 1975. Walrus ethology. I. The social role of tusks and applications of multidimensional sealing. *Can. J. Zool.* 53:590–613.

129. Miller, E. H. 1976. Walrus ethology. II. Herd structure and activity budgets of summering males. *Can. J. Zool.* 54(5):704–15.

130. Miller, E. H., and D. J. Boness. 1979. Remarks on the display functions of the snout of the grey seal, *Halichoerus grypus* (Fab.), with comparative notes. *Can. J. Zool.* 57:140–48.

131. Møhl, B. 1968. Auditory sensitivity of the common seal in air and water. *J. Aud. Res.* 8:27–38.

132. Møhl, B., J. M. Terhune, and K. Ronald. 1975. Underwater calls of the harp seal, *Pagophilus groenlandicus*. *Rapp. P.-v. Reun. Cons. Int. Explor. Mer* 169:533–43.

133. Nelson, C. H., and K. R. Johnson. 1987. Whales and walruses as tillers of the sea floor: side scan sonar studies of the Bering Sea. *Sci. Amer.* 256:112–17.

134. Oftedal, O. T., D. J. Boness, and W. D. Bowen. 1988. The composition of hooded seal, *Cystophora cristata*, milk: an adaptation for postnatal fattening. *Can. J. Zool.* 66:318–22.

135. Oftedal, O. T., D. J. Boness, and R. A. Tedman. 1987. The behavior, physiology and anatomy of lactation in Pinnipedia. In H. H. Genoways, ed., *Current Mammology*, vol. 1, pp. 175–246. New York: Plenum.

136. Oftedal, O. T., W. D. Bowen, E. M. Widdowson, and D. J. Boness.

1989. Effects of suckling and the postsuckling fast on weights of the body and internal organs of harp and hooded seal pups. *Biol. Neonate* 56:283–300.

137. Oliver, J. S., R. G. Kvitek, and P. N. Slattery. 1985. Walrus feeding disturbance: scavenging habits and recolonization of the Bering Sea benthos. *J. Exp. Mar. Biol. Ecol.* 91:233–46.

138. Øritsland, N. A., and K. Ronald. 1975. Energetics of the free diving harp seal, *Pagophilus groenlandicus. Rapp. P.-v. Reun. Cons. Int. Explor. Mer* 169:451–54.

139. Payne, P. M., and D. C. Schneider. 1984. Yearly changes in abundance of harbor seals, *Phoca vitulina*, at a winter haul-out site in Massachusetts. *Fish Bull.* 82(2): 440–42.

140. Payne, P. M., and L. A. Selzer. 1989. The distribution, abundance and selected prey of the harbor seal, *Phoca vitulina concolor*, in southern New England. *Mar. Mamm. Sci.* 5(2):173–92.

141. Perry, R. 1968. *The World of the Walrus*. New York: Taplinger.

142. Prieur, D., and R. Duguy. 1981. Les phoques des côtes de France. III. Le phoque gris *Halichoerus grypus* (Fabricius, 1791). *Mammalia* (Paris) 45(1):83–98.

143. Ralls, K., P. Fiorelli, and S. Gish. 1985. Vocalizations and vocal mimicry in captive harbor seals, *Phoca vitulina. Can. J. Zool.* 63:1050–56.

144. Ray, C. 1963. Locomotion in pinnipeds. *Nat. Hist.* 72(3):10–21.

145. Ray, C., and F. H. Fay. 1968. Influence of climate on the distribution of walruses, *Odobenus rosmarus* (Linnaeus). II. Evidence from physiological characteristics. *Zoologica* 53(1):19–32.

146. Ray, C., W. A. Watkins, and J. J. Burns. 1969. The underwater song of Erignathus (bearded seal). *Zoologica* 54(2):79–83.

147. Ray, C. E. 1976. Geography of phocid evolution. *Syst. Zool.* 25: 391–406.

148. Ray, C. E., F. Reiner, D. E. Sergeant, and C. N. Quesada. 1982. Notes on past and present distribution of the bearded seal, *Erignathus barbatus*, around the north Atlantic Ocean. *Ser. Zool.* 2(23):1–32.

149. Ray, G. C., and W. A. Watkins. 1975. Social function of underwater sounds in the walrus, *Odobenus rosmarus. Rapp. P.-v. Reun. Cons. Int. Explor. Mer* 169:524–26.

150. Reeves, R. R. 1978. *Atlantic Walrus, Odobenus rosmarus rosmarus: A Literature Survey and Status Report*. Wildlife Research Report 10. Washington, D.C.: U.S. Fish and Wildlife Service.

151. Reeves, R. R., and J. K. Ling. 1981. Hooded seal, *Cystophora cristata*. In S. H. Ridgway and R. J. Harrison, eds., *Handbook of Marine Mammals*, vol. 2, *Seals*, pp. 171–94. London: Academic Press.

152. Reidman, M. L. 1990. *The Pinnipeds: Seals, Sea Lions and Walruses*. Berkeley and Los Angeles: University of California Press.

153. Renouf, D. 1989. Sensory function in the harbor seal. *Sci. Amer.* 260:90–95.

154. Renouf, D., and M. B. Davis. 1982. Evidence that seals may use echolocation. *Nature* 300:635–37.

155. Repenning, C. A. 1972. Underwater hearing in seals: functional morphology. In R. J. Harrison, ed., *Functional Anatomy of Marine Mammals*, vol. 1, pp. 307–331. London: Academic Press.

156. Repenning, C. A. 1976. Adaptive evolution of sea lions and walruses. *Syst. Zool.* 25(4):375–90.

157. Repenning, C. A., C. F. Ray, and D. Grigoriscu. 1979. Pinniped biogeography. In J. Gray and A. J. Boucot, eds., *Historical Biogeography, Plate Tectonics and the Changing Environment*, pp. 357–69. Corvallis: Oregon State University Press.

158. Richard, P. R., and R. R. Campbell. 1988. Status of the Atlantic walrus, *Odobenus rosmarus rosmarus*, in Canada. *Canadian Field-Nat.* 102(2):337–50.

159. Richardson, D. T. 1975. Hooded seal whelps at South Brooksville, Maine. *J. Mamm.* 56(3):698–99.

160. Richardson, D. T. 1976. *Assessment of Harbour and Grey Seal Population in Maine*. Augusta: Maine Department of Marine Research.

161. Ridgway, S. H., ed. 1972. *Mammals of the Sea: Biology and Medicine*. Springfield, Ill.: Charles C. Thomas.

162. Ridgway, S. H., J. R. Geraci, and W. Medway. 1975. Diseases of pinnipeds. *Rapp. P.-v. Reun. Cons. Int. Explor. Mer* 169:327–37.

163. Ridgway, S. H., and R. J. Harrison, eds. 1981. *Handbook of Marine Mammals*. Vol. 1, *The Walrus, Sea Lions, Fur Seals and Sea Otter*. Vol. 2, *Seals*. New York: Academic Press.

164. Roff, D. A., and W. D. Bowen.

1983. Population dynamics and management of the northwest Atlantic harp seal, *Phoca groenlandica. Can. J. Fish. Aquat. Sci.* 40:919–32.

165. Ronald, K., and J. L. Dougan. 1982. The ice lover: biology of the harp seal, *Phoca groenlandica. Science* 215:928–33.

166. Ronald, K., B. L. Gots, J. D. Lupson, C. J. Willings, and J. L. Dougan. 1991. *An Annotated Bibliography on Seals, Sea Lions and Walrus*. Supplement 2. Copenhagen: International Council for the Exploration of the Sea.

167. Ronald, K., L. M. Hanly, P. J. Healey, and L. J. Selley. 1976. *An Annotated Bibliography on the Pinnipedia*. Charlottenlund: International Council for the Exploration of the Sea.

168. Ronald, K., and P. J. Healey. 1981. Harp seal—*Phoca groenlandica*. In S. H. Ridgway and R. J. Harrison, eds., *Handbook of Marine Mammals*, vol. 2, *Seals*, pp. 55–87. London: Academic Press.

169. Ronald, K., P. J. Healey, J. Dougan, L. J. Selley, and L. Dunn. 1983. *An Annotated Bibliography on the Pinnipedia*. Supplement 1. Copenhagen: International Council for the Exploration of the Sea.

170. Rosenfeld, M., M. George, and J. M. Terhune. 1988. Evidence of autumnal harbor seal, *Phoca vitulina*, movement from Canada to the United States. *Canadian Field-Nat.* 102(3):527–29.

171. Ryan, S. 1987. *Seals and Sealers: A Pictoral History of the Newfoundland Seal Fishery*. St. John's, Newfoundland: Breakwater Books.

172. Salter, R. E. 1979. Site utilisation, activity budgets, and disturbance responses of Atlantic walruses during terrestrial haul-out. *Can. J. Zool.* 57:1169–80.

173. Sarich, V. 1969. Pinniped phylogeny. *Syst. Zool.* 18:416–22.

174. Scheffer, V. B. 1958. *Seals, Sea Lions and Walruses: A review of the Pinnipedia.* Stanford: Stanford University Press.

175. Scheffer, V. B. 1967. Standard measurements of seals. *J. Mamm.* 48(3):459–62.

176. Scheffer, V. B. 1970. *The Year of the Seal.* New York: Charles Scribner's Sons.

177. Scheffer, V. B. 1976. *A Natural History of Marine Mammals.* New York: Charles Scribner's Sons.

178. Schevill, W. E., W. A. Watkins, and C. Ray. 1963. Underwater sounds of pinnipeds. *Science* 141:50–53.

179. Schevill, W. E., W. A. Watkins, and C. Ray. 1966. Analysis of underwater *Odobenus* calls with remarks on the development and function of the pharyngeal pouches. *Zoologica* 51:103–6.

180. Schneider, D. C., and P. M. Payne. 1983. Factors affecting haulout of harbor seals at a site in southeastern Massachusetts. *J. Mamm.* 64(3):518–20.

181. Selzer, L. A., G. Early, P. M. Fiorelli, P. M. Payne, and R. Prescott. 1986. Stranded animals as indicators of prey utilization by harbor seals, *Phoca vitulina concolor*, in southern New England. *Fish. Bull.* 84(1):217–20.

182. Sergeant, D. E. 1965a. Migrations of harp seals, *Pagophilus groenlandicus* (Erxleben), in the northwest Atlantic. *J. Fish. Res. Board Can.* 23:433–64.

183. Sergeant, D. E. 1965b. Exploitation and conservation of harp and hooded seals. *Polar Record* 12(80):541–51.

184. Sergeant, D. E. 1966. Reproductive rates of harp seals, *Pagophilus groenlandicus* (Erxleben). *J. Fish. Res. Board Can.* 23:757–66.

185. Sergeant, D. E. 1970. Migration and orientation in harp seals. *Proceedings of the Seventh Annual Conference on Biological Sonar and Diving Mammals*, pp. 121–31. Menlo Park, Calif.: Stanford Research Institute Biological Sonar Laboratories.

186. Sergeant, D. E. 1973. Feeding, growth and productivity of northwest Atlantic harp seal (*Pagophilus groenlandicus*). *J. Fish. Res. Board Can.* 30:17–29.

187. Sergeant, D. E. 1974. A rediscovered whelping population of hooded seals, *Cystophora cristata* (Erxleben), and its possible relationship to other populations. *Polarforschung* 44:1–7.

188. Sergeant, D. E. 1976. History and present status of population of harp and hooded seals. *Biol. Conserv.* 10:95–118.

189. Shepeleva, V. K. 1973. Adaptation of seals to life in the arctic. In K. K. Chapskii and V. E. Sokolov, eds., *Morphology and Ecology of Marine Mammals*, pp. 1–58. New York: Wiley. Translated from Russian by H. Mills for the Israel Program for Scientific Translations, Jerusalem.

190. Sjare, B. L. 1989. Observations on the breeding behavior of Atlantic walruses in the central Canadian High Arctic. *Proceedings of the 8th Biennial Conference on the Biology of Marine Mammals,* December 7–11, Pacific Grove, Calif. Abstract.

191. Sjare, B., and I. Stirling. 1991. I hear you knocking. *Nat. Hist.* 3:60–63.

192. Smith, T. G. 1973a. Management research on the Eskimo's ringed seal. *Can. Geogr. J.* 86:118–25.

193. Smith, T. G. 1973b. Population dynamics of the ringed seal in the Canadian eastern Arctic. *Fish. Res. Board Can. Bull.* 181:1–55.

194. Smith, T. G. 1976a. Predation of ringed seal pups (*Phoca hispida*) by the arctic fox (*Alopex lagopus*). *Can. J. Zool.* 54:1610–16.

195. Smith, T. G. 1976b. The icy birthplace and hard life of the arctic ringed seal. *Can. Geogr. J.* 93(2): 58–63.

196. Smith, T. G. 1980. Polar bear predation of ringed and bearded seals in the landfast sea ice habitat. *Can. J. Zool.* 58:2201–9.

197. Smith, T. G., and M. O. Hammill. 1981. Ecology of the ringed seal, *Phoca hispida*, in its fast ice breeding habitat. *Can. J. Zool.* 59:966–81.

198. Smith T. G., and I. Stirling. 1975. The breeding habitat of the ringed seal (*Phoca hispida*): the birth lair and associated structures. *Can. J. Zool.* 53(9):1297–1305.

199. Spotte, S. 1982. The incidence of twinning in pinnipeds. *Can. J. Zool.* 60:2226–33.

200. Stewart, R. E. A., and D. M. Lavigne. 1980. Neonatal growth of northwest Atlantic harp seals, *Pagophilus groenlandicus. J. Mamm.* 61:670–80.

201. Stirling, I. 1973. Vocalizations in the ringed seal (*Phoca hispida*). *J. Fish. Res. Board Can.* 30:1592–94.

202. Stirling, I. 1983. The evolution of mating systems in pinnipeds. In J. F. Eisenberg and D. G. Kleiman, eds., *Recent Advances in the Study of Mammalian Behavior,* pp. 489–527. Lawrence, Kans.: Special Publication, American Society of Mammalogists No. 7.

203. Stirling, I., and W. A. R. Archibald. 1977. Aspects of predation of seals by polar bears. *J. Fish. Res. Board Can.* 34:1126–29.

204. Stirling, I., and W. A. R. Archibald. 1979. Bearded seal. In *Mammals in the Seas,* vol. 2, *Pinniped Species Summaries and Reports on Sirenians.* Food and Agriculture Organization (FAO) Fisheries Series No. 5. Rome: United Nations.

205. Stirling, I., and W. Calvert. 1979. Ringed seal. In *Mammals in the Seas,* Vol. 2, *Pinniped Species Summaries and Reports on Sirenians.* Food and Agriculture Organization (FAO) Fisheries Series No. 5. Rome: United Nations.

206. Stobo, W. T., B. Beck, and J. K. Horne. 1990. Seasonal movements of grey seals (*Halichoerus grypus*) in the Northwest Atlantic. *Can. Bull. Fish. Aquat. Sci.* 222:199–213.

207. Stobo, W. T., and K. C. T. Zwanenburg. 1990. Grey seal (*Halichoerus grypus*) pup production on Sable Island and estimates of recent production in the Northwest Atlan-

tic. *Can. Bull. Fish. Aquat. Sci.* 222:171–84.

208. Sullivan, R. M. 1981. Aquatic displays and interactions in harbor seals, *Phoca vitulina,* with comments on mating systems. *J. Mamm.* 62:825–31.

209. Sullivan, R. M. 1982. Agonistic behavior and dominance relationships in the harbor seal, *Phoca vitulina. J. Mamm.* 63:554–69.

210. Summers, C. F. 1978. Trends in the size of British grey seal populations. *J. Appl. Ecol.* 15:395–400.

211. Tarasoff, F. J., A. Bisaillon, J. Pierard, and A. P. Whitt. 1972. Locomotory patterns and external morphology of the river otter, sea otter and harp seal (Mammalia). *Can. J. Zool.* 50:915–29.

212. Tarasoff, F. J., and H. D. Fisher. 1970. Anatomy of the hind flippers of two species of seals with reference to thermoregulation. *Can. J. Zool.* 48:821–29.

213. Tedford, R. H. 1976. Relationships of pinnipeds to other carnivores (Mammalia). *Syst. Zool.* 25:363–74.

214. Templeman, W. 1990. Historical background to the sealworm problem in eastern Canadian waters. *Can. Bull. Fish. Aquat. Sci.* 222:1–16.

215. Tenneson, M. 1991. Shy seal in a stormy sea. *National Wildlife* 29:22–27.

216. Terhune, J. M., and K. Ronald. 1971. The harp seal, *Pagophilus groenlandicus* (Erxleben, 1977), part 10: the air audiogram. *Can. J. Zool.* 49:385–90.

217. Terhune, J. M., and K. Ronald. 1972. The harp seal, *Pagophilus groenlandicus* (Erxleben, 1977), part 3: the underwater audiogram. *Can. J. Zool.* 50:565–69.

218. Terhune, J. M., and K. Ronald. 1985. Distant and near range functions of harp seal underwater calls. *Proceedings of the 6th Biennial Conference on the Biology of Marine Mammals,* November 22–26, Vancouver, B.C.

219. Thompson, D., M. A. Fedak, and P. S. Hammond. 1989. Grey seal movements and diving behavior in U.K. waters. *Proceedings of the 8th Biennial Conference on the Biology of Marine Mammals,* December 7–11, Pacific Grove, Calif. Abstract.

220. Thompson, D., and A. W. Mansfield. (rapporteurs): D. Beck, A. Bjorge, D. Bowen, M. Hammill, E. Hauksson, R. Myers, I. H. Ni, and K. Zwanenburg. 1990. Seal ecology. *Can. Bull. Fish. Aquat. Sci.* 222:163–70.

221. *Underwater World* factsheets: brief illustrated accounts of fisheries resources and marine phenomena in Canada, including the harbor seal, gray seal, harp seal, and hooded seal. Communications Directorate, Department of Fisheries and Oceans, Ottawa, Ontario, K1A OE6, Canada.

222. Venables, U. M., and L. S. V. Venables. 1957. Mating behavior of the seal *Phoca vitulina* in Shetland. *Proc. Zool. Soc.* (London) 128:387–96.

223. Wageman, R., R. E. A. Stewart, W. L., Lockhart, B. E. Stewart, and M. Povoledo. 1988. Trace metals and methyl mercury: associations and transfer in harp seal (*Phoca groenlandica*) mothers and their pups. *Mar. Mamm. Sci.* 4(4):339–55.

224. Watkins, W. A., and W. E. Schevill. 1979. Distinctive characteristics of underwater calls of the harp seal, *Phoca groenlandica*, during the breeding season. *J. Acoust. Soc. Am.* 66:983–88.

225. Watkins, W. A., and D. Wartzok. 1985. Sensory biophysics of marine mammals. *Mar. Mamm. Sci.* 1:219–60.

226. Wilson, S. 1974. Juvenile play of the common seal, *Phoca vitulina vitulina*, with comparative notes on the grey seal *Halichoerus grypus. Behavior* 48:37–60.

227. Wilson, S. C. 1978. Social organization and behavior of harbor seals, *Phoca vitulina concolor*, in Maine. Springfield, Va.: National Technical Information Service.

228. Wilson, S., L. Miller, M. Hursey, M. Frantz, and J. Gorte. 1985. The social development of a captive grey seal (*Halichoerus grypus*) pup for the first six months. *Aquat. Mamm.* 11(3):89–100.

229. Winn, H. E., and J. Schneider. 1977. Communication in sirenians, sea otters, and pinnipeds. In T. A. Sebeok, ed., *How Animals Communicate*, pp. 809–40. Bloomington: Indiana University Press.

230. Wyss, A. R. 1989. Flippers and pinniped phylogeny: has the problem of convergence been overrated? *Mar. Mamm. Sci.* 5(4):343–60.

231. Zapol, W. M. 1987. Diving adaptations of the Weddell seal. *Sci. Amer.* 256(6):100–107.

232. Zwanenburg, K. C. T., and W. D. Bowen. 1990. Population trends of the grey seal (*Halichoerus grypus*) in Eastern Canada. *Can. Bull. Fish. Aquat. Sci.* 222:185–97.

III. MARINE MAMMAL AUDIO-VISUAL SOURCES

Distributors for titles listed below have been taken from the most up-to-date source information available, but distribution ownership may change. Some older films are included for historical purposes.

FILMS, SLIDES, FILMSTRIPS, AND VIDEOS

Adaptation in Animals. 1963. 16mm, 13 minutes, color. Stresses adaptations leading to survival of species; includes convergent evolution of fish and whales. CRM Films, 2233 Faraday Avenue, Carlsbad, CA 92008.

After the Whale. 1971. 16mm, 29 minutes, color. Documents the plight of whales today as technological improvements in the whaling industry have brought them nearly to extinction. Shows the behavior and physiology of whales and offers recordings of their underwater "songs." Includes filming off South Africa, Bermuda, at California's Sea World and the Whale Research Lab in London.

Time-Life Films, 100 Eisenhower Drive, Paramus, NJ 07652.

And So Ends. 1972. 16mm, 25 minutes, color. Provides historical view of whaling and presents a plea for the preservation of the whale. Pyramid Films, 2801 Colorado Avenue, Santa Monica, CA 90404.

Beluga Days. 1968. 16mm or videocassette, 14:52 minutes, color. Documents a "roundup" of Beluga whales in the lower St. Lawrence River by Canadian Indians. National Film Board of Canada, 1251 Avenue of the Americas, New York, NY 10020.

The Best of Provincetown Whale Watching. 1989. Videocassette, 53 minutes, color. Scenes of all the whales common to the Gulf of Maine. Cetacean Video, Box 1052, Mechanicsburg, PA 17055.

Between Worlds: Alaska's Killer Whales. 1988. Videocassette, 30 minutes, color. Examines population dynamics of killer whales in Prince William Sound, Alaska, research efforts at Sea World, San Diego, and Sea World of Florida to learn more about the whales. Includes discussion of opposition to captivity of whales for research purposes, and conflicts between the killer whales and Alaska's fishing industry. Production of the University of Alaska.

Beyond Belief: The Humpback Whale. 1988. Videocassette, 50 minutes, color. Breaching, group feeding, close boat approaches, and other approaches that bring out the various personalities of the humpback whale. Cetacean Video, Box 1052, Mechanicsburg, PA 17055.

Bottlenose Dolphin. 8mm, silent loop, 3:55 minutes. Birth of a dolphin, mother guarding it, dolphins at play. Walt Disney footage. Doubleday Multimedia, Box 11607, Santa Ana, CA 92705.

Capture of a Smile. 1968. 16mm, 13 minutes, color. One of the *Living World of the Sea* series; shows capture, care, and training of an Atlantic bottlenose dolphin. Films, Inc., 5547 Ravenswood Avenue, Chicago, IL 60640.

Cetacean Anatomy: A Basic Introduction. Videocassette, 50 minutes, color. Provides visual information concerning the location and a brief description of the major organs of cetacea: whales, dolphins, porpoises. An Alden Mead production.

Conquering the Sea. 1967. 16mm, 25 minutes, color. One of the CBS *Twenty-First Century* series; describes experimental communications between man and porpoises and the possibility of the animals' living and breathing under water. CRM Films, 2233 Faraday Avenue, Carlsbad, CA 92008.

Discover: The World of Science, Program 4—What Man Can Learn From Dolphins. 1987. Videocassette, 15 minutes, color. Dolphins learn parts of their body through a trainer's hand language and demonstrate their ability to learn new instructions. PBS Video, 1320 Braddock Place, Alexandria, VA 22314.

Do Animals Reason? 1975. 16mm, 14 minutes. Explores the intelligence of dolphins and other species. National Geographic Society, 17 and M Streets NW, Washington, D.C. 20036.

Dolphin. 1979. 16mm, 60 minutes, color. A film by Hardy Jones and Michael Wiese; explores the close relationships possible between humans and dolphins in enclosed areas in the wild. Films, Inc., Public Media Inc., 5547 Ravenswood Avenue, Chicago, IL 60640.

Dolphins. 1974. 16mm, 22 minutes, color. One of the *Last of the Wild* series; explores exceptional intelligence of the dolphin, its "language" and communication system, and ability to perform sophisticated tasks. Films, Inc., 5547 Ravenswood Avenue, Chicago, IL 60640.

Dolphins. 1983. Videocassette, 15 minutes, color. Introduction to dolphins, including demonstrations of their intelligence. National Geographic Society, 17 and M Streets NW, Washington, D.C. 20036.

Dolphins and Men. 1972. 16mm, 25 minutes, color. BBC film for *Nova* series; reveals the results of recent studies of dolphin behavior. Time-Life Films, 100 Eisenhower Drive, Paramus, NJ 07652.

Dolphins That Joined the Navy. 1964. 16mm, 27 minutes. Shows the Navy's extensive research with dolphins and future applications of the researchers' findings. U.S. Navy Film MN 10199, Title 277695. National Audiovisual Center (GSA), Washington, D.C. 20409.

The Great Whales. 1981. 16mm, 59 minutes, color. Whale anatomy, communication, and behavior patterns are discussed, as well as the urgent need for protection. National Geographic Society, 17 and M Streets NW, Washington, D.C. 20036.

The Humpback: New England's Spectacular Whale. Videocassette, 40 minutes, color. Great footage of humpbacks in the southern Gulf of Maine feeding ground. Cetacea Research Unit, Box 159, Gloucester, MA 01930.

The Humpback Whale: Winter—A Time for Singing. 1978. 16mm or videocassette, 22 minutes, color. Underwater photographs follow the humpback whale in its winter home off the coast of Hawaii. Moonlight Productions, 2243 Old Middlefield Way, Mountain View, CA 94043.

The Humpback Whale: Summer—A Time for Feeding. 1979. 16mm or videocassette, 21 minutes, color. Follows whales to their summer feeding grounds along the Northwest Coast. Moonlight Productions, 2243 Old Middlefield Way, Mountain View, CA 94043.

Killer Whales: Lord of the Sea. Filmstrip. Educational Images, Ltd., Box 267, Lyon Falls, NY 13369.

Land of the Long Day, Part II: Summer and Autumn. 1952. 16mm, 16 minutes, color. Canadian Indians spot belugas and harpoon one as part of their lifestyle. International Film Bureau, 332 S. Michigan Avenue, Chicago, IL 60604.

Last Days of the Dolphins? 1974. 16mm, 261 minutes, color. Sad saga of the tuna/porpoise problem, with shots of the fleets in action. Environmental Defense Fund, 475 Park Avenue South, New York, NY 10016.

Life on Earth (21): Theme and Varia-

tions. 1981. 16mm or videocassette, 20 minutes, color. Some of the differences between mammals, including whales and porpoises, are explored in this program from the BBC *Life on Earth* series. Penn Communications Inc., Box 10, Erie, PA 16512.

The Magnificent Whales. 1986. Videocassette, 54 minutes, color. Marine Mammal Fund production. Excellent footage of whales, dolphins, seals, and the sea otter with narration and natural sounds. Smithsonian Books, Washington, D.C.

Mammals: Seals & Otters. Videocassette, 30 minutes, color. Part of the Oceanus educational series, this program discusses the three main groups of marine mammals: cetacea, pinnipeds, and sirenians, with special focus on seals and sea otters. RMI Media Productions, 2807 W. 47th Street, Shawnee Mission, KS 66205.

Mammals: Whales. Videocassette, 30 minutes, color. Part of the Oceanus educational series, this program gives an overview of whales, porpoises, and dolphins, including vocalizations and prospects for survival of species. RMI Media Productions, 2807 W. 47th Street, Shawnee Mission, KS 66205.

Marine Life. 1953. 16mm, 11 minutes, color. Shots of various marine life forms, including porpoises, seen in their relationships to each other. Encyclopedia Brittanica Educational Corp., 310 S. Michigan Avenue, Chicago, IL 60604.

Marine Mammals of the Gulf of Maine: An Introduction to Species Identification. 1991. Videocassette, 24 minutes, color. Video field guide to marine mammal species in Gulf of Maine. Tells the story of Allied Whale and presents information learned during 20 years of marine mammal research in the Gulf of Maine. Allied Whale, College of the Atlantic, Bar Harbor, ME 04609.

The Marvel of Whales. 35mm slides and text of the whales of the New England coast. Connecticut Cetacean Society, Box 9145, Wethersfield, CT 06109.

Moontrap. 1964. 16mm, 84 minutes, b&w. Feature-length film that tells the story of villagers of L'Ile-aux-Coudres, a small island in the St. Lawrence, who revived the practice of corralling beluga whales in primitive tidewater traps. Museum of Modern Art, 11 W. 53rd Street, New York, NY 10019.

Portrait of a Whale. 1976. 16mm, 12 minutes, color. Footage of the rare right whale flippering, lobtailing, and breaching. National Geographic Society, 17 and M Streets NW, Washington, D.C. 20036.

Private Life of the Gray Seal. 1974. 16mm, 26 minutes, color. Presents discussion of the Atlantic gray seal: its distribution, physiology, mating habits, as well as the controversy surrounding its exploitation. Time-Life Films, 100 Eisenhower Drive, Paramus, NY 07652.

Prowling with the Mighty Polar Bear. 16mm, 24 minutes, color. Includes footage of travel south to the Gulf of St. Lawrence, where baby harp seals are observed. Document Associates Inc., 211 E. 43rd Street, New York, NY 10017.

Return of the Great Whales. 1982. Videocassette, 60 minutes, color. A Hardy Jones film, Living Ocean Society. Spectacular footage of humpback whales in the area of the Farallon Islands off San Francisco. Includes footage of the killer whale, Risso's dolphin, bottlenose whale, blue whale, Pacific white-sided dolphin, northern right whale dolphin, Dall's porpoise, elephant seal, California sea lion, and the California gray whale on its migration down the Pacific coast. Discussion of the whaling industry off Farallon and conservation measures to preserve species. Films, Inc., 5547 Ravenswood Avenue, Chicago, IL 60640.

The Right Whale: An Endangered Species. 1976. 16mm or videocassette, 24 minutes, color. Footage of right whales as studied by Dr. Roger Payne. Behavior, physiology, conservation. National Geographic Society, 17 and M Streets NW, Washington, D.C. 20036.

Seal Song. 1974. 16mm, 17 minutes, color. Film shows the annual migration of harp seals off the coast of Newfoundland, where they await birth of their pups. Produced for the International Fund for Animal Welfare; makes a strong plea for preservation of the harp seals. Mobius International Film Library, Box 315, Franklin Lakes, NJ 07417.

Signs of the Apes, Songs of the Whales. 1983. Videocassette, 57 minutes, color. *Nova* series program explores language and communication in the animal kingdom, including studies with dolphins, sea lions, and whales. Time-Life Films, 100 Eisenhower Drive, Paramus, NJ 07652.

The Smile of the Walrus. 1978. 16mm or videocassette, 22 minutes, color. One of *The Undersea World of Jacques Cousteau* series; Capt. Cousteau studies the walrus in its annual migration to the Arctic and its importance to isolated Eskimos. Churchill Films, 12210 Nebraska Avenue, Los Angeles, CA 90025; Pacific Arts Video, 50 N. La Cienega Boulevard, Beverly Hills, CA 90211.

The Smithsonian's Whale. 1963. 16mm, 15 minutes, color. Documents the design and construction of a full-sized model of a blue whale in the Smithsonian. Smithsonian Institution, Museum of History & Technology, Washington, D.C. 20560.

Surface Breathers: The Mammals. Filmstrip, 12–14 minutes. Part of the *Sea Life* sound filmstrips. National Geographic Society, 17 and M Streets NW, Washington, D.C. 20036.

Swimming with Whales. 1990. Videocassette, 58 minutes, color. In this *Nova* program researchers observe humpback, killer, and gray whales in Vancouver, British Columbia. Includes discussion of whaling in the mid-1960s and the impact of environmental hazards. Coronet/MTI, 108 Wilmot Road, Deerfield, IL 60015.

Talking with Dolphins. 1970. 16mm, 16 minutes, color. Describes experiments at the U.S. Naval Undersea Research and Development Center with electronics and dolphins. U.S. Navy Film, Title 732620. National

Audiovisual Center (GSA), Washington, D.C. 20409.

Voyage of the Mimi. 1984. WNET production for classroom use. 13-part series, 30 minutes each, color. Series combines dramatic episodes and documentary "expeditions" in an attempt to open the worlds of science and math to children ages 8–12. Episodes follow a seaborne scientific project of student assistants and young scientists on board the *Mimi* to track and study humpback whales. (Not currently in distribution.)

The Warm-Blooded Sea: Mammals of the Deep. 1982. Videocassette, 58 minutes, color. A Jacques Cousteau Film, from the *Cousteau Odyssey* series. Traces the evolutionary history of seals, dolphins, whales, and other marine mammals as Cousteau visits locations in North and South America. Includes discussion of the tuna/porpoise problem. Warner-Elektra, 4000 Warner Boulevard, Burbank, CA 91522.

Watching the Whales. 1985. Videocassette, 30 minutes, color. Surface and underwater footage of whales and dolphins. Soundtrack of whale sounds. Marine Mammal Fund, Fort Mason Center, Bldg. E, San Francisco, CA 94123.

Whale Hunting. 1977. 16mm or videocassette, 9:35 minutes, color. Six Inuit hunt for beluga whales near Frobisher Bay, Northwest Territories. National Film Board of Canada, 1251 Avenue of the Americas, New York, NY 10020.

Whale Rescue. 1988 *Nova* special. 16mm or videocassette, 52 minutes, color. Chronicles the struggles of volunteers and professionals to rescue pilot whales stranded in Cape Cod Bay on December 3, 1986, efforts by the New England Aquarium to rehabilitate three of the whale calves, and attempts to return them to the wild. Scheduled for re-release in March 1992, to include the June 1991 mass stranding of pilot whales. WGBH-TV, 125 Western Avenue, Boston, MA 02134. (Not currently in distribution.)

Whalers out of New Bedford. 16mm, 24 minutes. Historical whaling in the open-boat days as re-created by the Russell-Purrinton panorama in the New Bedford Whaling Museum. New Bedford Museum, Johnny Cake Hill, New Bedford, MA 02740.

Whales! Videocassette, 60 minutes, color. National Audubon Society special; highlights a recent study of the North American right whale. PBS Video, 1320 Braddock Place, Alexandria, VA 22314.

Whales and Dolphins. Slides of Richard Ellis paintings. Educational Images, Ltd., Box 267, Lyon Falls, NY 13369.

The Whales Are Waiting. 1976. 16mm or videocassette, 17:42 minutes, color. This film presents the dilemma of the whale: its questionable value to certain industries and as a source of food versus the possibility of its extinction. National Film Board of Canada, 1251 Avenue of the Americas, New York, NY 10020.

Whales: Can They Be Saved? 1978. 16mm or videocassette, 22 minutes, color. From the *Wide World of Adventure* series; examines the behavior of many types of whales and explains the steps people must take to save this nearly extinct species. Encyclopedia Britannica Educational Corp., 310 S. Michigan Avenue, Chicago, IL 60604.

Whales, Dolphins and Men. 1973. 16mm or videocassette, 52 minutes, color. *Nova* series documentary on the various types of whales and dolphins; presents results of scientific experiments that prove their remarkable intelligence and gentle dispositions. Also examines the whaling industry and threats to whales. Time-Life Films, 100 Eisenhower Drive, Paramus, NJ 07652.

Whales Surfacing. Super-8mm, silent loop, 1:25 minutes. Whales as they surface and dive, close-ups of barnacles and the diving action. Disney footage. Doubleday Multimedia, 1371 Reynolds Avenue, Santa Ana, CA 92705.

Whalewatch: A New England Adventure. Eye to Eye with the Great Whale. 1989. Videocassette, 48 minutes, color. A video composite of New England whalewatch experiences. Benta/Wassner Productions, Cambridge, MA.

Where the Bay Becomes the Sea. 1985. Videocassette, 30 minutes, color. The unique ecosystem of the Bay of Fundy is presented, tracing the intricate interrelationships within the food chain from tiny plankton to whales and humans. Includes footage of the rare right whale. Bullfrog Films, Oley, PA 19547.

Wild Seas, Wild Seals. 1985. 60 minutes, color. *Survival* series program #504, produced by Survival Anglia for PBS. Film team captures the fascination of an orphaned baby seal that becomes part of their "family" for six months; spectacular surface and underwater footage. Warner Home Video, 9000 Warner Boulevard, Burbank, CA 91522.

The Wonder of Dolphins. 1980. 16mm, 11 minutes, color. Underwater footage of dolphins in their ocean habitat; includes discussion of their bahavior, communication system, and intelligence. Centron Educational Films, 108 Wilmot Road, Deerfield, IL 60015.

RECORDS AND TAPES FEATURING VOCALIZATIONS OF WHALES, DOLPHINS, AND SEALS

And God Created Great Whales. Alan Hovhaness symphony with whale sounds. André Kostelanetz, conductor. Columbia.

Beneath the Waves. A recording of humpback whale vocalizations. Total Recording Co., Ltd., Box 309S, Mt. Albert, British Columbia, Canada.

Callings: A Celebration of the Voices of the Sea. Paul Winter Consort. Living Music Records, Box 72, Litchfield, CT 06759.

Colors of the Day. Judy Collins; includes "Farewell to Tarwathie" and humpbacks. Elektra.

Deep Voices. The second whale record produced by Roger Payne. Capitol Records ST-11598.

Inside II. Paul Horn on flute; "Haida," an orca, sings along. Epic KE 31600.

Northern Whales. Music Gallery Editions, 30 Patrick Street, Toronto, Ontario, Canada M5T 1V1.

Ocean of Song: Whale Voices. PET Records, Box 1102, Burbank, CA 91507.

Songs and Sounds of the Humpback Whales. Total Recording Co., Ltd., Box 309S, Mt. Albert, British Columbia, Canada.

Songs of the Humpback Whale. Available on CD. Living Music Records, Box 72, Litchfield, CT 06759.

Songs of Yankee Whaling. Old songs sung by Bill Bonyun. American Heritage.

Sound Communication of the Bottlenosed Dolphin. Biological System, Inc., P.O. Box 26, St. Augustine, FL 32084.

Whale and Porpoise Voices. Compiled by William Schevill and William Watkins. Woods Hole Oceanographic Institute. Available to qualified scientists only.

Whales Alive. Paul Winter Consort. Living Music Records, Box 72, Litchfield, CT 06759.

Whalescapes. Interspecies Music, Vol. 1. The Gallery, 30 Patrick Street, Toronto, Ontario, Canada.

Whale Songs and Whales. Interview on tape with Roger Payne; includes humpback songs. Pacifica Tape Library, 2217 Shattuck Avenue, Berkeley, CA 94704.

ADDENDA

The following references were added at proof stage and are not included in the species guides to the bibliography.

CETACEANS, "BONUS" SPECIES, AND PREY SPECIES

Agler, B. A., K. A. Robertson, D. Dendanto, S. K. Katona, J. M. Allen, S. E. Frohock, I. E. Seipt, and R. S. Bowman. 1992. The use of photographic identification for studying individual fin whales (*Balaenoptera physalus*) in the Gulf of Maine. *Rep. Int. Whal. Commn* 42:711–722.

Amos, B., J. Barrett, and G. A. Dover. 1991. Breeding behaviour of pilot whales revealed by DNA fingerprinting. *Heredity* 67:49–55.

Baird, R. W., and P. J. Stacey. 1991. Status of Risso's dolphin, *Grampus griseus,* in Canada. *Canadian Field-Nat.* 105(2):233–242.

Baraff, L. S., P. J. Clapham, D. K. Matilla, and R. S. Bowman. 1991. Feeding behavior of a humpback whale in low-latitude waters. *Mar. Mamm. Sci.* 7(2):197–202.

Campbell, R. R. 1991. Rare and endangered fishes and marine mammals of Canada: COSEWIC Fish and Marine Mammal Subcommittee Status Reports: VII. *Canadian Field-Nat.* 105(2):151–156.

Clapham, P. J. 1992. Age at attainment of sexual maturity in humpback whales, *Megaptera novaeangliae*. *Can. J. Zool.* 70(7):1470–1472.

Clapham, P. J., and I. E. Seipt. 1991. Resightings of independent fin whales, *Balaenoptera physalus*, on maternal summer ranges. *J. Mamm.* 72(4):788–790.

Eckert, S. A. 1992. Bound for deep water [Leatherback turtle]. *Nat. Hist.* 3/92:28–35.

Gaskin, D. E. 1992a. An update on the status of the harbour porpoise, *Phocoena phocoena*, in Canada. *Canadian Field-Nat.* 106(1):36–54.

Gaskin, D. E. 1992b. An update on the status of the common dolphin, *Delphinus delphis*, in Canada. *Canadian Field-Nat.* 106(1):55–63.

Gaskin, D. E. 1992c. An update on the status of the Atlantic white-sided dolphin, *Lagenorhynchus acutus*, in Canada. *Canadian Field-Nat.* 106(1):64–72.

Hain, J. W. 1992. The fin whale, *Balaenoptera physalus*, in waters of the northeastern United States continental shelf. *Rep. Int. Whal. Commn* 42:653–669.

Hoek, W. 1992. An unusual aggregation of harbor porpoises (*Phocoena phocoena*). *Mar. Mamm. Sci.* 8(2):152–155.

Kastelein, R. A., and N. M. Gerrits. 1991. Swimming, diving and respiration patterns of a Northern bottlenose whale (*Hyperoodon ampullatus*, Forster, 1770). *Aquat. Mamm.* 17(1):20–30.

Knowlton, A. R., J. Sigurjonsson, J. N. Ciano, and S. D. Kraus. 1992. Long-distance movements of North Atlantic right whales (*Eubalaena glacialis*). *Mar. Mamm. Sci.* 8(4):397–404.

Lohmann, K. J. 1991. How sea turtles navigate. *Sci. Amer.* 266(1):100–106.

Martin, A. R., and T. G. Smith. 1992. Deep diving in wild, free-ranging beluga whales, *Delphinapterus leucas*. *Can. J. Fish. Aquat. Sci.* 49:462–466.

Mitchell, E. D., Jr. 1991. Winter records of the minke whale (*Balaenoptera acutorostrata acutorostrata* Lacepede 1804) in the southern North Atlantic. *Rep. Int. Whal. Commn* 41:455–457.

Nelson, D., A. Desbrosse, J. Lien, P. Ostrom, and R. Seton. 1991. A new stranding record of the pygmy sperm whale, *Kogia breviceps*, in waters off eastern Canada. *Canadian Field-Nat.* 105(3):407–408.

Norris, K. S. 1992. Dolphins in crisis. *National Geographic* 182(3):2–35.

Reeves, R. R., B. S. Stewart, and S. Leatherwood. 1992. *The Sierra Club Handbook of Seals and Sirenians*. San Francisco: Sierra Club Books.

Robinson, J. 1992. *The Whale in Lowell's Cove*. Camden, Maine: Down East Books.

Scott, M. D., and J. G. Cardaro. 1987. Behavioral observations of the dwarf sperm whale, *Kogia simus*. *Mar. Mamm. Sci.* 3(4):353–354.

Shane, S. H., R. S. Wells, and B. Wursig. 1986. Ecology, behavior and social organization of the bottlenose dolphin. A review. *Mar. Mamm. Sci.* 2(2):34–63.

Smith, R. J., and A. J. Read. Consumption of euphausiids by harbor porpoise (*Phocoena phocoena*) calves in the Bay of Fundy. *Can. J. Zool.* 70(8):1629–1632.

Smith, T. D., D. Palka, K. Bisack,

and G. D. Nardo. 1991. *Preliminary estimates of harbor porpoise abundance and by-catch.* Northeast Fisheries Science Center Reference Document 91–04, Woods Hole, Mass.

Smith, T. G., D. J. St. Aubin, and M. O. Hammill. 1992. Rubbing behaviour of belugas, *Delphinapterus leucas,* in a high Arctic estuary. *Can. J. Zool.* 70:2405–2409.

Stone, G. S., S. K. Katona, A. Mainwaring, J. M. Allen, and H. D. Corbett. 1992. Respiration and surfacing rates of fin whales (*Balaenoptera physalus*) observed from a lighthouse tower. *Rep. Int. Whal. Commn* 42:735–745.

Tershy, B. R., and D. N. Wiley. 1992. Asymmetrical pigmentation in the fin whale: a test of two related hypotheses. *Mar. Mamm. Sci.* 8(3):315–318.

Wenzel, F., D. K. Matilla, and P. J. Clapham. 1988. *Balaenoptera musculus* in the Gulf of Maine. *Mar. Mamm. Sci.* 4(2):172–175.

Whitehead, H., S. Brennan, and D. Grover. 1992. Distribution and behaviour of male sperm whales on the Scotian Shelf, Canada. *Can. J. Zool.* 70:912–918.

SEALS

Bowen, W. D., O. T. Oftedal, and D. J. Boness. 1992. Mass and energy transfer during lactation in a small phocid, the harbor seal (*Phoca vitulina*). *Physiol. Zool.* 65(4):844–866.

Bowen, W. D., W. T. Stobo, and S. J. Smith. 1992. Mass changes of grey seal *Halichoerus grypus* pups on Sable Island: differential maternal

investment reconsidered. *J. Zool.* (London) 227:606–622.

Stenson, G. B., R. A. Myers, M. O. Hammill, I.-H. Ni, W. G. Warren, M. C. S. Kingsley. 1993. Pup production of harp seals (*Phoca groenlandica*) in the northwest Atlantic. *Can. J. Fish. Aquat. Sci.* In press.

FILMS, SLIDES, FILMSTRIPS, AND VIDEOS

Dolphins, Whales and Us. 1990. Videocassette. Emphasizes the ways in which humans and dolphins interact and conservation issues affecting the future of cetacean populations. Produced by Stanley M. Minasian for the Marine Mammal Fund.

In the Company of Whales. 1992. Videocassette. Roger Payne visits important research projects on whales and dolphins and discusses highlights of his own career. Produced for the Discovery Channel.

Private Lives of Dolphins. 1992. Videocassette. An outstanding Nova film documenting research on social behavior of bottlenose dolphins at Monkey Mia, Australia, and Sarasota Bay, Florida. Penn State Audio-Visual Services, Special Services Building, 1127 Fox Rd., University Park, PA 16803–1824.

Talbot—The Video: Dolphins and Orcas. Videocassette. Lovely images of swimming and breaching put to music by Mannheim Steamroller. No narration. Available from Bob Talbot Photography, P.O. Box 3126, Rancho Palos Verdes, CA 90274.

INDEX